THE DOOR IS OPEN

The Door Is Open

MEMOIR OF A SOUP KITCHEN VOLUNTEER

Bart Campbell

ANVIL PRESS • VANCOUVER

THE DOOR IS OPEN

Copyright © 2001 by Bart Campbell

Printed and bound in Canada
Cover design: Rayola Graphic Design
Interior photos & cover image: Marina Dodis
2nd Printing: August 2004

CANADIAN CATALOGUING IN PUBLICATION DATA

Campbell, Bart.

The door is open

ISBN 1-895636-36-1

1. Campbell, Bart. 2. Downtown-Eastside (Vancouver, B.C.)—Biography. 3. Homeless persons—Services for—British Columbia—Vancouver. 4. Poverty—British Columbia—Vancouver. I. Title
HV4510.V35C34 2001   362.5'09711'33   C00-911580-3

Represented in Canada by the Literary Press Group
Distributed by University of Toronto Press

The publisher gratefully acknowledges the financial assistance of the B.C. Arts Council, the Canada Council for the Arts, and the Book Publishing Industry Development Program (BPIDP) for their support of our publishing program.

The Canada Council | Le Conseil des Arts
for the Arts | du Canada

BRITISH
COLUMBIA
ARTS COUNCIL
Supported by the Province of British Columbia

Anvil Press
P.O. Box 3008. MPO
Vancouver, B.C. V6B 3X5   CANADA
www.anvilpress.com

CONTENTS

for Pina, Cary, Aaron, and Neil

"Writing a book is hard, because you are giving yourself away. But if you love, you want to give yourself. You write as you are impelled to write, about man and his problems, his relation to God and his fellows. You write about yourself because in the big run all man's problems are the same, his human needs of sustenance and love."

— Dorothy Day
(from her autobiography, *The Long Loneliness*)

SELECTED FACTS:

The downtown eastside of Vancouver makes up most of the V6A forward sortation area, which has the lowest median income of all 7000 of Canada's postal prefixes.

Because of their poor financial demography, downtown eastside residents receive almost no junkmail, except for flyers from high-interest money lending companies and cheque cashing stores.

The downtown eastside houses less than 3% of the city's population but was responsible for 17% of all Fire Department responses and 22% of all police calls in 1999.

Half of the unattached elderly in Canada are poor.

Over 70,000 Canadians visit food banks every month.

1 in 5 Canadian children are poor.

Canadian volunteers serve more than one billion hours annually. Their unpaid services are estimated to be worth $13 billion, or about 8% of our nation's GDP.

PROLOGUE

WHEN MY wife and I separated I sought comfort and solace in the usual ways of divorcing men—wrapped in the arms of a different woman, and by drinking too much and too often—but my depression just got steadily worse. I was waking up in the middle of the night screaming, ringing in my ears, weeping in the hallways, rapid weight loss and night sweats, depressed. My life had become a very scary thing for me and I've worked around enough busy Hospital Emergency Rooms as a Medical Laboratory Technologist to know that kind of deep depression can be fatal.

And then one afternoon on my way home from work I pulled my bicycle up to the curb at the front of a long bread line I had indifferently commuted by hundreds of times before, and asked a stocky man with a broom if he needed any help. It was as casual as that. It just sort of happened without a plan or a reason, like this book just kind of happened—while I was sitting on the steps of a skid row drop-in centre, smoking cigarettes, talking, listening, watching, and writing down what I remembered when I got home.

Writing down my feelings and immediate impressions is a habit I developed during my dizzy childhood to cope with my family making seventeen cross-country moves before I was fourteen years old. Recording my feelings onto paper made them last longer and helped impart context to the whirligig of my childhood which lacked any other sort of geographical or personal connections. The confused, messy scrawlings on scraps of paper stuffed into shoeboxes on the top shelf of my bedroom closet were the word maps that I used to try and understand my life. And I've never lost that childhood habit of writing something down everyday about the world I am currently living in— because I know very well that things won't stay the same forever, and if I don't get it all down right away, I might not be able to believe myself later.

The counsellor I sometimes saw during the early, painful days of our separation once asked me why I had chosen that particularly chaotic time in my life to begin volunteering at a skid row charity. I had absolutely no idea how to reply. That unanswerable question irritated me, and I began delving into the notes I had written after my shifts at The Door Is Open, looking for the real reason why I went back there every Monday and Wednesday evening.

But after reading through all the disjointed, out of sequence notes in one sitting, I still hadn't learned why I hung out so often at the drop-in centre. Seemingly, I started every new shift at the drop-in centre expecting something to happen, but then nothing ever did. But I did recognize that in the beginning I kept going back because I was trying to seek peace beyond my loud, angry divorce proceedings—living the forgiveness of my debt and debtors in a place where I could perform acts of quiet kindness without expectations of gratitude. And that was the best part of it. No one knew me down there, so my good deeds became less complicated, and more than just the atonements I was making to ease my guilty conscience for being such a failure as a husband.

I also saw that I had found more friendship than I had ever known before in that blustery community of alcoholics and homeless people, and that the personal lessons I learned from them have resonated throughout my life and permanently changed me.

To tell a long, complicated story briefly: My wife and I reconciled after seventeen months of legal separation. That was six years (and two more kids) ago, and we still have tender spots—old wounds whose scabs rip off occasionally and bleed a little into our lives—but we find creative new ways to work them out.

Once I overheard my wife describe our surprising reconciliation to a friend by saying: "It was like in this recurring dream I have where my family is driving down a bumpy road and we get into a car accident and we are flipping end over end over a cliff in slow-motion and then I blink and suddenly we are all ok and our car has landed right side up on a smooth highway and we just keep rolling happily along. The kids are ok, and everybody's singing 'Baby-Beluga-in-the-Deep-Blue-Sea' at the top of their lungs."

But she was only ducking a difficult question and I know about all the hard things we both went through before we reconciled, and that it probably never would have happened if I hadn't started hanging out at The Door Is Open and let the experience change some of my entrenched outlooks on life, and teach me some things—like that often the best way to help yourself, is by helping others, and that the more you give of yourself, the more you forget yourself in work or in love, to that extent you will become happy.

DIARY EXCERPTS:

I am going to start volunteering at a skid row drop-in centre called The Door Is Open. It has been closed for renovations for one month, but Brother Tim MacDonald hopes they'll be reopening next week. He gave me and a few other volunteers a tour of the construction-tangled rooms and proudly showed us a seventy foot-long wall mural of a colourful mountain meadow filled with life-sized wild animals. An elementary school class and their teachers recently painted it.

The drop-in centre was closed a couple of months ago when city inspectors threatened to condemn the building unless extensive repairs were made. Brother Tim was the only applicant for the job of cleaning up the place, which is kind of ironic because he dresses more like a sloppy, colour-blind New York City taxi driver than a religious brother. When I asked him if he ever wore a frock or a roman collar he growled: "Naw, because then I'd be a walking advertisement. To some people those things symbolize authority and they might want to knock my block off!"

My third shift, and a very quiet evening. Most of our patrons were reminiscing about the good times they had at the Stanley Cup riots downtown last night. Vic came by. He was the native guy who trained me my first night. Many of the rice winos are his cousins. He gave them all the extra sandwiches that Sister Maura dropped off, which wasn't very fair (or kind) in front of a roomful of hungry men who weren't related to him.

Tonight Vic smelled really bad, so he stripped down to his boxer shorts in the janitor's closet and hosed himself off over the scummy, slow-draining sink. He told us that he collected $67 in empty beer cans and bottles amidst the riot mayhem last night. "That's why I stink," he explained.

One of his cousins started bragging about the great jeans he scooped from a smashed store window on Robson Street.

"Man," Vic complained, "I got so caught up with all the beer cans I was finding I didn't even think to steal nothing."

His cousin laughed at him and said, "Since you're so rich, how about buying a couple of bottles of rice wine and some skunk weed and we can party in my room."

"Ok," Vic said, and they left.

It wasn't until closing time that I realized that Vic and his cousin must have doubled back and broken into the Sisters' clothing room. I recognized his old, smelly jeans and T-shirt that were hanging off the smashed padlock.

Vic came back to my place after our shift tonight. He was quietly rolling a cigarette at the kitchen table while I fried us some steaks and onions and potatoes for dinner, when out of the blue he said: "Now there's a sound I miss."

"What's that?"

"A clock ticking, the sound of a home."

CHAPTER ONE

Precarious Addresses

A LARGE BRASS plaque upon the wall of an old Canadian Imperial Bank of Commerce building at 300 W. Hastings arrogantly proclaims:

> *"Here stood Hamilton,*
> *First Land Commissioner,*
> *Canadian Pacific Railway,*
> *1885.*
> *In the silent solitude*
> *of the primeval forest*
> *he drove a wooden stake*
> *in the earth and commenced*
> *to measure an empty land*
> *into the streets of*
> *Vancouver."*

Another, smaller plaque on the wall of a boarded-over detox centre a few blocks away suggests:

> *"Already the folds had*
> *worn through, tearing long*

*slashes in the map, names began
to disappear along its tattered
edges, eventually whole sections
of the city tore away . . ."*

Before and after mottoes for the same strange place?

The downtown eastside makes up most of the V6A forward sorta-tion area, which has the lowest median income ($5900) of all 7000 of Canada's postal prefixes. More than 10,000 poor people live there. Yet it is also Vancouver's oldest neighbourhood with many lifelong residents. Once you get used to it the place can cast a peculiar spell and some people stubbornly stay on for years, decades, lifetimes. They stay because the rent is cheaper than everywhere else, and because the winters are warm, and because the downtown eastside is that rarest of places, a cheap slum with picturesque mountain and har-bour views. And they stay because they feel at home there.

But the downtown eastside is no place special, really. There are skid rows in every other Canadian city. They are usually located downtown some place, with borders on the main business district, in neighbourhoods that were affluent and full of busy hope during their horse and buggy days. That is before the old mansions were convert-ed into cheap rooming houses.

The name "skid row" originated over a century ago in Victoria amongst lumberjacks who patronized one seedy neighbourhood for heavy drinking and brothel visits when they came to town at the end of the logging season. They nicknamed the place "skid road" after the greased log runways down which they slid lumber to the rivers in the logging camps. "Skid row" suggests fast, slippery descent, an unstable way of life, a hopeless address.

&- &- &-

According to a BC Housing Study from 1998, males make up 83% of downtown eastside residents. But such uneven gender ratios are noth-ing new here. Ever since Vancouver was called Stamp's Landing or Hastings Mill, Gastown or Granville, the population of the neigh-bourhood has been overwhelmingly male, single, robust, and rowdy. When Vancouver was a frontier town there was no limit of pick and shovel work for them to do, digging up stumps and grading roads and excavating basements and digging ditches for sewers and water mains—or else their strong backs were needed for the sawmills, slaughterhouses, granaries, canneries, shipyards, or for dock work—or for seasonal, hard-ass sweat labour in the logging camps up the coast.

During the 1930s Depression, thousands of unemployed men wintered in downtown eastside hobo jungles because of the mild weather. They gathered in transient villages of crowded lean-tos and forts built from soggy cardboard, old carpets and flattened tin cans, located along the mucky False Creek Flats and at the Hastings Mill hobo jungle on Burrard Inlet. All the hobo jungles reeked of sewage and mildew and the pissy smell of wet wool clothing, because Vancouver's mild winters are also very wet and people living outside for a few weeks discover curious moulds and fungi growing in their armpits and crotches.

When I first moved to East Vancouver in 1988 the neighbourhood beer parlours and small bacon-and-egg cafés were filled with elderly pensioners who had lived off and on in remote coastal logging camps all their lives (except for the winter lay-ups and summer fire seasons when they came down to town to blow their stakes on booze and gam-bling and women). Every Canadian skid row used to be filled with old guys like that when I was a kid: Quiet, heavily accented old men who did all the hard, bull labour that built this country. Shy strangers who often never married and never had anything to show for all those years of hard work. Often not even citizenship.

Most of them have passed on now, but you can still find pockets of those gnarly old men here and there around the downtown eastside—huddled together around beer parlour tables all day long, just reading the newspapers and watching the hockey games and telling each other stories about what it was like when they were young and could take quite a bit more knocking around than they can now.

Many of those old guys hang around in the beer parlour at the Marr Hotel. It is located at the northeast corner of Powell and Dunlevy, in one of the oldest buildings in Vancouver, across the street from the sawmill site that was the birthplace of Vancouver, and across the park from the Franciscan Sisters of Atonement who operate their bread line and other ministries from the oldest building in Vancouver (being the only house to survive the big fire in 1886).

I've gotten to know the Marr Hotel beer parlour over the years because Brother Tim used to send me there to look for replacements when we were short a volunteer. Even though someone redecorated when they tried to turn the place into a stripper bar a little while ago, the Marr has a refreshingly simple décor for a Vancouver bar—without plants or glowing lights and stupid props, without aspirations to be anything but what it is—a place for drinking until drunk. It is a cool, dim, quiet, simple room with a television above the bar and a clientele of old men who usually have multiple glasses of draught beer arranged in rows on their tables beside their cigarettes and ash tray. Their entire afternoons already laid out at their fingertips.

I like the Marr Hotel beer parlour because it is a simple, one-bartender establishment where anyone who wants to can always earn a free glass of beer by collecting the empty glasses, or emptying the ashtrays into a coffee can. And the place makes me feel nostalgic for the taverns in small rural Manitoba towns that my grandfathers used to take me to when I was a kid. They were cool caves where we could while away the hot afternoons between our daily dawn and dusk fishing excursions. Each place had a coin-operated pool table and air hockey board and not much more on the menu but beer, rye whisky, and pickled eggs, and everyone followed a very rigid drinking code:

No one drinks alone.

No one buys a beer for himself, without buying one for a friend.

No one accepts a drink from a friend, without buying him one in return.

No one deserts an unconscious drinking companion.

Just like in those small-town Manitoba taverns, everyone in the Marr is included in the general conversation and flow of things, even though they may be sitting at separate tables, or complete strangers, and incoherent. I like to go there and ask the old-timers questions about what the downtown eastside was like in the 1930s, when my grandfathers lived in the Vancouver hobo jungles for a few seasons. And it usually doesn't take long before nearly everyone in the tavern is remembering some long ago moment and telling stories and anecdotes, some of which could even be true.

Many of the old-timers at the Marr Hotel live in rooms above the beer parlour so they don't have far to commute every morning. I've been upstairs a few times and except for the inconvenience of shared bathrooms, the rooms themselves are nicer than in most of the other downtown eastside hotels. They are broader, and longer, with ten-foot ceilings, and a sensible kitchen nook by the big, bright windows. No matter how neglected the hotel may be now, the class it was built with still shows through.

The mouldy, flaking patches of gray and light blue stucco on the outside walls may make the building currently resemble a big, soggy, burnt marshmallow. But that doesn't mean that the Hotel wasn't really something in its day. It was called the Stanley Hotel when it was built in 1890. Back then it had broad, wraparound balconies outside the second and third stories and cedar shake walls that gave it a young, open-faced, optimistic look. The Stanley tried to cater to the train and ship travelers arriving just a little down the road, but mostly it was a semi-permanent address for employees of the Hastings Sawmill, and a seasonal pasture for sailors and loggers blowing all their stakes on another rowdy trip to town.

The Secord Hotel (as the Stanley was renamed by new owners in 1898) was the type of place that Martin Grainger described in

Woodsmen of the West, his informative book about BC logging camp lifestyles that he published in 1908.

"A fellow can't do better than go to a good, respectable hotel," Grainger wrote. "Where he knows the proprietor and the bartenders, and where there are some decent men stopping. Then he knows he will be looked after when he is drunk; and getting drunk, he will not be distressed by spasms of anxiety lest someone should go through his pockets and leave him broke. There are some shady characters in a town like Vancouver, and persons of the underworld."

Single, transient men have always occupied the Marr Hotel, and they've seen a lot of interesting history because of that address. The beer parlour windows face out over Oppenheimer Park, which was formerly called the Powell Street Grounds—the assembly point of all the city's violent riots and labour strikes. A couple thousand Relief Camp Strikers gathered there for the news and to get their daily assignments when they occupied Vancouver for three months in 1935—and it was their assembly point when they left town en masse on commandeered freight trains as part of the doomed "On-to-Ottawa" trek. The Powell Street Grounds was also where the unemployed assembled before they marched off to occupy the Main Post Office in 1938, and then became the martyrs of Vancouver's murderous "Bloody Sunday."

Oppenheimer Park has always been a breeding ground for lost causes. So when I step out onto the sidewalk outside the Marr Hotel beer parlour after hearing about those tumultuous times from the old-timers inside, the long bread line outside the Franciscan Sisters of the Atonement looks a lot like an angry mob to me, gaining momentum for violence.

   & & &

Most of the men and women you see in the soup kitchens live in single occupancy hotel rooms (SROs) and rooming houses. The number one reason for going to soup kitchens is simply "no money." But the second most common reason cited is, "No cooking facilities," a sad statement when you realize that in downtown eastside hotels a hot plate or an electric frying pan rate as cooking facilities, and every shady windowsill is a refrigerator.

Over my years at the drop-in centre I have visited many SRO Hotels. All my tours were remarkably similar. You just don't get much for $350 a month. Fat, cigarette-butt size cockroaches scurried over every surface of every building I visited. The light bulbs in most of the stairwells were burnt out or missing; the communal toilets were usually plugged, the shower stalls were black with mildew, often with mushrooms sprouting from the ceilings. And all the hotel rooms were small (usually 5' x 9', the same dimensions as jail cells, unintentionally making many of the tenants feel at home). Several of the rooms were windowless, and living in them must have seemed a little like living in a tomb, or a sewer.

Many of the landlords of the hotels and rooming houses use out of country addresses. I met one owner of two skid row hotels on the loading dock of a large downtown department store where he worked as a shipper. He explained that officially he was the building manager and his mother in the Philippines was the landlord. I guess such legal sleight-of-hand is necessary in a business where most hotels sell phoney rent receipts. The operator of the Grand Trunk Hotel on Powell Street was caught with nineteen phantom welfare tenants on his books in 1998.

But such arrests are rare. Very little effort is exerted by City Authorities in policing the slumlords; perhaps because they expect the hotels and rooming houses will soon be demolished, or redeveloped. More than one thousand downtown eastside Single Room Occupancy units were converted into tourist backpacker hotels in the last three years, and over four thousand units of low-cost housing have been demolished in a little more than a decade, mostly around the neighbourhood's softening borders. Five or six city blocks of hotels and boarding houses along False Creek (the downtown eastside's southwestern corner) were bulldozed for Expo 86. When the fair ended, a steep canyon of tall, glassy, expensive condominiums rose up in their place. Strathcona (the neighbourhood's southeastern rim), is rapidly being gentrified, and high rise condominiums are under construction in Gastown (the northwestern corner).

The exuberant real estate agents in the Gastown condominium sales offices claim that the downtown eastside will be completely redeveloped within five years. When I asked one of them where all the people in the bread lines across the street will go, he glibly replied, "Surrey," Vancouver's largest suburb.

But in the meantime police respond to distress calls at certain Hastings Street hotels all day long, and every door is pockmarked with boot prints and crowbar scars from generations of break-ins.

One old pensioner complained to me: "I got robbed four times in two months. The last time, they tied me up and whipped me with an extension cord until I told them where I hid my wallet."

And I've heard many similar stories about poor people robbing other poor people. The downtown eastside houses less than three percent of the city's population but provides more than twenty percent of the murder victims, and suffers four times the robberies of all other Lower Mainland zones combined. And frighteningly, such dismal crime statistics don't take into account the fact that crimes are much less likely to be reported in the downtown eastside because of victim's fear of retaliatory assaults. The old man who complained to me about being whipped reported none of his recent robberies.

    ❧ ❧ ❧

Poverty has become a much more personal issue for me since I have started hanging out at The Door Is Open. Instead of commuting numbly through the downtown eastside as I used to, now I know that "Pete" lives under that loading dock ramp, and "Bill" lives in that alley doorway. I now consider a cardboard box in a weedy, vacant lot, or a shallow cave carved into the steep, berry bush-covered embankments of the Grandview Railway Cut, to be legitimate addresses. And I have learned to differentiate a little between the various styles of homelessness. Only a small portion of the homeless shuffle from place to place pushing shopping carts stuffed with all their possessions.

Many people live in vans and cars that barely run. They are forever limping from parking spot to parking spot as the police harass them and move them along.

"Squatting" is breaking open a door or smashing a window and moving into some vacant building for a few days. Squatters are like ghosts, haunting the ruins of our crumbling urban landscapes. Most experienced squatters start by constructing barricades of heavy junk—car doors, bed springs, bicycle frames, freight pallets—that make their new-found space difficult to get into, and easy to get out of if you understand the secrets of the maze. The more junk they pile up, the less easily they can be evicted. If it is a good squat, and they can stay a week or more, they will steal garden hoses and run them from the water mains.

The winter weather is mild (if very wet) in Vancouver, so sleeping in the parks and hedges isn't too uncomfortable. But for the truly down and out, there are 250 beds in downtown eastside emergency shelters, although they are not very restful places to sleep. Many of the men who stand in line every evening outside The Look Out (70 beds and four couches), or Triage (28 beds), The Crosswalk (25 sleeping bags on the concrete floor), Catholic Men's Hostel (80 beds), or Dunsmuir House (10 emergency cots inside the Salvation Army Cafeteria), are mentally ill wanderers or sick, delirious, substance abusers, or both. Somebody's always screaming in their sleep.

෴   ෴   ෴

While talking to homeless people, you soon realize that all those years of living completely in the present make chronology difficult for them. They often can't tell you if the event they are describing occurred last year, or five days ago. Everything is completely arbitrary; there is no emotional sequence.

But sometimes when I watch an ancient bag lady feasting on a sandwich of stale bread and gamey luncheon meat, I feel envious of her grateful here-and-now dependence upon providence. I am slowly learning the Christian values of giving, and of open-hearted, non-judgemental acceptance—and learning to appreciate the human talent for adaptation. I am learning to see the homeless as individuals who have been inventive in their struggles for survival.

"But such here-and-now philosophies can be very frustrating," Brother Tim complained to me once. Then he told me a story about giving a wool blanket to someone who was sleeping on the steps of the drop-in centre.

"It's hard enough to have nothing to give a homeless person but an old blanket," he said. "But I got kind of pissed off when I opened up in the morning and saw that the blanket had been discarded in a puddle in the curb lane."

And then the same guy came back that night and asked Brother Tim for another blanket.

"Why didn't you keep the blanket I gave you last night?" Brother Tim complained. "Or at least you could have left it by the door so I could have brought it in and it wouldn't have been ruined, and I'd have something to give you now."

"But I didn't know I'd need it," the man explained.

"Do those guys in the sandwich line ever think about their future?" Brother Tim frequently wonders.

☙ ☙ ☙

The best insight about homelessness that I ever heard came from a sandwich line patron: "If you take the time to think about it, you gotta realize that homeless people are not stupid, 'cause nobody stupid is gonna survive on the street. You gotta be smart and strong when you're homeless."

He has been living outdoors ever since he lost his good factory job in southern Ontario when the auto parts plant he worked in for twelve years closed up and moved south. His name is "Paul" and he is that quiet type of bum nobody pays much attention to, even in soup kitchens. Paul is so lonely he is almost invisible, his life cancelled retroactively, like an annulled marriage. One day he "disappeared" from his life and was slowly forgotten by his former friends, co-workers, family. And ever since he has been living on the fringes, away from the action, unable to work through the riddles of his own life.

"I chose to live this way," he told me once, "and now there is no way home for me."

But he wept as he told me how he had left his wife and mother in Hamilton when the Unemployment Insurance ran out. He actually believed when he abandoned them that he'd find a good job in a B.C. logging camp or a sawmill, send for his wife, and send some money to his mother. But all his leads turned out to be rumours and he just started drinking and drifting, and stopped writing postcards.

"That was about six years ago," he told me. "I wonder what happened to them?"

DIARY EXCERPTS:

Tonight "Jimmy" (a big, sinister looking regular who often gives himself mottled looking hair cuts with a disposable lighter on the front steps of the drop-in centre) came in barefoot and covered from head to foot in fresh, smelly human excrement. He wouldn't say how he got that way. We made him walk around the block to the alley door in back and I hosed him off while Brother Tim looted the sisters' clothing room.

"You've been having a bad day," I suggested, trying to make conversation.

"Not really, shit washes off," Jimmy shrugged.

"Words to live by," Brother Tim quipped as he arrived with a towel and soap, some jeans and underwear, a flannel shirt, a sports jacket, and some running shoes.

"I couldn't find any socks," he apologized.

᠅   ᠅   ᠅

The Door Is Open is as popular as it is because the place shows movie videos (from the 1800 titles in the collection Brother Tim has begged, borrowed, compiled, numbered, and catalogued) instead of the usual situation comedies and sporting events that most other drop-in centres show on their televisions. And Brother Tim distributes free program listings of the movies he will be screening a month in advance, with regularly scheduled popular events like showing that week's most popular "Just Released" video one afternoon and evening a week.

Since nearly all popular movies nowadays have bad language and sex scenes Brother Tim doesn't worry about censorship and he schedules most of the Action and Comedy movies his patrons request, with the sole exception being the Sunday at noon time-slot which is always a Disney film just in case one of the senior parishioners of St. Paul's chapel next door should happen to peek in from the common porch and be offended.

(Incidentally, Die Hard is the most popular movie at The Door Is Open.)

☙ ☙ ☙

I overheard a guy in the sandwich line say: "Yea, I'm grateful for the free sandwiches the sisters give me. They alleviate just about one percent of my problems for fifteen minutes or so. Yea, tell the sisters I really fucking appreciate it."

☙ ☙ ☙

The most depressing thing about being a volunteer in a skid row charity is that although you want to help, you end up saying "no" eighty percent of the time.

"No, we don't have any more sandwiches."

"No, there is no sugar or milk or coffee, only tea."

"No, they didn't leave me the key to the clothing room."

CHAPTER TWO

Christian Charity

EVERY AFTERNOON around 2:30 a couple hundred very aggressive sea gulls begin to land on the right and centre fields of the
baseball diamond in Oppenheimer Park. The birds have been trained
over generations. They know that precisely at 3:30 the Franciscan
Sisters of the Atonement sandwich line opens for business, and they
fly down from murky Burrard Inlet for their fair share of the daily
bread. Any pick-up softball games in progress have to be postponed,
because these are tough birds that won't share an inch of territory with
puny mammals they outnumber 30 to 1.

The sandwich line began accidentally in 1932 when a hobo popped
his head through the kitchen window of St. Paul's church rectory and
told Sister Antoinette that he was starving. Good Franciscan that she
was, she gave him the sandwich she was about to eat for lunch. The official ministry of the Sisters at the time was working with the poor
Japanese who lived on small fishing boats and in the crowded tenements
of "Little Tokyo"—ministering to the old or sick, teaching English, and
running a free day care and kindergarten for exhausted mothers who
spent sixteen-hour days working in the numerous canneries along the
industry cluttered shores of the busy port a few blocks north.

The next day the hobo returned with two friends and Sister
Antoinette made sandwiches for them all. The day after that a dozen

hungry men showed up for lunch and the sisters have been in the bread line business ever since.

Unfortunately the sisters' sandwich lines are longer today than ever before, because poverty in Canada affects more people today than ever before, and is more permanent.

The bored, bread line patrons shuffle single file from the church garden window with two sandwiches wrapped in wax paper, a piece of fruit, and a styrofoam bowl of rice or chili, and many sit down in the park in a broad circle around the flock of noisy gulls and feed them their crusts and leftovers. It's one of the better soup kitchen meals around town except for the "fish" sandwiches that are made from donated salmon that the sisters tin themselves. Those are an acquired taste, and since a fifth of every day's production is usually fish sandwiches, many of them are tossed whole to the delighted gulls. It is the reason why they come.

"The sisters should try eating what they serve," is a common bread line complaint about fish sandwiches.

There are only eight sisters left in the Vancouver order because no one seems to get vocations for a religious life anymore. The youngest is fifty-eight, and the rest are over eighty—old enough for many of them to have known Sister Antoinette personally. But they still manage somehow to scavenge and prepare all that donated food every day with an ever-shrinking volunteer base. Their slowest time is the day after Welfare Wednesday when they hand out as few as two hundred lunches. Then the numbers of free meals served daily climbs steadily until it reaches over one thousand in the cold, broke days just before the next Welfare Wednesday.

One Sunday a month the sisters prepare a hot, sit down meal for one thousand, and serve it to one hundred diners at a time. They also run a popular free used clothing room and an unlisted emergency food bank. But the sisters are nothing very special. There are fifty-nine other poverty programs in the downtown eastside because it is a neighbourhood desperately in need of some Christian charity.

Christian charities become established in skid row neighbour-hoods because there is a large need for them, and because the people who work in them sincerely want to help in some small, Christ-like fashion. Creating and maintaining soup kitchens is a compassionate response to the shock of seeing hungry, homeless people on the streets—people who have so visibly fallen through the broad cracks of our welfare system.

&- &- &-

Poverty is extraordinarily complicated. After paying $350 rent for a crummy, five- by nine-foot hotel room, a single person trying to live off the remainder of their $496 per month welfare cheque has to memorize the business hours of every soup kitchen or they will starve, especially if they smoke and need to occasionally buy tobacco. Breakfast, lunch, and dinner are a matter of persistence—of queuing in the right place at the right time. And it is easy to get trapped in the bread line shuffle because at least it gives the security of a nearly full stomach. Knowing where your next meal is coming from can be a relief, even when it comes from a barred window in a church garden with a hundred or so hungry men in line in front of you.

A small sampling of the free food available in the downtown eastside begins with coffee at The Dugout (59 Powell) when it opens at 7:20 a.m., and you can have a cup of soup and a bun there at 7:40 if you have enough patience to stand in the same line twice. First United Church (320 E. Hastings) serves hot soup at 8:30, and Harbour Light (119 E. Cordova) serves coffee at 9:30, and then a hot lunch at 11:00. The Door Is Open (373 E. Cordova) serves bowls of hot, homemade stew when they open at 11:00 everyday. St. James (303 E. Cordova) serves a hot meal at 1:30 on Tuesday, Wednesday, and Saturday. Union Gospel Mission (616 E. Cordova) serves coffee and muffins after their bible study classes at 2:00. The Franciscan Sisters of the Atonement serve their hearty picnic lunch at 3:30 and then it is back to The Dugout for more soup and buns at 5:00, and Harbour Light at 6:30 for a hot dinner every evening except Tuesdays and Thursdays. At 8:00 the last hot meal of the day is served at Union Gospel, but the Street Church (175 East Hastings) serves soup and sandwiches at 9:00.

Simple.

One old alcoholic roguishly told me, "Where would I be without religion, eh? I'd have starved to death, for sure!"

A few years ago the Franciscan Sisters of the Atonement were audited by some Catholic social workers. Their report recommended that the sisters give up their sixty-five-year-old sandwich line and concentrate their meagre resources on more "empowering" programs. The social workers subtly accused the sisters of perpetuating the deviant lifestyle of alcoholics living in Oppenheimer Park and the vacant lot across the street from The Door Is Open—foggy men and women who depend upon the sisters for their one and only meal every day. The report cited several examples of malnourished men who have stood in their sandwich line for more than a decade, and reasoned that nothing ever changes if nothing ever changes.

Unfortunately nobody seems to have asked the bread line patrons for their point of view about closing their soup kitchen. If they had they would have discovered that the bread line shuffle beats most of the other ways to pass a day with no money. Who after all wants to go home when that is a cheap hotel room that is sprayed for vermin once a month, and it isn't enough? Who wants to hang out alone in their five- by nine-foot room when the surfaces of everything are often alive with roaches?

Soup kitchens serve a large social need for the very lonely poor. There are hardly any public community centres in the downtown eastside except for the Carnegie Library, which has become so dangerous that they hired bouncers to man the front door. Many more people buy drugs there than read books. The soup kitchens, and the sidewalks outside them, have become areas for socializing—safe places to josh with your line mates and pass around bottles of rice wine.

Soup kitchens are popular not because of their free food, but because they are one of the only places left for the poor urban nomad to find social acceptance—sort of like warm public living rooms where they are never treated as specimens of some disease.

Acceptance is so paramount that soup kitchen protocol insists you don't stare at people who may be pacing, laughing out of context, or talking to themselves. Everyone at a table is included in the general conversation—no matter how shy, drunk, insane, or obnoxious—because total acceptance is the only thing that can connect with such a restless, transitional society, where so many people leave town daily chasing rumours of jobs, and many more arrive for the same reason. In studies performed in skid rows all over Canada, approximately sixty-five percent of soup kitchen guests change every three to six months, largely because so many have recently been in jail, are awaiting a trial date, or are currently engaged in breaking the law—precarious lifestyles that necessitate periodic escapes in the middle of the night. Only the alcoholics and untreated mentally ill seem to stubbornly stay put for years.

And most soup kitchen patrons generally appreciate the accepting atmosphere. To have a problem in common is as close to love as some poor and homeless people are likely to get, and I've heard more than one guy say, "When I'm rich again, the sisters will get a big cheque from me. Hell, they've fed and clothed me for almost three years now!"

       ⅌ ⅌ ⅌

Brother Tim describes his own drop-in centre simply: "It's a place for people to keep out of the rain, and a place to rest and be safe because the staff will not allow violence or bottles." Around 350 people have hot cups of tea there every afternoon and evening, and watch television, or play cards.

When Brother Tim was transferred to Vancouver they gave him a condemned building, a storeroom full of stale tea bags and mice, and a budget of zero dollars. Less than two months later he had somehow gutted, refinished, and repainted the building with begged and borrowed materials. He managed to recruit hundreds of volunteer tradespeople because Brother Tim has an effervescent, entrepreneurial type of personality that many people have trouble saying "no" to.

Once when a pious volunteer asked Brother Tim why he refused to start up a bible study class, or form a prayer group, like in many of the other Christian Charities, I overheard Brother Tim reply flatly: "Because I'm not an asshole."

And then he told us about how on his first night in Vancouver he went for a free supper at one of the Pentecostal missions. He was incognito, checking out the competition down the block, when suddenly the yelping preacher was wagging his righteous forefinger in his face and howling, "You are a piece of garbage in the sight of God!"

When Brother Tim began to chuckle because he has been a faithful friar since 1954, the preacher yelped, "Go ahead and laugh, Satan! I got your number now, and you will cause no more mischief in my house."

And then the preacher strutted back up to his pulpit and began to spout a half dozen different homilies—all at the same time. That was when Brother Tim leaned over and asked his pew-mate, "So what do you gotta do to get fed around here?"

"Take Jesus into your heart, brother," was the bored, insincere reply.

The Door Is Open is popular because Brother Tim learnt his lesson and does not force God into the routine. Under his directorship, there is only one small, token crucifix left on the walls of the drop-in centre. But sometimes new people are bewildered that they do not have to sing about Jesus for their meagre lunches, as in many of the other Christian Charities. A while ago an old native man offered to shake my hand. I think he was intending to thank me for the unexpected, freshly baked muffin he was munching, so in my best hail-fellow-well-met manner I said, "My name's Bart, what's yours?" and he became instantly flustered and angry.

"I was raised a Cat'lic in a residential school in the Cariboo," he spurted, "and it is none of your business what my name is. I got a right to a free cup of tea just like any other Cat'lic, don't I? I paid my dues."

I tried to tell him that you didn't have to be Catholic or even remember your name to have a cup of tea here, but he would not be consoled. And I think that says something about fire and brimstone missionaries to the poor. Harsh words like "sin" and "sinner" imply that the poor deserve their fate—and by focusing on poor people's bad behaviour, they hide the poverty causing the behaviour, and blame the victims. After all, who amongst us wouldn't fornicate more casually, drink too much, or do hard drugs if we had to live in desperate poverty, without hope, and little faith in human institutions? If you cannot even envision a secure future, let alone plan for one, it becomes inevitable that you begin living in the present, because within such a bleak personal landscape there is neither real fear of HIV or addiction, nor any hope of heavenly salvation.

º º º

There are sixty poverty programs in the downtown eastside. Each addresses facets of specific problems without collaborating with the other agencies or working together in a comprehensive manner. The communication between program workers is almost intentionally fragmentary, inconsistent and territorial—too often because they are in direct competition for the same limited funds, and because non-profit organizations seem to have a need to justify the funding they are receiving by doing much of their work "on their own."

But different as the skid row programs are, they share many features. They are usually formed through trial and error and depend upon peer support. They are small and employ few experts. And miraculously they survive for long periods. Many of the programs are run in large church basements—the abundant space recalling an earlier, happier time when congregations were wealthy and numerous and the church played a central role in the social life of the neighbourhood. Nowadays the downtown eastside churches have more pew than flock, more history than future, and most of the soup kitchen volunteers live outside of the community. Of the estimated seventy parishioners of St. Paul's (the small chapel beside The Door Is Open), only four actually live within the parish borders.

One strange thing I have noticed talking to the various skid row program managers is that they seem to cope with their jobs better than the public poverty workers I've met. Public health nurses, welfare and social workers, the police and probation officers all seem to wrestle with burnout problems. But religious workers hardly ever do—perhaps because they see at least part of their mission in life as service to the poor.

Or maybe it's because very religious people have one basic thing in common with the homeless: They can't live in the real world! Nuns often situate themselves in rough places where no one else will go, and thrive. Much of their strength stems from their ability to reach into the poorest sections of society and, simply by giving food and clothing and a cheerful daily greeting, provide real solace.

Soup kitchen workers regularly work in situations where they are outnumbered 200 to 1 by "guests" whom most of society labels as unstable and dangerous. This would seem to be very stressful but it seldom is. Every soup kitchen, when it opens its doors and feeds as many hungry people as it can without infantilizing stuff like forms, eligibility requirements, or demands for change, creates an instantaneous sense of community.

One of the regulars at The Door Is Open summed it up best when he told me: "I got enough people telling me what a mess I've made of my life. I've heard it all before from coast to coast and I don't want to listen to it anymore. No one can tell me something I don't already know. I hang out in soup kitchens because nobody there reminds me what a loser I'm supposed to be."

The only soup kitchen workers who occasionally do get punched out are the ones who preach, so I never understood the thankless, evangelizing impulse of some of my fellow skid row charity volunteers until one night when "Billy" stumbled into the drop-in centre after being released from Vancouver Pre-Trial down the block. Billy is a famous jailhouse storm trooper serving life on the instalment plan— six months here, fourteen months there, two-years-less-a-day some-place else. Hundreds of crude blue and green tattoos cover his face and long, muscular forearms. The stories about his many barroom brawls are terrifying for their brutality and viciousness.

Billy started loudly boasting to all of us that he was a two-time, cold-blooded murderer and he was looking for a good fight. No one dared to even mutter the usual:

"Shad-up, already. I can't hear the TV."

It was the only time I was truly frightened for my own safety at the drop-in centre. I knew if Billy started a fight it would be my responsi-bility to try and break it up. And if he knocked me down to the floor and started raking me with his Dayton motorcycle boots, he would show no mercy. Well-intentioned white liberals like me have no value in his apocalyptic world.

Billy stared each and every one of us down. When no one was will-ing to fight him, he screamed, "Jesus Fuck!"

That was when one meek, tiny, malnourished hobo stood up and said with uncanny authority and firmness: "Jesus CHRIST! You should say Jesus Christ, ok? He was the Saviour of Man and deserves respect!"

For a few painful seconds Billy stared at that one scrawny bum who had the guts to stand up to him. Then he turned his back and walked quietly away and the entire room breathed a long, loud sigh of relief. Watching this sublime event it occurred to me that is why so many Christian zealots man the skid row soup kitchens. They come not necessarily to convert, but because it is the only place they can be truly open about their embarrassing Christianity. In a soup kitchen their zeal is tolerated, their blind faith is accepted, just as long as it respects certain limits. Joyous Christians are welcomed—just as are alcoholics, junkies, and the untreated mentally ill—in the same open, patient way that everyone else is accepted.

When I first started volunteering at the drop-in centre I did not seem to be religiously motivated and soon there were rumours that I was a cop, or a pervert. Now the regulars have stopped asking me why I come. It is enough that I am dependable and harmless.

In the beginning, I suppose I came back on Monday and Wednesday evenings because I wanted to feel needed, or I wanted to make my own life more meaningful, or for some other equally selfish reason. But I know now that all that separates me from the homeless men and women I serve is a couple of paycheques. You just need to sit still and let the world of the poor flow around you to get a sense of its moods and rhythms—and ask questions, as in any other world—and you'll hear how fragile the human condition is, and how lives can come crashing down in a heartbeat because of some accident, layoff, illness, death of a loved one, or a divorce.

℣   ℣   ℣

The sudden urge to do good deeds is not uncommon. Well-intentioned people often come by the drop-in centre wanting to help. But then they see the ugly, open, physical and psychological wounds of some of the patrons and they recoil. Brother Tim gives all the new volunteers the same hopeful speech he gave me and they usually schedule their first shift for the next week. But they often never come back. Of the ones who stay awhile Brother Tim asks only that they be gentle and kind and unjudgmental, and he patiently lets them find their own peculiar styles of service.

Often volunteers arrive with strange mandates. One zealous volunteer went through nearly 2000 or more videotapes in the film library that Brother Tim has collected for his popular movie nights. She marked all the "pornographic" ones with a large black X and then wrote the archbishop a letter about the dirty movies being shown in a Catholic charity. Later, during one of the frequent interruptions that were common in my interviews with Brother Tim, I reached up and randomly pulled down three of the X'd videos from the office shelves: *All the President's Men*, *The Muppet Movie*, and *Stand by Me*.

Brother Tim told me, "Unfortunately, volunteers who arrive with secret agendas are more common than I expected they would be when I first started. And you can't always tell who the crackpots are at first. I caught one volunteer and his wife baptizing people under the back stairwell. When I suggested that they go see a priest and get it done right, the volunteer got mad at me and said: 'That just proves that you're not a real Christian.' "

And I can think of six or seven examples from my own volunteer experience, of feverish people who claimed to see the Holy Spirit working in the most unlikely situations, who desperately wanted to become divine instruments, and then left after only one or two shifts.

Take "Albert." He's a normal enough seeming, middle-aged guy who is often invited by small Catholic prayer groups around the Lower Mainland to give his inspiring talk about the evangelization work he does down at The Door Is Open. I've heard him speak three times and it is powerful (if repetitious) stuff, full of inspirational stories about long-lost sons reunited with good Catholic mothers dying of cancer back in Northern Ontario, and alcoholics who never drank again because he prayed over them, and numerous prostitutes who gave up their awful careers because of rosaries he pressed into their hands on Christmas Eve. (Remarkably, Albert's former "harlots" always seem to marry well.)

But Albert isn't actually a volunteer at the drop-in centre. Nor has he ever been. In fact I've only seen him down there once, trying to get people to sign a petition demanding Brother Tim's dismissal because he refused to let a charismatic choir come in and pray over his patrons.

There are only fourteen volunteers at The Door Is Open—not very many considering it's open every day and most of us have jobs and families and donate only four or eight hours of our time every week. Brother Tim bridges the manpower gap with the 1500 hours of community service time that is served there annually. Last year nearly 200 people worked off their debts to society cleaning and polishing and painting at the drop-in centre a couple days a week.

Brother Tim told me once, "In many ways the community service hour guys are easier to manage than the volunteers because they have no secret agendas except for maybe sneaking a joint in the staff washroom. Last year only two did not work out. They do their time and leave and that is an attitude I can appreciate from my prison experience." (Brother Tim's favourite gig so far—until he was pushed off a balcony during a riot—was the ten years he spent as a prison padre at Riker's Island. Because of that hard fall he is stone deaf in the right ear, and has lost sixty percent of the hearing in his left.)

And then Brother Tim said, "When I first started here I was worried that I was taking advantage of a slave labour pool. But a lady at the Elizabeth Fry Society (a non-profit organization that runs dozens of correctional programs in Vancouver, and seventeen other Canadian cities), helped me see the point of community service hours. They are meant to be a strong warning to people who have made one or two relatively non-violent mistakes. And cleaning toilets in a skid row mission can be a strong personal lesson.

"The drop-in centre is better because of community service hour servers," Brother Tim insisted. "Our patrons get more interaction with more varied people. Some of the community service staff make strong one-on-one connections down here."

One electrician who served his community service time for driving while intoxicated by replacing the depression-era wiring of the cavernous drop-in centre, has now become a sort of unofficial labour manager, lining up his building contractor friends with his skid row buddies—guys who held his ladder and handed up tools during the three solid weeks he spent crawling around in the mice infested ceiling. I watched him do it, and believe me, he repaid his debt to society.

Another community hour server painted luscious cloud murals on the walls of Sister Maura's sobriety centre upstairs and served over one hundred additional hours doing it. He joked with Brother Tim that he wanted those extra hours held in his account just in case he got in trouble again.

&ε&   &ε&   &ε&

A fellow volunteer at the drop-in centre summed up the bread line shuffle best when she told me: "Problems sort of compound themselves in the downtown eastside. The whole neighbourhood is poor and it's easy to be poor there. The missions and bread lines don't change people's lives. They just feed and clothe them and help them survive a little more humanely. For most, the downtown eastside is a good place to spend what little money they have on cheap booze or drugs and forget about all their problems for a little while longer while waiting in line for another free meal."

Brother Tim agreed that helping the poor survive is usually the best he can do. But then he said, "Soup kitchens are really just a visible sign that something is wrong with society. But they are also the glue that holds compassionate communities of poor people together."

DIARY EXCERPTS:

Once Brother Tim came back late from a Police Community Liaison meeting and found over twenty-five men standing in line outside his locked office door.

"Hey, hey, Bro!" several guys in line called out to him when he walked through the front door.

"Tim, Tim, over here! Remember me?" one old guy near the end of the line called. "I hope you got enough so I can get some."

"Enough what?" Brother Tim asked him. "I got nothing to give away."

"But someone said you was going to give away something good when you get back," the old man complained.

Brother Tim asked the deflating mob if anyone knew what it was he was supposed to give them? Not one of them did.

&   &   &

Some graffiti spray-painted in crimson red across the windshield of a Salvation Army van proclaims: "Charity is not Justice!"

&   &   &

Ten people died of heroin overdoses in the Lower Mainland last weekend. On Thursday, February 22nd (1996) there were five fatal overdoses, and then four more on Friday. One more man died on Saturday the 24th before the purity was readjusted and things reverted to the usual four or five fatal overdoses per week.

Because of such brisk business of bodies needing disposing they have a lot of funerals for overdose victims at St. Paul's Chapel. But usually not a lot of mourners come, so Brother Tim sometimes asks drop-in centre volunteers to stand in as a congregation. This evening's funeral was for a handsome twenty-four-year-old man. His mother's short, sad eulogy went precisely as follows:

"In a way I'm glad he's dead. At least now I can go to sleep at night a little easier because I know where he is. And I can buy a new TV because I know he won't steal it. That sounds awful, doesn't it?"

CHAPTER THREE

Rice Wine, Heroin, and Crack

"... of a thousand dreams
of a thousand hopes
of a thousand yearnings for real community
lost to us
but memorialized today
brought finally into a unity
here in this community park
this park which is the geographical heart
of the downtown eastside
these thousand crosses are a protest
against the abandonment of powerless
and voiceless human beings . . ."

—Bud Osborn (from his poem "A Thousand Crosses in
Oppenheimer Park" which the poet read aloud during a memorial
service to mourn the drug overdose deaths of more than one thousand
downtown eastside residents in less than four years.)

VIC WAS talking with a frantic cousin on the kitchen telephone at
the drop-in centre. The cousin was hysterical, screaming over
the phone lines, and half the drop-in centre could hear every word of

her bullshit spilling out from the cheap phone receiver. She wanted Vic to run right over to the Sunrise Hotel and help her look for her five-month-old baby. She said she left him with someone while she was smoking crack but now she couldn't remember whom.

"I'm sure it's someone we're related to," she insisted. "I don't think I'd leave my baby with a stranger no matter how stoned I got. I'm a good mother."

But when Vic began coldly explaining to his cousin that she shouldn't call the police because they would put her in jail and put her kid in a foster home and she'd lose the extra $363 per month in welfare income her baby generated, I had to leave the kitchen. Some lives are just too stupid and depressing to eavesdrop on.

I wandered onto the front porch for a cigarette break. But instead of relief all I had to look at was a hard-boiled looking woman cradling her drunken boyfriend who had collapsed on the sidewalk in a puddle of his own piss and vomit. He struggled for a moment, and then went limp in her arms, sobbing helplessly, hiding his face in the nape of her tattooed neck.

"What's the matter? Ain't you never seen a man puke before?" The woman angrily hissed at me.

"He'll be all right," I suggested.

"Sure," she bitched, "the damned selfish bastard is indestructible, but I'm not! I . . ."

And she began to weep right along with him. I lit a cigarette and ignored them because I'd seen it before.

When I first started volunteering at the drop-in centre I looked upon drunks as a break in the monotony. But they soon became boring because they are all so much alike. Cleaning up after some rice wino's mucky party seems to be the major part of my job description, since about half of soup kitchen patrons are alcoholics. Alcoholism and drug abuse are the most common reasons cited for living in extreme poverty, and seemingly the cause of most of the social, physical, and mental health problems of skid row neighbourhoods.

The soup kitchens and drop-in centres seem to intentionally take on an "enabler's" role with the alcoholics—feeding, clothing, and seldom judging, comforting without really helping, perpetuating their existence, but expending very little real effort in trying to help them achieve a new position in life.

Alcoholics impact every health and service facility in the downtown eastside. They monopolize the system with their immediate needs, and seemingly receive what they want on their own terms. All of life's necessities (and binge money, too) are readily provided by a plethora of sixty competing services. And sometimes you can't help but think that some of these drunks are doing it on purpose—that there is nothing at all wrong with them except selfishness and self-pity, viciousness and fear. Sometimes it is difficult to tell whether some skid row alcoholics are psychologically damaged or just extremely selfish.

To be fair, part of the difficulty in helping skid row alcoholics is that their harsh social environment makes them very resistant to treatment. Homelessness and unemployment make every skid row alcoholic into a complicated case, with a multiplicity of needs. Most of the drinkers I know from the drop-in centre have lived in isolated islands of dangerous single room occupancy hotels for at least five years—unable to really remember whether their heavy drinking is a way of coping with the misery of their lousy address, or if the hovels they live in are the result of their heavy drinking.

But skid rows are also amicable places for alcoholics. They like to cluster in neighbourhoods like the downtown eastside because they are so disaffiliated from the rest of us that a bunch of drunks getting drunker around a bonfire in a vacant urban lot might be the only community left for them—the only place where they are still welcomed.

   ℇ ℇ ℇ

Brother Tim tells all the volunteers never to give money to anyone because they'll probably just get drunk or stoned with it. But sometimes you can't help yourself. Some stories are just too sad—and not to respond would make you feel inhuman. Still, I've seen a little of the frustration that Brother Tim is trying to protect us from.

One time I palmed $5 to an old woman with a dirty four-year-old boy because she said she was his grandmother and needed to buy some milk and Kraft Dinner for his supper. But ten minutes later I saw her guzzling from a bottle of rice wine in Oppenheimer Park and her kid greedily nibbling on a small bag of potato chips. They were both laughing, happy in the moment, and I felt used and angry, until I remembered what hollow comfort a box of macaroni is.

Many of my friends from the drop-in centre are unrepentant drunks. They've taught me useful things like how to strain canned-heat through a cotton T-shirt, and rubbing alcohol through stale bread. When I first started volunteering, most downtown eastside alcoholics drank Chinese cooking wine, which is a fermented rice and fruit juice stew that has been flavoured by bitter spices. That was until a public health and police campaign against rice wine forced the skid row alcoholics to rely on more expensive sources for their booze: government liquor stores, beer parlour off-sales, and bootleggers. (And you can still buy rice wine if you know where to look.)

Rice wines contain anywhere from 25- to 55-percent alcohol and before the police campaign, nearly every corner store used to sell it for between $3 and $8 a bottle, depending upon the time of day or month, how desperate their drunken customers looked, and whether or not they thought they might have enough coordination left to stumble down the street to the competition.

One of the rice wines is called "Ginseng" and it is a little more expensive and much more hallucinatory than the others. I took a sip off a circulating bottle of Ginseng once and it made my tongue vibrate like a tuning fork. Some of the rice winos periodically like to spend a week or two drinking Ginseng—taking alcoholic spirit-quests to rattle the rust from their souls. But you can't drink Ginseng for very long because it short-circuits your nervous system. I've been taught to recognize the Ginseng drinkers in the drop-in centre from their distinctive jerky gait, a condition called "Ginseng legs" by downtown eastside alcoholics.

"That stuff makes your brain get wet," one rice wino explained. "That's when you start noticing that your legs tremble every time you try and walk, and your feet start shaking, and your knees just jerk out from under you, and you end up flat on your chin on the sidewalk."

The very worst rice wine—and the one with the highest alcohol content—is nicknamed "Salty" because of its blood-blanching, high salt content that clogs the liver and corrodes the kidneys, and of course makes you thirsty with a capital T. One of the famous old men of the downtown eastside is a hulking warrior they call the Caveman because of his broad, sloping forehead. He has been drinking Salty for five months now and his mind has been twisted like a tar-stained pipe cleaner. He can't talk because his thinking has become too random to articulate. His stumbling body is a cadaver bag of short-circuited reflexes. Nothing is left but a personality of tics propped up on crutches.

From my shoeboxes full of diary notes, I distilled a three-year survey of sorts, of a few score rice winos that I met in the drop-in centre. Most of them described lives of steady-state drinking. Their average daily consumption was six bottles of rice wine, and a few cans of beer. Most downtown eastside alcoholics are male, but the less numerous women tend to drink more than the men. The average daily consumption amongst nine women I know was eight bottles of rice wine, and at least six beers.

All of the rice winos I talked with looked much older than the ages they claimed to be, but over half of them were between 35 and 45 years of age. The next most common age grouping was between 25 to 34. There are many skid row alcoholics who are over 50, but their rough, hard-drinking lifestyle has taken its toll: most of the older alcoholics I talked to were very sick (forty percent had been hospitalized during the past month), or dying from a variety of alcohol-related diseases.

The most surprising thing I discovered about the alcoholics I talked with is that two-thirds had entered some type of alcohol treatment program before, and averaged five admissions each. Over half of them told me they had completed a treatment program at least once.

℈ ℈ ℈

I attended a few Narcotics' Anonymous gatherings up in Sister Maura's Sobriety Centre, and some AA meetings at another nearby drop-in centre. Many of the people who sat around me were very drunk, or stoned, and smiling like Cheshire cats, trying to fool everyone, including themselves, I guess.

I asked a guy at a meeting with a five-year pin on the lapel of his jean jacket why abstinence programs worked for some people, but not for others. He defensively replied: "Before a guy can see anything, he's got to have his eyes opened. He's got to want to see."

When I pointed out that most of the people at that night's meeting seemed more interested in the free coffee and doughnuts than sobriety, he got mad and sputtered: "And how do you know that coming to these meetings when you're drunk won't do some good eventually? I used to come just to keep out of the rain, just like a lot of the guys here tonight. But then one evening I was sneaking out early and what a woman was saying began to make a lot of sense to me, so I sat back down and I started listening more closely. What I was hearing got me thinking that there might be hope for me to quit drinking, and now I got a good job and a car and an apartment and a nice girlfriend and I keep coming to meetings down here because I know how sometimes you can hit one of these guys with exactly the right line at the right time, and he goes for it."

And perhaps he's right. That's the way redemption works, one tortured soul at a time.

᠊᠊᠊   ᠊᠊᠊   ᠊᠊᠊

There are nearly one hundred pawnshops in East Vancouver. Many of them also operate as 24-hour convenience stores, conveniently allowing thieves to fence stolen goods day and night. A few of the pawnshops trade drugs directly for TVs and other loot. According to the Vancouver Police B&E Squad, as much as seventy percent of all break-ins are committed by drug addicts.

Crack and heroin are very easy to purchase in the downtown eastside, and cheaper than beer. You simply can't walk down the sidewalk on East Hastings without being approached by nearly every shifty-eyed adolescent you pass and asked: "Smoke? Down? Up? Rock? Powder?"

In many of the Vietnamese restaurants and Karaoke Bars on Hastings Street all you have to say to the waitress who comes to serve you is, "Down, please," and she will unblinkingly respond, "Show me the money." (Or you can say "Up" if you want cocaine, and "Rock" if you want crack.)

When you hand her $20 she will palm you a couple of chicklet-sized paper squares of beige-coloured heroin.

"You go now," the waitress will then sternly insist as she pockets your money.

Illicit drugs are the leading killer of British Columbians between the ages of thirty and forty-four. Over 336 people died of heroin overdoses in BC in 1993 when the ninety percent pure "China White" was circulating. And then there were 246 more BC heroin deaths in 1994, 175 in 1995, and 256 in 1996. (And the majority of those 1013 corpses had downtown eastside addresses.)

It wasn't until BC Ambulance Services dedicated two units to OD calls only and paramedics started administering Narcan (a narcotic antagonist that can reverse complete respiratory depression if injected into the overdosed patient quickly enough) that Lower Mainland heroin overdose deaths began to fall—to 145 in 1998, and 91 in 1999. But more responsible than Narcan for the lower death rates were the efforts of grassroots educators who encourage addicts to use the buddy system when fixing so that someone will be on hand to call 9-1-1 if they should stop breathing.

"Sure, we can bring them back now," one Paramedic I know from the hospital I work at complained to me. "But now we are getting calls for the same people over and over again."

DIARY EXCERPTS:

This man I know was weeping on the steps of the drop-in centre.
"What's wrong? Why are you crying?" I asked him.
"You know Johnny? That big ugly guy that always drinks with me?"
"Yea?"
"Well, he just raped my wife while I was passed out on the couch."

☙ ☙ ☙

A competing downtown eastside drop-in centre parks their large cube
van at the curb beside the sisters' sandwich line every afternoon. The
logo on the back door of their van boasts about "Feeding BC's Needy."
But they don't actually contribute any food or labour to the sisters' enter-
prise. So it seems they park there at that time because they're hoping to
take some fraudulent credit for feeding the long line of hungry men and
women. They must hope that the few commuters who might still be
moved by the sight of a bread line will mistakenly call the phone number
stencilled on the van box if they want to make a donation.
But the sisters can't really complain about people taking advantage of
appearances. I notice that for identical shock advertisement reasons,
they insist the sandwich line forms on the hot, sunny sidewalk in the first
place, rather than in the shady alley.

☙ ☙ ☙

Recently I heard a woman say: "I'm so glad we're finally winning the war against poverty."

She belonged to a suburban prayer group that drives into the city one Tuesday morning a month and makes sandwiches for the sisters.

"But didn't you drive through the neighbourhood on your way here?" I incredulously asked.

"Yes, but all those gross drug addicts and sleazy hookers don't count because they chose to live that way. You just can't help some people, so they don't count."

& & &

Sometimes I wonder if some of these guys I see night after night sitting in the same chairs, staring at reruns of the same stupid, mind-numbing television programs and old movies, ever get tired of trying to maintain all the common skid row fictions I hear them tell each other. I'm talking about all the stories people tell others (and themselves) to explain why they hang out in soup kitchens in the first place. As the years roll by it must get harder and harder to believe that your alcoholism (and poverty) is only transitional, that your skid row flophouse addresses are only temporary.

& & &

"You have to go now, it's closing time," I told a man I had just shaken awake.

"What good are you?" he angrily muttered. "Why do you people bother coming down here at all? You don't do nothing."

& & &

Every year or so Brother Tim takes a vacation and he asks me to take notes for him at the monthly Vancouver Food Providers Coalition meetings which are often held at The Door Is Open. The meetings are usually rather slow moving, with lots of long personal opinions expressed by many diverse grass-roots experts. A perverse thing I've noticed about poverty-related professions is that the more dangerous, useful, and necessary the work is, the less it pays, and the less training it requires.

While listening to the earnest, idealistic people who operate poverty programs talking about their problems, I began to notice that some of them are crackpots with some pretty weird and reactionary theories. But I've also noticed that colourful characters are often drawn to long-term poverty service careers because you need a forceful personality to run decent programs with inadequate funding and staffing, year after year after year. A strong sense of purpose, and a busload of faith in your own ingenuity and ability to make it up as you go along, seems to be the most essential job requirement.

At one of the meetings, a Native Elder asked if the police were responsible for nearly all the public pay phones in the neighbourhood being removed. (Because BC Tel demands $200 deposits from all new downtown eastside accounts, people in the neighbourhood rely heavily on pay phones.)

The police department officials present told the meeting that they only asked for two pay phones in Chinatown to be removed, and that they are being used as scapegoats by the telephone company who are using the opportunity to remove unprofitable and frequently vandalized pay phones.

And then the Native Elder told us about how a stranger had died in his arms a few days ago: BC Tel had removed all the pay phones on Hastings Street and his wife had to run five blocks to the Jackpot Bingo Parlour to call an ambulance but the man died just before the first panic vehicle arrived.

"A million fucking commuters whizzed by a man in the curb lane with a big fucking butcher knife sticking out of his belly," the Elder complained, "and not one of them dialled 9-1-1 on their fucking cellular phones. That's bullshit, man. That's white man's world."

CHAPTER FOUR

If You Can't Beat Them, Join Them

A BALD TEENAGED girl sitting on the pavement outside my neigh-bourhood banking machine in East Vancouver asked me: "Spare any change or cigarettes?" I recognized her spiky-haired boyfriend sitting beside her. He is a squeegee punk who works a split shift washing windshields for spare change during the morning and afternoon rush hours at this same busy intersection.

"No, sorry," I mumbled and strolled quickly by them.

"Hey," she shouted after me, "you're starting to piss me off!"

I stopped and turned back to face her. This was against the law. Panhandlers cannot harass people, or impede their progress. If you complain about a panhandler the Vancouver Police will respond quickly to a "Priority 2" call—the same as for a burglary or assault. Several other pedestrians also paused mid-stride and stared at her.

"Why do I piss you off?" I asked.

"I see you giving money and cigarettes to my friends on the other corners. But you never give me nothing. What the hell is wrong with me?"

I was stunned. It never occurred to me that panhandlers studied the competition—and compared the effectiveness of tactics. I was amazed that they could tell they were being ignored by one person, when most of the world ignores them.

"Yea, man, what's wrong with her?" her boyfriend loudly agreed and leaned forward, seemingly ready to leap to his feet.

His intimidating growl made me angry. This has been my neighbourhood for over a decade, and I usually feel safe here.

"Both of you have got big frigging swastikas tattooed on your forearms," I complained, "and that insults me, ok?"

"Oh, that's all right then," he said, chuckling a little as he reclined back against the brick wall. "Just as long as it's not personal."

But the weird thing is, swastika and all, I still somewhat respect him because he doesn't sit on the sidewalk and beg like his girlfriend. He works very hard scrubbing the windshields of impatient rush hour commuters who get caught by the long First Avenue traffic lights. "Squeegee Punks" are mostly young men, and need all their young man's energy and ambition to survive the dangerous gymnastics necessary to work amidst so many slowly moving, potentially bone-crunching vehicles. And the black leather jackets and paratrooper boots and fierce facial tattoos are an important part of their uniform. I've noticed that nine out of ten times squeegee punks will pick on cars with a single woman driving them first, because they are the most likely to feel vulnerable and intimidated by the jarring sight of a dirty, skin-headed brute suddenly beaming at them through their windshield, mere inches above their face. And I've noticed the ones who look the most frightening usually get the biggest tips.

But his girlfriend is right. I do occasionally give to other panhandlers as the spirit moves me. I give to buskers a lot because they are at least singing for their suppers, and I give cigarettes to nearly everyone who asks for one because I know how cranky and weird-thinking I can get when I have a real craving for nicotine. But the murmurs of runaway children sitting cross-legged on the cold, hard pavement are getting fainter and fainter to me and I hardly ever give them anything.

I don't seem to be alone with my increasing indifference to poverty. At the Holy Rosary Cathedral on Dunsmuir Street they posted signs on the inside of all the doors that proclaimed: "Please!—do not give to those who beg outside (or inside) the Cathedral. Unfortunately it only encourages them to use this method, and bypasses our efforts to assess the legitimate needs of those who are unfortunate in one way or another. For some, especially the elderly, to not be able to enter the Church without being harassed for money is intimidating—Giving without being able to take time to assess each person to whom one gives often encourages begging for the wrong reasons."

"But what are the right reasons?" I asked myself after reading that sign, and then looking directly at a half-dozen homeless men camping in sleeping bags and cardboard boxes in the breezy concrete amphitheatre of Cathedral Square Park across the street. On the other corner, a block-long line of hungry men and women stood outside the Salvation Army cafeteria.

     ❧ ❧ ❧

A few blocks away on Robson Street, a long downtown avenue of expensive fashion boutiques and restaurants, the merchants have responded to the blight of panhandling in a much more aggressive fashion. They've hired private security guards to patrol their building perimeters and evict poor people for loitering.

The Robson and Downtown Business Improvement Associations pressured city council for nearly a decade for evermore severe panhandling bylaws. And in April 1998, Vancouver City Council finally succumbed to their lobbying and decreed it illegal to panhandle from sunset to sunrise, or to beg within ten metres of an automated bank machine, bus stop, or liquor store.

The city hoped that they had solved the panhandling problem. Then several anti-poverty groups united and launched a court challenge of the new bylaws, calling them discriminating to the poor and an attack on their freedom of speech. And ironically, while the charter case meanders through the courts, panhandlers have become more numerous and aggressive on Vancouver streets. They know that the only response the police can make right now is to gently encourage them to change locations and suggest alternatives to begging with a brochure listing the addresses and hours of operation of all the free food and bed facilities available in the city.

Things were a bigger mess than before city council tried to fix things, so they started looking at their math again. The estimated direct costs to health care and law enforcement budgets due to drug use was $96 million in B.C. in 1997. And also there was that embarrassingly high overdose body count, and the highest rates of new HIV and HCV infections of all the cities in the western world, and an open drug bazaar on Hastings Street operating 24 hours a day, with people fixing everywhere, in the parks and sidewalks and on the front porches of private homes. City Council finally realized that they couldn't afford to sit idle anymore, and so they began looking at some unusual new strategies.

&   &   &

The Vancouver Agreement is a $30 million, five-year commitment from the City and Provincial and Federal governments to a four-pillar approach to the drug problems in the Lower Mainland (those pillars being: Harm Reduction, Treatment, Enforcement, and Prevention). Not surprisingly, the largest proportion of the money and focus will be spent on the downtown eastside.

The thirty-one recommendations of the Vancouver Agreement are modelled after successful programs in Portland, Frankfurt, Merseyside in Liverpool, and Switzerland.

Harm reduction related recommendations include safe injection sites, more accessible methadone therapy, and street-drug testing to inform the public about changes in drug quality. The treatment goals of the plan are increased detox beds, increased primary care facility participation, more residential and home-based withdrawal management programs, more ongoing medical care at the street level, more temporary and emergency housing, more entry points for employ-ment services and life skills training, and more support for the families of addicts.

The Enforcement portion of the proposal gives the Vancouver police a sweeping mandate to attack the street drug culture and make the city streets (particularly around Main & Hastings) as safe and clean and drug-free as the Canadian Charter of Rights will allow. The agreement proposes to deal with the increased arrest rates with the formation of specialized drug courts that will give stiffer penalties for mid- and high-level dealers, and steer drug users into treatment facili-ties rather than jail.

The Prevention pillar proposes citywide drug and drug abuse education in all schools, and encourages neighbourhoods and com-munities to fight drug abuse under the coordination of a Drug Action Team.

Now that's a pretty severe about-face in attitude for a mayor and city council that only the year before had thought they could make many of their poverty problems disappear by stopping people from begging.

☙ ☙ ☙

I attended one of the six town hall meetings that the city held to invite public commentary on their "Framework for Action." The mayor and six of the eleven city councillors were present, and as I looked around the large meeting room I saw many of the same faces I used to see at the Vancouver Food Providers Coalition meetings at The Door Is Open.

One of the panel of experts made a twenty-minute "power point" presentation of the proposal. After that, four panel members were sup-posed to give five-minute speeches about each of the "pillars" of the strategy. But when it was time to speak about Enforcement, the police department representative announced: "The Vancouver Police will not support three of the thirty-plus recommendations. We cannot allow safe consumption facilities. Nor will the police department publicly announce street drug testing results. And we feel that the recommendation calling for prescription heroin should be removed from the draft discussion paper completely."

And then he folded his arms over his chest and stubbornly refused to say anything else for the rest of the meeting except that, "Heroin and cocaine are illegal in Canada, and until the Controlled Drugs and Substances Act is changed, the Vancouver Police Department will enforce it to the best of their capabilities."

And then the video camera was turned towards the microphone stand at the back of the room where people had lined up to speak and ask questions. Many of them talked about their poverty programs and small grass-roots organizations. There seemed to be quite a few drug prevention educators, some of them openly pitching their services. One guy who read his website address into the public record apologized to the whole room: "I hate making everyone listen to my sales pitch like this. But no one can tell me what the correct channels for submitting new program ideas are." Seemingly, no one on the panel of experts could either.

"What is the strategy for finding all the little grass-roots organizations?" one young woman asked the panel. She wanted someone to pay for the coffee and doughnuts and blankets her half-dozen friends give out every Saturday night when they patrol the downtown eastside alleys from midnight to dawn.

When I first started volunteering at The Door Is Open in 1994, there were sixty downtown eastside charities and poverty-related programs. Now there are seemingly hundreds of small groups wanting their fair share of the $30 million government commitment to the new drug strategy. Everyone seems to have a program or two that addresses facets of some of the problems, but no one mentions all the redundancy and duplication of services that already exists in the downtown eastside. They just want to plaster it on a little thicker.

There is no real coordination of poverty programs in the downtown eastside, partly because so many are run by well-intentioned amateurs and self-taught experts who feel quite territorial about their pet programs. As they took their turns at the open microphone, everyone politely praised the mayor and city council and the new proposal. But then their transparent sales pitches began, as many of those strong individualists who run addiction and poverty programs seemed unable to resist embracing this vast new pool of funding as a lucky opportunity to finally "launch" their own personal, divergent "solutions" for all the social problems of the neighbourhood.

After leaving the public forum I was left with the unsettling perception that there was no real central coordination for the bold new plan, and probably never could be. And without realistic management of the health care and law enforcement components of the strategy, harm reduction could make things worse for the downtown eastside. Those autonomous European city-states we are haphazardly imitating have thousands more treatment and detox beds than Vancouver, and their safe consumption facilities are directly integrated with primary care medical facilities and not harassed by the Police as Vancouver's pilot sites apparently will be. And the poor of Frankfurt and Switzerland have adequate housing and diets, and the addicted mentally ill don't live on the streets.

DIARY EXCERPTS:

On Granville Street today I was waiting for my transfer and a pan-handler asked a well-dressed man for a quarter and the man sneered: "Get a job!"

And then the panhandler punched him in the nose and ran away.

☙ ☙ ☙

A lonely single mother of a busy toddler complained to me, "It is very depressing to have to decide whether to risk meeting a friend for a cup of coffee, or saving the $2 just in case I need to buy some children's aceta-minophen.

"And it was very hard," she insisted, "to get over all the useless middle-class values I had before I became a single mother. It was very hard for me to learn to stop going through life expecting to get whatever I wanted."

"I never thought I would end up on welfare," is quite a common sentiment amongst drop-in centre patrons. They are normal human beings with dreams and ideals and yearnings—but they live in an impoverished world which is small and petty—limited at every turn.

☙ ☙ ☙

Trying to supplement inadequate social assistance cheques makes wel-fare parents into bottom-feeders—perpetually searching for refundable cans and bottles wherever they walk, clicking coin return levers at every pay phone and newspaper box, scrounging from friends and family.

Nearly every welfare recipient I've talked with admitted cheating in some small way. Cleaning houses for undeclared cash, waiting restaurant tables during busy lunch and dinner rushes for tips and take-out food for their children, storing hundreds of pounds of smelly marijuana while it cures, and taking "loans" from casual "boyfriends" are just some of what I've heard about. They all claimed that they had to cheat to survive. This stark truth was confirmed by a BC Benefits caseworker who told me: "Of course we know everyone cheats on welfare, otherwise they'd be dead."

℞ ℞ ℞

Dumpster diving can be a practical and profitable way to pass another day without money. It gets you out of the downtown eastside for a few hours and you get lots of fresh air and exercise and you can work your own hours. Vic has been teaching me and my kid some of the nuances of the profession in exchange for a ride in my car out to distant, profitable neighbourhoods. All you really need is lots of spare time and some work gloves, a stick or cane to poke and push around garbage bags, a razor or pocket knife to slash the bags open if they look interesting, and a sturdy sack to carry away your salvage. In a couple of hours we found nearly $20 in refundable beverage containers, some sealed tin cans of tuna and chili, clothing, money, books, magazines, and working power tools. Vic cut off the electrical cords of all the discarded appliances we came across and tied them to his belt because he sells them to a scrap metal dealer for their copper wire.

CHAPTER FIVE

But the Harder I Work, the Poorer I'm Getting!

S OME OF US were loafing on the front steps of the drop-in centre one warm summer evening when a chubby cop jogged by. You could tell he was a police officer because of the black handle of a riot baton that stuck out from the top of his lumpy knapsack.

"Evening, constable," someone called after him.

The chubby cop gave him a suspicious, sideways glance and then barked: "Get a life!"

"I got a life," the hobo laughed. "What I need is a good job like you got."

☙ ☙ ☙

Nine out of ten jobless Canadians qualified for (Un)Employment Insurance in 1989, but because of the harsh, systematic changes to eligibility requirements since then, only three in ten Canadians who lost their jobs in 2000 qualified. Those that did qualify found that the length of time they could receive benefits (and the bi-weekly sum of their pogey cheques) was now half of what it used to be.

The BC Ministry of Human Resources responded to the huge

increase of unemployed workers applying for welfare during that time by redesigning their social assistance bureaucracy, and giving it a tough new mandate to increase the "diversion rate" of all applicants to fifty percent. The first thing they changed was their name, to "BC Benefits," and then they used the excuse of a new letterhead to rewrite all their forms in more opaque and confusing language, making them longer and more personally intrusive. Now they make all new welfare applicants join job-search programs and attend mandatory "pre-eligibility" information sessions. All parents applying for welfare must submit to a home visit by a caseworker, which in itself is enough to scare away many single mothers who are rightfully fearful of the BC government's bad reputation for child apprehensions from poor families.

But just what are you supposed to do when you have lost your job and discover, after weeks of standing in lines and filling out forms, and attending information seminars and keeping appointments with petty government clerks, that you don't qualify for either (Un)Employment Insurance or welfare, and the rent or mortgage payment is past due, and there is no food in the fridge, and your cranky kids haven't eaten anything but salted soda crackers and tap water since yesterday morning?

(And if you think it can't happen to you, Statistics Canada announced in June 2000, that the average Canadian is only two months away from welfare if they should lose their job.)

&   &   &

Only one in five Canadian women have steady full-time jobs with annual incomes over $30,000. A statistical composite of Canada's most typical working poor would be a young, divorced, single mother.

Like "Cindy." She is a small woman in her early thirties who just began working again after ending up on welfare two years ago when she left her physically abusive husband.

A few days ago, I watched her park her badly dented, late model Toyota at the curb beside the school playground and pull herself out through the open, passenger door window. None of the car's doors will open since the time her seven-year-old son popped the parking brake and coasted the vehicle into the brick wall of his little sister's day care. The car's bumper is tied on with twisted coils of wire clothes hangers, and the hood is tied down with a pink skipping rope.

Cindy spread her lips apart with a thumb and forefinger and blew a loud, mournful whistle across the nearly empty school grounds. Then she saw me playing basketball with my kids and came over and asked if I had seen her son. I told her that he was playing on the tire swings a little while ago, and we both scanned the schoolyard horizons for him. He was nowhere in sight, and Cindy was getting anxious.

"I bet you think I'm a bad Mom, don't you?" she said. "For leaving my kid to play here unattended after school every day." She began to weep, and turned her face away so I couldn't see her tears.

"Man, I fucking hate my life," Cindy moaned. "Every fucking minute it's hassles, hassles, hassles, all day fucking long, like a long slow fucking death by a thousand fucking cuts."

And then in a run-on swoosh of expletives and complaints she told me all about her life's predicaments, about her problems with her children and men, and about some of the things she had always wanted in her life and was now afraid she would never have—like a good job, a nice home, a real car, money in the bank, one dependable man to grow old with.

She told me that when she was trying to get off welfare and looking for a job, her caseworker promised to provide some support in the form of day-care subsidy. But when she found a part-time office job (28 hours a week) for $16.15 an hour she discovered that BC Benefits would only give her a day-care subsidy of $300 per month. Cindy has to make up the difference for the real cost of her daughter's day care ($500 per month) out of her small paycheque, and must leave her seven-year-old to play unattended in the school playground after school and go to the food bank every Tuesday morning. And she's still worse off than she was on welfare.

"And my office manager is getting really pissed at me," she told me, "because I'm always late for the morning staff meeting and I have to make a lot of personal phone calls to mooch last minute free childcare from my friends whenever one of my kids has a dentist appointment or there's a professional development day at school, or something else."

I suggested that she should consider going back on welfare until her daughter is in kindergarten. Cindy told me that if she quit her job, BC Benefits would penalize her and wouldn't give her any money for at least two months, and she wouldn't qualify for (Un)Employment Insurance because she worked part-time.

"I'm really mad at the whole welfare system," she complained. "When I applied for BC Benefits in the first place they made me take a Job Search Training Program for two months. It was just a bunch of stupid, meaningless pep talks that never took into account the harsh realities of being one of the working poor, or what it's like to have to live on welfare. They build up people's confidence and expectations and promise to help you and then they don't, and they're really just setting everyone up for failure and making them feel like real losers."

"Wait," I interrupted her with some good news. "I think I see your son. He's over there, kicking a soccer ball with those kids behind the portables."

"I gotta go," she said. She sprinted across the playground to grab her son so they could rush off together to pick up his sister at the day care and then go home where Cindy would cook them supper and help them with their homework and bathe them and read them bedtime stories and then do all the laundry, the dishes, the vacuuming the endless, unshared drudgery of single parenting. Her daily death by a thousand cuts.

☙ ☙ ☙

If you're an unemployed male and are not afraid of some hard labour with a pick and shovel you can go hang around on a "cash corner" early in the morning and try to get a casual job on one of the many small construction sites around the city.

There are many "cash corners" around East Vancouver. The term is left over from the 1930s Depression and refers to any place outside one of the numerous temporary employment agencies in town. Every weekday morning at 5:30, dozens of ambitious, broke men begin gathering outside some of the agencies a full hour before they open. They do this because many builders can't be bothered filling out paper work and hire their crews from the sidewalk.

I got up early one summer morning and hiked over to a nearby "cash corner." I noticed that the ugliness of my city is much more obvious before the sun rises and warms up the muck, and that for the employed commuters who gawked as they drove by, a block-long line-up of sullen men waiting outside a temporary employment agency serves as an abject lesson about what happens to people who lose their jobs.

The first thing I noticed was that nearly everyone in line with me had come prepared for work, and were wearing steel-toed boots and heavy work clothing. Some of them carried optimistic hard hats and thick leather gloves. A few of them had lunch boxes.

They were all a little rough in appearance, but were trying to work their way through their tough times and I can respect that. They come to "cash corner" early every morning hoping to earn some quick under-the-counter cash from some contractor who needs a few strong backs for a day or two to cut brush, paint a house or dig a ditch for drainage tiles.

"Hard ass, sweat labour," one of the old guys I met down there called it. "But any building site is better than factory work."

And most of the guys agreed with him. It seems many small factories hire them to work in dangerous conditions that their permanent workers won't accept. One of the guys showed me large pink scars from chemical burns on his hands and forearms.

I told some of the guys that this was my first morning at a "cash corner" and they helpfully explained to me how things worked. They told me that most of the building contractors who recruit their crews outside the employment agencies are solid, hard working guys who respect the value of backbreaking work. They pay at least $7 an hour in cash and sometimes feed the guys a hearty lunch and give them a ride home at the end of the day, and occasionally tip the good ones— and that's fair treatment. There are only a few bastards who underpay because they know you have no one to complain to, and you catch on pretty quick who those employers are. If the other guys won't get in the truck, then you probably don't want to work for that contractor either.

The disappointed remainder, the ones who didn't get on with any of the building contractors cruising "cash corner" that morning, shuffled into the employment office when it opened and registered themselves. I had lots of time in line to read the glossy company brochure, because first-timers have to fill out more forms and stand in more lines than the regulars. Apparently temporary labour wrangling is becoming big business. "Labour Ready," where I was that morning, filled more than 6.5 million worker orders in 1999 with 650,000 temporary labourers in their 831 branch offices in 47 US States, Canada, Puerto Rico, and the United Kingdom.

But the guys sitting in plastic orange chairs in the bleak waiting room with me explained that the temporary employment wranglers are second best to the rough handshake of a contractor outside. That's because they leave paper trails that the (Un)Employment Insurance and BC Benefits offices can easily follow. And all the labour wranglers have limited success rates. Too often you waste your time sitting around their offices re-reading old magazines, waiting all morning to hear your name called over the intercom.

By noon most of the guys had given up and left. I wandered over to the receptionist. She told me they had placed 28 of the 81 men who showed up for work that morning. The day before they placed 16 of the 99. When I asked her if those were considered good or average scores, she told me that they were pretty good because it was summer, which is the busy season for manual labour. During the long, rainy winters the construction work disappears and they average 150 to 180 men a day and place very few of them.

Hanging around a "cash corner" is a pretty depressing business. But hard as the work usually is, temporary manual labour beats most of the other ways to kill another day without money or choices. You can only stand in so many bread lines, or spend so many hours dozing in drop-in centres, before going nuts from the boredom. And best of all, a pocketful of wages differentiates you from your neighbours in skid row boarding houses. It tells everyone that you are a workingman and not another bum. And nothing quite beats the good feelings you have about yourself when your muscles buzz with residual aches left over from some tough, physical job. A couple of cold beers at a tavern on the way home taste great when you've paid for them with honest sweat.

While I was walking home from the temporary employment agency I recapped the morning in my mind. The most surprising thing I had learned was that several guys waiting around for temporary jobs with me had full-time jobs to go to later. One guy who worked midnights as a security guard complained to me: "It doesn't matter even if you are working, because I'm working full-time and I still can't make it on my paycheque." And several other resentful people told me similar stories about being unable to live off the low salaries they were paid.

Most of the conversations that killed time on "cash corner" that morning had been about the job they were on yesterday or the day before, and how the guys planned to spend the money they will earn the next time they luck into a longer-lasting job. They all wanted new televisions and portable stereos—skid row status symbols. I thought the guys were just dreaming aloud to keep warm, but then I learned that some of them had better TV's than mine. They told me about several "rent-to-own" stores where for only signing a couple of papers and paying just a "few" dollars a week, some of their material ambitions can be instantly realized.

I went to a rent-to-own store on East Broadway and told the sales-man my television was recently deceased. He showed me a 27-inch Sanyo they would instantly deliver to my home for just $74.99 a month if I would sign his 24-month rental agreement. "No credit has-sles!" was the statement he used to punctuate nearly every sentence.

When I asked him if I would own the TV free and clear after mak-ing all my rental payments for two years, he said no, but I could buy it at any time merely by paying off sixty percent of the remaining lease plus all the relevant office and service charges. When I asked him to explain the buy-out charges he got very vague. When I pushed him for an answer he finally admitted: "No one has ever asked me that before."

So I called their Surrey store and got an even more high-pressure salesman who wanted to fill out all the contracts over the phone. He promised to deliver the television to my home by dinnertime. He, too, was vague about buy-out charges and also constantly repeated, "No credit hassles." The company mantra. And then he wanted to charge me $84.99 a month for the same make and model TV. Ten dollars more than the East Vancouver store.

I shopped around. London Drugs offered a similar 27-inch Sony for $897, and Video Only had an even better JVC model with a very cool "picture in picture" on sale for $729. In comparison, the rented 27-inch TV ends up costing $1800. And you don't even get to keep it.

Listening to the aggressive rent-to-own salesmen I became grateful for my own good credit rating and the VISA card in my wallet. Even paying seventeen percent interest on my credit card, I will still pay much less for my television than any poor man with a bad or no credit rating who has to shop at one of the various rent-to-own stores because no one else will serve him. It is expensive to be poor.

I went back to Labour Ready on another morning and asked a cou-ple of guys I recognized why they were willing to pay twice as much for a television as the rest of the world. No one *needs* a TV and they are not stupid men; they could pass the time reading library books until they saved up enough money to buy a television.

Many of them said that they got lonely at night and if they didn't have their TV's to watch they would get bored and probably end up watching TV in some beer parlour and drinking away all their wages. Watching television gave them something to do at night and saved them money in the long run. Besides, very few of them had bank accounts since there was never money left over from a paycheque to save.

When I asked them how much television they watched every day I learned that when they didn't find work, they would often spend whole days at it. They sit alone in their small boarding house rooms and watch other people's exciting lives—their zest, their humour, their intimacy with each other, their tanned and beautiful bodies, their freedom, and their seemingly never-ending supply of money and choices.

I thought about how my own life never seems to measure up to those enchanting lives I see on the flickering blue screen in my living room. I thought about how watching too many "episodes" from successful people's lives can make you gradually feel that you are among the few who are missing out on life, freedom, laughter, love, intimacy. Television can deactivate you, and make you feel even more lonely because it portrays life as something to look at, something that is happening somewhere else, to other people.

The young, ambitious, manual labourer shows up at a "cash corner" every morning and works hard—hoping to impress his boss-of-the-day enough so that maybe he will hire him on full-time. He is ever-looking for that lucky break, that regular paycheque, that good job, that chance to open a bank account and get a small apartment in a nicer neighbourhood so he can begin consuming his fair share of the good life he watches and envies on his rented TV every night.

And I guess $74.99 a month is not too much to spend on your only dependable friend in the world.

DIARY EXCERPTS:

"The food bank is ok for some things," a welfare mother in line for the food bank depot that operates at The Door Is Open told me. "But I have to shoplift all my milk and eggs and butter because they never have enough."

Not surprisingly, over seventy-five percent of Canadians who use food banks are on welfare because it's impossible to live indoors and eat off a welfare cheque. Food banks are a phenomenon that is less than twenty years old in Canada, but it seems to be a growth industry. Since 1989, the number of food banks has tripled (there are currently 625 Canadian food banks), and the proportion of the population relying on them has doubled. The Lower Mainland's 16 food bank distribution depots feed 9,000 people per week, 2,700 of whom are children.

☙ ☙ ☙

Thirty-seven percent of downtown eastsiders get paid on the third Wednesday of every month, which makes Welfare Wednesday into a sacred skid row holiday, and very big business. Cheque cashing stores have line-ups around the block. Government liquor stores put on extra staff. Taxi companies can't keep up with the demand. Many Hastings Street taverns offer discounted beer, and on this, their busiest day, 1,300 people will visit the needle exchange at 223 Main Street. Most of the Christian charities take the day off because there is little demand for their secondhand charity.

A perverse and popular voyeur's sport in the Lower Mainland is cruising up and down Hastings Street on Welfare Wednesday. Paying poor people only once a month creates a feeding frenzy that some people find entertaining to watch. Staggering drunks stumble blindly through traffic, roving gangs of thugs rob the old and disabled on the sidewalks, people pass out on bus benches with needles still sticking from their arms. Driving down Hastings Street on Welfare Wednesday can be like weaving through a drunken, violent Mardi Gras of lunatics. Behaviour really does seem to be determined by economics, and poverty frees some skid row residents from ordinary standards of behaviour, just as money frees other people from work.

But a more accurate image of welfare is the thick, simmering atmosphere of impatient desperation engulfing the over half million Canadian welfare mothers waiting by their mailboxes for letter carriers to deliver their cheques. More than a million Canadian children live in families on welfare.

   ℞ ℞ ℞

A forty-seven-year-old friend named "Anna" was diagnosed with pancreatic cancer. The doctor (accurately) suggested she could expect less than three more months to live. Just like that her life was nearly over, and her fourteen-year-old son would soon be an orphan.

Her sympathetic welfare caseworker gave Anna a taxi authorization number to help her get to all the necessary hospital treatments, and doctor visits—but the first taxi driver refused to let Anna into his cab when he saw the welfare chit in her hand.

"You're supposed to tell the dispatcher that it's a welfare ride when you call for the cab!" He drove away without her.

When Anna called the dispatcher to complain, he told her that welfare authorization numbers were useless during rush hours or busy times and she would have to wait until after six if she still wanted a cab. Anna was furious and told him off. (Usually taxi drivers are the only people that the poor can boss around, providing they have the money for the fare.) The indignant dispatcher told her he was entering her name and phone number on their computer's black list and they would never respond to another of her calls again. As he hung up, the dispatcher hissed at Anna, "Get a job, you bum!" And just like that her taxi authorization number was worthless.

CHAPTER SIX

50,000 Government-Apprehended Children

I PHONED MY kid sister last weekend to see if she could lend me some more money, and she asked me if I was taking my medication, because if I was she didn't think I was taking enough, or it was the wrong kind." The words had gushed out in a sudden, breathless stream from the perplexed looking young woman sitting beside me on a couch at the community centre playroom for toddlers. I glanced around and was surprised to realize that she must be talking to me.

"So I told my sister that she's a bitch, and that she's been a bitch ever since she was born, and I told her that medication wouldn't change the fact that we had no money and would have no money for another week because there is five fucking weeks between welfare cheques this month. And then I told her that I was very depressed from worrying about our situation all the time. About worrying how to feed Charlie good food so he will stay healthy. And my sister hung up on me, the bitch!"

I noticed that a couple of young First Nations women sitting together across the toy and toddler cluttered room had stopped talking and were staring at us.

"Then it turns out my stupid sister called the psych nurse that my caseworker makes me see," the perplexed woman continued to rant, "and my sister told her that I needed more and better medication, and she told her that I spanked Charlie, which I did, twice, a few weeks ago. Two separate, individual spankings. And then that psycho-fuck nurse didn't even call me to hear my side of the story. She just turned around and told my caseworker that Charlie was having a difficult time with me, and that I was arguing with the home support people."

And the young woman began to loudly weep and blubber, publicly suffering the stress and frustration and depression of raising children alone in poverty.

"So last night, Car 86, a police cruiser manned by a social worker and a psychiatric nurse, came by my apartment to see if I really was losing my mind, or abusing my kid, and they wouldn't go away until after two hours of asking me the same fucking questions over and over again. They even made me wake Charlie so they could see if he was bruised up or brain-damaged or something.

"So thanks to my bitchy kid sister," the woman mumbled bitterly, "this has been one fuck of a week so far and I still don't have 48¢ to buy a can of food for the fucking cat. And the unfair part is my sister just did it out of spite, and if I had money she never would have got away with it! I bet middle class people never have to worry about their kids being taken away by the fucking government in the middle of the night."

"You're lucky," one of the First Nations women across the room interrupted, and then she told us how the Ministry of Children and Families had apprehended her two kids a month ago, because she yelled and swore at them too much, and her nosy neighbours tape recorded her and called the cops.

"That must be really tough," I said stupidly. I just couldn't begin to imagine the despair I would be feeling if my own children were taken away from me and I was accused of being a bad parent. And with three young boys bouncing off the walls like caged, wild animals at my place day and night, I'm yelling myself hoarse all the time.

"It's very tough," the First Nations woman complained. "I'm a good mother, but I can't get anyone to believe it. And the unfairest part of all is my lawyer told me this kind of thing almost never happens to white girls. They just have to bat their baby blue eyes and curtsy and the social workers and judges almost always give them one more chance, just like what happened for that white bitch."

I learned a little later how right both their intuitions about personal persecution were. Half of all BC children in care are Aboriginal, although First Nation's people comprise only five percent of BC's population. Aboriginal women have the lowest level of education, employment, and income in the country, and suffer the highest rates of poverty, rape and violence, incarcerations, child apprehensions, and—not surprisingly—suicide. I also learned that over $1 Billion was spent on Canadian foster care in 1999, and there were more than fifty thousand Canadian children and youth in care, and nearly all of them came from poor families. Apparently if you are on welfare you are very visible within the child apprehension system, and subject to a level of scrutiny that the rest of society is not. Welfare parents—living on incomes that are less than half the poverty line—are being judged by middle-class standards and blamed and punished for the deprivations that their children suffer along with them.

❦ ❦ ❦

Traumatized, freshly apprehended children are routinely baby-sat in hotel rooms for days, while weary, overworked social workers try to find an empty bed in one of BC's five thousand foster homes for them. But with twelve thousand kids in provincial care, it's not easy to find a space, especially if the kids have emotional or developmental problems. Problem teenagers are sometimes left living in hotel rooms for months because many are just plain dangerous around smaller children.

Kids arrive at foster homes with little or no clothing, and often bruised and malnourished, hosting lice and scabies. Their background is usually a shadowy secret to the foster home workers since the Ministry discloses as few details as possible. And since nearly all the social worker's time is squandered making court appearances, they are often too busy to properly assess the children. It's up to the foster home workers to guess what's going on with the kids and direct them into the appropriate resources and counselling.

A group foster home worker told me that when resource workers call her they often say things like: "I got a couple of four-year-olds in the bank, can you take one?" As if they were NSF cheques, requiring processing.

"Foster home workers have the most direct contact with the kids, but the least training, autonomy, and decision-making power," she complained to me.

The foster care system is so overextended that they encourage nearly anyone who expresses interest in becoming a foster parent, to try it for a while. The only qualifications people need to become foster parents are that they be between nineteen and sixty-five, and willing to submit to a medical exam, a criminal record check, and an interview in their home by a Ministry social worker to discuss family history, interests, lifestyle, and previous child-care experiences. And then they have to take a short Ministry sponsored course on child development and foster parenting.

From the outside looking in, foster parenting can seem to be reasonably lucrative. If a child is placed in the care of a relative, the BC Ministry of Children and Families will pay them $574 per month for children under eleven, and $669 for children between twelve and nineteen years of age. A foster parent receives $638 per month for each child eleven and under and $732 per month for children over twelve, and $989 per month if the child has physical or developmental disabilities, emotional or behavioural disorders. And foster parents don't have to pay taxes on most of that income if the children are living with them in their own home.

But the job is not as easy as it looks. Purely profit motivated foster parents usually drop out when they discover that raising traumatized, problem children is a lot of hard, thankless drudgery, and that being a good parent means surrendering yourself to others with an abundance of love, no matter what. Not everyone can do it. Not everyone can survive it.

                ≿ ≿ ≿

Robyn Stoy is one of the longest serving foster home operators in BC, with twelve years continuous service. One hundred and thirty foster children have passed through Robyn's Nest, her emergency group home in East Vancouver, and she has formed some strong opinions from her accumulated experiences.

"The Ministry just hired three hundred more social workers to deal with the huge backlog of contested court cases, but they are not putting any money into real resources for the kids and the families they come from," Robyn explained to me. "There's simply not enough counselling available. The waiting list for a psycho-educational assessment is over two years long, and parents and children in crisis still have to wait more than six months for family counselling.

"For all the new money the government is throwing into the system," she observed, "all the social workers really have to support reunited families is some home-support like day-care and housekeeping and taxi authorization numbers. And that just sets those families up for failure. If there was more counselling available, there wouldn't be so many repeat kids in the system."

Robyn is a confident woman in her thirties with bushy brown hair, flashing dark eyes, and a deep, contagious laugh. Most people find her very attractive. When I asked her to describe herself for this book, she said: "I'm a strong woman with a big voice. And my kids love that about me because it makes them feel safe and protected."

An average of fifteen kids a year pass through Robyn's Nest—a broad cedar A-frame house with a long, sloping tile roof on a quiet suburban street with a big city park across the way. When I visited her emergency group home with my own kids I noticed the clean laundry piled up in baskets along the wide stairwell, the sink and kitchen counter full of dishes, toys littered across every floor space, little handprints on the television screen and all the windows and mirrors. They made the place look, sound and smell exactly like my house does, on a good day.

But as soon as I crossed the kitchen threshold I overheard a frail four-year-old girl lisping into a telephone: "Are you sleeping? Did you remember to eat today? You're not drinking too much, are you?"

The bony little child seemed to be taking on the worrying role for her whole family, since seemingly her parents don't, won't, can't.

"I encourage my kids to have as much positive interaction with their parents as possible," Robyn explained to me in a whisper in the next room. "But often that is only a daily phone call. It takes some parents a couple of weeks to realize that their babies aren't away at summer camp. That they fucked up and better get their lives together for the sake of their children."

A common complaint amongst foster home workers is that many parents are angry at being placed in the position of having to ask permission to see their own kids. It often takes a long time before a civil, working relationship can develop between parents and the people raising their kids in the foster homes.

"At first the parents usually view me as M-I-N-I-S-T-R-Y," Robyn explained. "But somehow I always find a way to make connections with them for the good of their child. I am nonjudgemental and fair and very fucking honest, and eventually they begin to see that I'm taking good care of their kids, and they learn to respect me."

When I asked her to describe a composite of the parents she deals with, Robyn replied: "Every family is unique, so it's impossible to make broad generalizations like that, but a lot of the parents I get are alcoholics. They go on a binge for a few weeks a month and the whole household becomes a big party, and kids just don't fit into that kind of life. Kids can't really feel safe in homes like that. With no regular meals, no laundry, no school, no trust of anyone. For kids raised that way it is a very scary world without a lot of boundaries.

"And many of them come from generations of alcoholism and just don't seem to have the emotional or cognitive abilities to understand the long-term implications of their actions because those personal skills were never taught or encouraged when they were kids," Robyn observed. "Their own parents never taught them how to work their problems out, just how to temporarily escape them with alcohol and sex.

"But all every kid really wants is their Mom and Dad back," Robyn insisted. "No matter what. Even when home is a bug-infested slum."

All five of Robyn's current foster children have been with her more than a year, even though Robyn's Nest is supposed to be an emergency (short-term) group home. Two of the kids are permanent wards of the Ministry and they have been with Robyn since they were babies. The other three kids have been with Robyn so long because they are contested court orders, which automatically involve a complicated legal process.

"Parents who humbly admit their guilt get their kids back much faster," Robyn explained. "Just telling the judge that you fucked up and learned your lesson, and now want to rebuild and move on and be forgiven, is all it really takes to get your kids back quickly. That and some sort of sobriety or anger management program."

Having lived with 130 foster children, Robyn has learned that resource workers usually disappear pretty quickly after they "drop" a kid. So she has learned to ask a lot of questions when they call her on the phone. She keeps a photocopied list beside the kitchen telephone: Name? Age? Clothing? Have they been "medicalized" yet? Why were they removed from their parents? Sexual or Physical abuse? Neglect? What are the court ordered conditions for parental visits? Will this be a short- or long-term kid?

Robyn keeps a written log of all the daily events that go on with her kids: the phone calls and disclosures, their interactions with their parents, and whether or not Mom and Dad were sober when they visited. She also documents what the social workers are doing (or not doing). "I have to protect myself," Robyn insisted, "because foster parents are called to testify in court all the time, and we can be sued twenty years later."

Robyn closely watches every new child's interaction with the other group home kids, both in front of her and when they think she's not looking. She knows that children look at things very directly and simply and are great learners and manipulators.

"They're always watching and learning weird behaviour patterns from their parents, siblings, and other children they come in contact with," Robyn explained. "But I trust children. I believe they would never say or do anything to intentionally hurt you. They are not that complex yet. It's your own stuff you see reflected back in their bad behaviour. Children are honest even if you don't always want to hear it."

Robyn's Nest is structured with daily, healthy, interactive chores and routines. The more experienced kids help the transition process for the new kids. Robyn and her two full-time staff members and two part-time floaters try to build trust by treating all the kids in a consistent, loving, but firm manner, and by encouraging them to make their own choices about things that affect them.

"I have clear rules of behaviour at "The Nest." Kids live with me, I don't live with kids," Robyn insists. "But giving kids choices is even more important than the consistent day to day routine and structure we try to provide. A lot of kids that come through here don't even know what OK behaviour is. All their life they've been yelled at and beaten up and locked in closets and starved. Children have a natural sense of joy in life, but that soon wears off when they've been raised like that, with nothing but beer in the fridge, and their parents are always yelling at them, and the television is their only friend and teacher.

"Every kid has potential, no matter what they've been through," Robyn believes. And if there is any "trick" to successful Foster

Parenting, she insists that it is in the uncovering of every kid's natural talents and encouraging them.

"I really try and teach my kids about the tremendous power of their own voices, and the value of their own ideas," she told me. "Because lives transform and expand when natural gifts are developed. When a kid learns how to draw or play a musical instrument or play a sport, it gives a real sense of movement to their lives. It teaches them to believe in themselves, and helps them to realize the importance of practice and continuous learning and having a personal focus in life. And that injects some spirit back into them."

Robyn likes to believe that once her kids have been "Robynized" they'll understand what right and wrong is, and want all their rights and responsibilities as humans.

"The only rights anyone has are the ones that they know about," she explained. "And when my kids go back to their real parents, I encourage them to try and be strong enough to insist upon clear conditions about how they want to live. Because now they know how a normal life is supposed to be—with school, meals, and safety—and because now they want communication, and they want to make their own choices about things that affect them."

Robyn's biggest complaint about the foster care system is that there is usually no transition process for the return of foster children to their real parents or relatives.

The worst thing that happened to Robyn during her foster parent career was the time she had to deliver a five-year-old girl to a relative the child had never met before. Robyn was the only mother figure the little girl had ever known, and suddenly she was supposed to be delivered to a stranger on a day's notice.

"The exchange took place at the Calgary airport," Robyn remembered, "and I only had four hours before my return flight, because the Ministry refused to let me layover, or pay for a hotel room.

"I only decided to go at the last minute because the kid was too frightened to go with the social worker who was supposed to bring her," Robyn said. "I was hoping to explain things to her on the plane, but I guess I didn't know how to say them in a way she could understand."

And Robyn's strong, clear voice began to soften and stutter as she told me what happened: "Her aunt was waiting for us at the gate, and to her I was 'Ministry' with a capital 'M'. She just grabbed her niece away from me before I could even say goodbye. I heard that child screaming 'No-No-No! Robyn, Get Me!' as her aunt dragged her from one end of the airport to the other. I had been her only secure thing in life, the only mother figure she could remember, so how could that child not feel abandoned by me for just standing there and watching her be dragged away by a stranger? And all I could do was stand there and watch it happen and think of about a million other ways we could have done that transition better."

Robyn learnt her lesson then, and won't allow transitionless custody exchanges anymore with any of her foster children. Every time they try to do another one she immediately informs the provincial Child Advocates Office, and they pressure the Ministry on her behalf so that the money can be found for a proper transition.

But not all foster parents are as confident and system-wise as Robyn. She would like to see the Ministry formalize an official, graduated transition process for all foster kids—beginning with day visits, and then overnight and weekend visits, so that the parents and their kids can learn to cope with each other again.

When Robyn was pouring us some coffee at her kitchen table she surprised me by announcing that she was not renewing her contract with the Ministry when it came up next time. She explained that her emergency group home will survive (under a different name). "The Ministry doesn't want to lose my central location and this big house full of kid-proof furniture, toys, games, and closets full of children's clothing and shoes in all sizes."

I asked Robyn, "Why now, after twelve years at the job?"

She replied: "I just don't like what's happening to the system, the lack of care about the kids, the political bullshit. I don't like how it was starting to make me feel. But I don't feel like I'm quitting, or running away. That caregiving energy is still a big part of who I am. I'm just moving on."

And then she poured some milk into a half-dozen plastic cups and called for her kids and mine to come and join us for some cookies.

Postscript: Robyn purchased a 25-acre ranch and farmhouse on top of a bald Okanagan Valley mountain and is living there with her two long-term foster kids and her 80-year-old aunt, Gracie. They are currently raising pigs, chickens, turkeys, barn cats, three dogs, three goats, a donkey, a pony, two horses, and two cows. Last summer she invited my entire family to camp beside her barnyard for a few days and my kids had the best vacation of their lives. One night while we were drinking wine around a bonfire I asked if she missed her old city life and she replied, "No, I don't miss it anymore. In fact, when I look back through the old log books now I'm amazed I managed to survive the experience. One hundred and thirty foster children in twelve years was a lot to go through. I think I must have had a much bigger ego when I was younger. I wanted to have a big impact on the world so I opened up an emergency group home in my twenties. I'm a very giving person, and I wanted to find some way to use my talents to their fullest, and boy did I get lots of opportunities to learn about what that means.

"But even though I only have two kids with me now, I think I use my love powers much more efficiently than before. It's better for me to have a really big effect on a few people, than a smaller effect on many. Here in our mountain top nest it really feels like we are a family, and in a way we're even closer than that because we all choose to be here with each other."

DIARY EXCERPTS:

Tonight on the drop-in centre steps a burly man flattened a short, chunky woman with a sucker punch. And then as "Perry" (another volunteer) and I pulled him away from her, he tried to kick her in the head.

"Let's take a break," Perry earnestly suggested to the brute as he pushed a cigarette into his surprised hand. "Let's have a smoke, and talk about it."

Perry bizarrely tries to defuse all explosive situations at the drop-in centre by offering the combatants my cigarettes. This time it actually seemed to distract the burly man long enough that I could go and help his bewildered girlfriend to her feet. Perry mimed a few chugs of an invisible bottle to warn me that the man was drunk.

"I feel like shit, and it's all because of her," I heard the man complain to Perry.

The woman he had knocked down seemed catatonic, punch-drunk, mute. She just lay on the sidewalk, staring sightlessly down the block. I pulled her up into a sitting position on the bottom step and tried to get her to say something, but then her boyfriend lunged at us with an unexpected kick that just missed the back of her head, and she collapsed again into a foetal position on the sidewalk.

Perry and I cornered him near the top of the steps, far away from her, and I shouted into Brother Tim's office window that he should call 9-1-1. Like most people, I have no idea how to deal with domestic violence—except to call the police. Domestic disputes make me feel uneasy, and I always want to cringe and look away if I can.

"The cops will be here soon," Perry and I continuously reassured her.

"They'll help you."

But the woman would not get up from the sidewalk. She just seemed to tremble a little harder every time we spoke to her, or when her boyfriend bellowed.

When a police cruiser showed up thirty minutes later (the Main Street Police Station is two blocks away) one of the cops immediately complained, "Shit! It's Franky and Annie," and he handcuffed Franky and tossed him into the back seat as his partner slowly helped Annie up to her feet.

"Annie? Do you hear me, Annie?" he kept softly repeating, trying to gently coax her from her blind, trembling stupor, while the first cop told Perry and me that this was a frequent occurrence.

"Franky has a restraining order," he explained, "but we can't enforce it when Annie goes looking for him."

It seems that every time they arrest Franky for beating up Annie, she goes down to Pre-Trial a few hours later and insists on visiting with him.

But even so, I was horrified to watch the cops leave without Franky only ten minutes later, when Annie came out of her stupor. As soon as they let him out of the back seat Franky backhanded her across the mouth and said, "That's for nagging me and making me lose my cool, you stupid cunt." And then, even though he was assaulting her in their presence, the police officers drove away. Franky respectfully waited until they turned the corner before he punched Annie solidly in the abdomen and she fell down on all fours, breathless.

Perry and I made a lunge for Franky, but he dodged into oncoming traffic and sprinted across Cordova Street giving us the finger before turning on his heels and strutting away.

"Wait for me," Annie croaked and stumbled after him. "Franky, wait for me."

☙   ☙   ☙

Whenever an unescorted woman enters the drop-in centre the entire roomful of bored men will cock their heads in unison like a pack of wild dogs picking up a scent. Their yellow, calculating eyes will follow her as she crosses the room to the tea urns. It happens every time.

Skid rows are especially dangerous places for women. In the downtown eastside, single women sometimes find their hotel room doors being battered down in the middle of the night, and then they are raped. If they call the police, they are often accused of being a prostitute complaining about a bad trick. If they complain to the hotel manager, they can be evicted for being troublemakers. One fifty-four-year-old woman told me that the same man had raped her six times in the last year.

A community hour server told me that since his divorce he has had sex with a prostitute every second Wednesday. (Payday.)

"Every time I pick up a different one," he bragged. "I drive up and down all the downtown eastside streetwalker tracks for about an hour, because I really like to take my time choosing the right one. It's like ice cream: 101 flavours! And I want to try them all. I've been doing it for over three years, but I could quit anytime if I really wanted to. Just like when I quit smoking."

A fifty-seven-year-old woman crossing Woodland Avenue with the lights was run over by a man who made a right-hand turn right over top of her because he was distracted by a prostitute.

CHAPTER SEVEN

Gentrification, Johns, Pimps, and Working Girls

ONE NIGHT at the drop-in centre I watched a barely pubescent native girl drink a cup of tea and eat a stale sandwich while her fifteen-year-old "boyfriend" whispered in her ear. Her name is "Lisa" and she is a runaway from a Northern BC Reserve. She had shown up at The Door Is Open the week before with a different boyfriend.

After several cajoling minutes, Lisa shuffled obediently out to the funeral home parking lot across Cordova Street and huddled against a parking meter, too frightened to run away because her boyfriend was watching her from the shadows of Oppenheimer Park. A maroon mini-van stopped at the curb and Lisa slowly got in, pulling open the passenger door as if it were her own coffin lid.

And when she drove away with her first "date" it occurred to me that I had just watched the entire initiation process and done absolutely nothing to stop it. When I came back for my next shift, only five days later, Lisa was already a corrupt, bubble gum popping streetwalker dressed in a short, tight, yellow leather mini-dress. She unzips and flashes her small pink tits at every car that slows down near her. She will open her legs or mouth for anyone with a little money or drugs.

Her rapid transformation bothered me, and on my way home that night I decided to take a couple of months off from the drop-in centre to regain some perspective. I wasn't doing anyone any favours hanging around there.

☙ ☙ ☙

My wife and I occasionally hire a baby-sitter and take a walk over to Hastings Park to bet on the horse races. One evening we were running a little early so we stopped for some beers at the Princeton Hotel. An angry parade of nearby homeowners were marching up and down the sidewalk outside the pub's broad front window. They were protesting against the visual pollution of streetwalkers in their neighbourhood—the open solicitations with teasing, sudden flashes of bare tits and ass, the leering curbside negotiations, the traffic jams—the curious blendings of the shocking, the titillating, and the boring that goes with streetwalkers. They were expressing middle-class anxieties about the effect of prostitution on their property values, and its influence on their children. "Not in My Neighbourhood," was the recurring motto on their placards.

My famously impulsive wife muttered something about this being her neighbourhood too and she gave the enraged mob the finger and some of them started throwing eggs at the window in front of us. I guess they thought she was a bar prostitute, and that I was a john negotiating the prices of her sexual services.

I noticed that one of their placards claimed they had picked up over four hundred used condoms from the playground and the sidewalks around Sir William MacDonald Public School up the block. I admired their thoroughness but I gave them the finger too, because the prostitutes were working this neighbourhood long before they started gentrifying the area, and they had no right to pass the problems off onto some other place.

I have lived in various addresses in East Vancouver for over a decade. Long enough to know that no matter what curve balls the imaginative but fleeting community groups throw, the johns just keep coming. Public embarrassment is an inconvenience, not a deterrent to them.

During the Mount Pleasant: Shame the Johns Campaign in 1995, 250 cars an hour used to cruise the narrow residential streets of that small neighbourhood next to mine. That community group copied down the licence plate numbers from the cars that stopped to pick up streetwalkers, then researched the names and addresses of the car owners and sent them letters stating that at a given time, on a given day, the driver of the vehicle was seen picking up a prostitute.

Sometimes the vigilantes took photographs of surprised johns caught in the act and enclosed the incriminating prints in their envelopes. They blew up the best photos and unveiled them at a local community college auditorium and attracted a lot of television news attention.

Their very public campaign was successful for a few days. But when the TV news camera crews stopped coming, the interest of the vigilantes flagged, and less than a month later many of the same prostitutes were back on their old corners, and much of the john pool had returned. Business as usual: lonely drivers circling the same streets, shopping around for the prostitute they prefer, using the driving time around the short blocks to make up their minds. A river of traffic made up of the curious, and serious buyers.

Streetwalkers are not easily pushed off busy corners because they know that is where their customers will come looking for them when they want to rent their sexual services. They cluster, just as book and antique stores, used car lots, and little art galleries tend to congregate within the same few blocks of a busy street. Clustering allows speciality businesses to attract more people to the area than one shop could attract alone.

I think that is a big part of the reason why community groups hate the johns so vehemently. The bad reputations of their neighbourhoods prompt johns to make assumptions about nearly every woman walking in the area. My wife has had more than a few cars pull up to the curb beside her when she is walking home from a friend's apartment after dark. Leering men pop their heads out of the passenger side window and say, "Get in," or "How much for half and half, baby?"

≈   ≈   ≈

Fourteen Canadian cities have begun encouraging the men they catch buying sex to attend "John Schools" where they are publicly lectured and berated by former prostitutes, community groups, cops, crown attorneys, psychologists, and health professionals. The ironic logic behind the programs is that men caught buying sex will be humiliated enough by the process to become less misogynistic. But one graduate told me all he learned was how not to get caught.

Whatever the effectiveness, the "John Schools" have compiled an interesting profile of men who buy sex. Canadian johns come from every age, ethnic, and economic status group. They are good and bad neighbours, husbands, fathers, brothers, sons. Ordinary men.

The most common answer to why these men regularly went to prostitutes for sex goes something like: "I enjoy making it with a hooker once in awhile because after we have agreed upon a price, I have no more obligations to the woman. I can relax and enjoy myself." They want a contractual, rather than personal, association with a woman.

The next most common reason for visiting prostitutes seems to be a fulfilment wish for some sexual fantasy, a craving for "kicks" and adventure. The third most common reason is "loneliness."

My wife and her girlfriends believe that johns do it because it is just too easy for them to get away with it, and they are probably right. The johns have very little risk of being caught, or punished. Section 213 of the Criminal Code of Canada (Communicating for the Purposes of Prostitution) is almost impossible to enforce: ninety percent of Vancouver men who have been charged with it during the last five years have received either conditional or absolute discharges.

Johns have even less chance of getting caught if they shop around skid row. The downtown eastside provides one-third of the charges against sellers, but less than one percent of the men who were charged for trying to buy sexual services were caught doing it in the downtown eastside.

Prostitution arrests (unless theft or assault are involved) are put low on the list of police priorities because of the built-in futility of trying to enforce an almost unenforceable law. So, ultimately, the largest risk to both sides in prostitution transactions does not come from the police or the legal system, but from each other—the johns and the working girls.

On a boarded-over window of the nameless hotel on the corner of Franklin and Woodland Streets a scribble of graffiti says:

Rapist alert!
Rape 3+
threaten 10
spit on 5
Very twisted!
White male pock-marked face
Orange van - white stripe
Camper style
SWL 141

"Bad trick" warnings are written upon countless other boarded-over windows, and lampposts throughout the neighbourhood. But the violence is a two-way street. "Grope and Grab" pickpocketings are quite common, as some streetwalkers try to supplement their incomes. Many of the ripped-off johns don't even report the thefts because of the inevitable, embarrassing questions. How do you explain to a police officer that you didn't feel your wallet being lifted because the girl had her other hand down your pants? And do you really want that written down on a public police form with your name and address attached?

℞ ℞ ℞

If there were not men willing to pay for sex, there would not be poor women willing to sell it to them. But those are not the only possible roles in the sex trade. There is also the pimp.

On the surface there does not seem to be very much to a pimp's job. They buy the drugs and lurk in the shadows while the girl is waiting for some john to stop and negotiate. When the girl gets into a car the pimp is supposed to write down, or memorize, the licence plate and model, just in case there is trouble. It is called "spotting." But of course they never remember anything, and if the girl does get beaten up by a date, the pimp just rushes off angrily into the night and returns several hours later, claiming to have hunted down the scum and snuffed him.

Many streetwalkers stop by The Door Is Open for a tea break after the first evening rush-hour. We keep a clean Ladies Room, and are pretty tolerant of their IV drug use, as long as they safely dispose of their own syringes. After getting to know some of the women, you soon learn that they're not really prostitutes—just desperate drug addicts renting their bodies for more drugs. Every morning, city sanitation crews sweep up hundreds of discarded syringes from the alley behind The Door Is Open.

I've noticed that many of the pimps that escort the streetwalkers seem to enjoy showing off their expensive clothing and jewelry in front of soup kitchen patrons. They can't help themselves—their vanity and arrogance are what make them good at their work. All the pimps I've met ooze self-esteem, and use it to seduce young girls with no self-esteem at all.

Many of them are braggarts and like to crow about their money and promiscuity and drugs and guns. Sometimes they compare recruiting tactics. It seems that since the average age of entry into streetwalker prostitution is fourteen, suburban shopping malls are a good place to look for new girls to train. They look for shy girls, and tell them that they are very pretty and try to make them feel special by affirming and praising them, using simple, jarring endearments the girl has probably never heard at home. Teenage runaways are supposed to be even easier recruits because they usually have nowhere else to go. The pimps only have to offer a girl like that food, drugs, and a place to sleep to win her loyalty.

Once he's seduced her, the pimp asks his new girlfriend to do him "a favour" and "spot" for the older girls. And usually it's only a week or less before the new girl will volunteer to try it out herself—with only subtle, basically non-threatening, coercion. The girls "volunteer" to do it because they think they owe their new boyfriend something for being nice to them, or because they think it's not fair for the other girls to do all the work, or they think that it's too late for them to go back home.

Becoming a pimp is not an accidental vocation like becoming a waiter, or a taxi driver, or laboratory technologist, I observed. Their cruelty must be imaginative and deliberate since the only essential step in the recruiting process is to reward the girls after—and during—each hard night's work by turning them onto hard drugs. The sooner the girls get hooked on heroin or cocaine, the better for the pimps. Once hooked, they become low-maintenance whores. Their addictions will keep them in line and obedient until their stoned, brittle minds finally snap from all the kaleidoscopic sexual and personal role-playing.

℣   ℣   ℣

At The Door Is Open I have become acquainted with several working girls as they take their tea breaks. The saddest thing I've discovered about them is that all my preconceptions concerning coercion and physical force were inaccurate. They suffer beatings and ugly copulations daily, and receive little financial reward; yet talking to these women you realize that they almost always enter the market willingly, and often choose to stay in the business because they don't think they deserve any better.

The end of a streetwalker's career is not a happy one. When their looks begin fading, a prostitute has to "discount" her prices to keep the johns from driving down the block and picking up the pretty teenagers who are her neighbourhood competition. Most have little to show for all the time they spent staring up at unlit car dome lights from beneath the heaving shoulders of sweaty strangers.

Streetwalkers are the very lowest in the loose hierarchy of prostitution because they are the most visible, have the highest risk of arrest, and suffer the most harm from pimps, customers, and competing prostitutes. It seems that as prostitution income increases, pimp involvement decreases, and the danger of arrest declines.

A friend of mine lives in a glassy high-rise condominium next door to an elegant downtown hotel. He has made friends with a couple of the doormen during his evening strolls about his neighbourhood. Through those doormen we have both met a few escort service prostitutes as they were waiting for cabs. All I can say about them is they are extraordinarily beautiful, well educated, and smart. One of them told us she made over $40,000 last year, tax free, and refuses to see more than two clients on weekday nights because she is a post-graduate student at Simon Fraser University and needs to spend a lot of time on her studies so she can get a "good" job when she graduates.

The saddest type of prostitution I know about are the live-in girls who occasionally work for the old men with good pensions who retire to skid row apartments. There are many tired, wasted, alcoholic women who can be hired as sort of "temporary wives." The wages of these temporary girlfriends depend on the woman's looks, which tavern she was found in, and how much of a drunk she is.

One apartment building we lived in when we first moved to East Vancouver was infested with old guys like that. We regularly got to meet some of their rental wives in the laundry room as they tried to be the perfect little woman that would never be tired, never be busy, never be interested in anything but pleasing "him." But no matter how hard the girls tried, when the men got tired of them they just booted them back out on the street and then went to a Hastings Street tavern to find a replacement.

DIARY EXCERPTS:

"Pigeon Park" is a greasy, oblong triangle of downtown eastside pavement where many brooding alcoholics and junkies hang around all day and night. A couple of people get stabbed there every week. A block and a half west of Pigeon Park there are $1,000. gold pens for sale in a lawyer boutique.

I absorb disparate facts like these about the downtown eastside very slowly; they're observations from a decade of daily bus commuting through the disintegrating neighbourhood on my way to and from work. The trip is not long in terms of time or miles—but in terms of landscape, attitudes, and shrinking possibilities, the distance is sometimes enormous.

On No. 14 Hastings buses I've often seen drunken men and women puking in the aisles, and people passed out in soggy puddles of their own urine. Public domestic disputes are a common occurrence. On three occasions I've witnessed cops boarding the bus and arresting belligerent people. No. 14 Hastings buses are the only ones with panic buttons under the driver's seat for calling the police.

And subconsciously I guess I must have been slowly discovering a sense of the place, incorporating maps of memory, merging my personal geography with the disintegrating landscape whizzing by outside the grimy bus windows. When I was a kid my grandfathers taught me that it was through the places we live, and how we relate to the landscape of our lives, that we learn about who we are. They showed me hundreds of Manitoba fishing holes. I can easily understand their love of green rural spaces, but I'm only beginning to comprehend my own preference for raunchy urban blight.

I think I first started volunteering at The Door Is Open not because I thought I could make a difference in any of the lives I glimpsed through grimy bus windows, but because I hoped the experience might become the antidote to my increasing indifference.

☙   ☙   ☙

This ex-con (14 weeks out) sat on the steps of the drop-in centre and bummed cigarettes off me and talked about how hard it was to go straight because he couldn't find a job because of his criminal record. A man I know sat down on the steps between us and started swigging off a bottle of rice wine. The ex-con asked me what time it was and said he had to go to some AA party down the block and meet his ex-wife. I watched him walk down to the traffic lights on the corner and then I went back inside to play some crib. But before I finished the first hand, the rice wino I'd just left outside on the front steps was clutching the back of my chair and bleeding onto my T-shirt. He told us the ex-con had doubled back, punched him out, and robbed him of his corduroy jacket and half-empty bottle of rice wine in full view of the early evening traffic.

On my way to get the first aid kit from Brother Tim's office, I popped my head out onto the porch but the ex-con was long gone. There was a puddle of fresh blood on the steps and I could see his crimson footprints escaping westwards along the sidewalk.

And I remember marvelling that he had seemed so normal and gentle when we were gossiping moments earlier. He had used all those comforting "R" words: Responsibility. Rehabilitation. Retribution. Reform. The same words he probably remembered to tell his parole officer.

☙   ☙   ☙

A popular skid row drop-in centre pastime is contemplating get-rich-quick schemes. You're always hearing guys saying things like: "Other people are lucky, so why not me? It could happen. I just gotta come up with the right idea at the right time."

Their desperate optimism reminds me of the way excited jackpot bingo players line up around the block in the rain, or how soup kitchen Christians try to make poor and homeless people believe that the meek shall inherit the earth.

Soup kitchen patrons cheer when mug-shots of their friends and acquaintances sometimes appear in televised Crime Stoppers "Most Wanted" segments.

CHAPTER EIGHT

Crime and Punishment

I GOT OFF a crowded No. 14 Hastings bus just south of movie row on Granville Street and heard the shrill shriek of a police whistle and then the angry, winded shout: "Stop him, he's a thief!"

I looked up and saw a chubby blonde teenager running towards me along the sidewalk with a policewoman on a mountain bike gaining ground fast behind him. A brown leather purse danced absurdly from the teenager's hard pumping right fist. Tears poured freely down his horrified face.

"Stop him," the cop shouted again, and a couple of middle-aged men in suits dutifully corralled him into the doorway of a boarded-over store. One of them held his briefcase protectively in front of himself at arm's length, but he need not have bothered; the policewoman had already leapt gracefully from the seat of her bicycle and quickly had the chubby purse snatcher in a shoulder-wrenching half-nelson. I glanced around and saw a dozen other fascinated rush-hour bystanders mutely watching the real life drama along with me.

The chubby boy was weeping and shaking hysterically now—openly despairing the unretractable impulse that had made him snatch a purse—and change forever the trajectory of his short life.

"Stop crying for Christ's sake," the policewoman barked as she snapped handcuffs around his wrists. "If you can't serve the time, then you shouldn't have done the crime."

Our crowd of bus-transferring, workaday commuters were respectfully silent, as if some great moral lesson had been expressed. Watching the tears rolling down the purse-snatcher's face as a paddy wagon arrived to take him away, it occurred to me that just like the policewoman had said, every criminal I've ever met at the drop-in centre knew what ill treatment they could expect if they got caught. But they committed their crimes anyway, and usually kept on doing it until they were caught in the act. Perversely, they seemed to want both the excitement of the crime and the punishment and suffering that goes along with it.

The criminal code offence rate for the downtown eastside is 540 per 1,000 people (compared to a citywide average of 202), and most of the arrest records of the guys that hang around The Door Is Open are absurd. Vandalism, Assault, Shoplifting, B&E's. Chump change stuff. Such stupid, pointless crimes that apparently they want to be caught and punished—if only to occasionally reinforce their poor sense of self and place. A jailhouse is, after all, a permanent address, and a prison number is some sort of identity. And for some people, a short jail sentence can be like a vacation from the monotony of their skid row lives—three square meals a day, a clean bed and clothing, plenty of exercise and cable television, lots of people to talk to, some kind of daily work routine to make them feel useful.

When I suggested to Brother Tim that there must be something more than mere poverty responsible for high skid row crime rates, he replied: "Yea, I think stealing is a little like sex for some people. The nervous tension excites them and they steal things of no real value just for the thrill of getting away with it. Just because they're bored.

"And sometimes," Brother Tim suggested, "they do bad things just because they like to be bad. There are a lot of little bastards running around."

&ε&   &ε&   &ε&

Brother Tim believes that the major reason why his drop-in centre is popular is because of all the downtown eastside charities, The Door Is Open most resembles the typical jailhouse common room—a big, windowless, cinder block room with a television high up near the ceiling at one end. Since many of his patrons have served jail time, Brother Tim thinks they feel at home there.

Before Brother Tim took over, The Door Is Open was run a lot like a cellblock and many of the volunteers were thugs that acted like prison trustees. The mostly unsupervised ex-cons managed things the only way that made sense to them: as profitably as possible. When after-hour donations of food and clothing came in, the volunteers took first pass, and then let their homeboys pick over the remainders. The sisters next door received very little of the evening donations that were intended for them.

Then Brother Tim showed up with all his new rules, and his locks and keys, and his eighty-hour work weeks. The original volunteers quit one after another because mopping up piss was no longer worth their while.

Whenever you ask Brother Tim about crime and punishment issues, he becomes very animated. With almost thirty years experience as a prison padre—beginning with a North Carolina chain gang in 1969, and then moving on to Riker's Island for a decade, followed by a hodgepodge of Canadian appointments at Vancouver Pre-Trial, Okalla, and a half dozen jails in southern Ontario—Brother Tim has developed a lot of strong opinions.

"Correctional Officers (COs) have strange careers," Brother Tim told me once. "Most of their time on the job is spent locking and unlocking doors and staring at people in cages. Can you imagine any job more boring than sitting in a guard tower at three in the morning watching a brick wall?

"The basic problem with our prison system is that in order to gain enough prisoner respect to rehabilitate them, you gotta wade right into the cell blocks," he explains. "And that doesn't happen, because as soon as a CO is hired he begins to do his best to escape the prisoners he was hired to watch.

"The Housing Unit Officer is considered the low man on the totem pole, when in all fairness the reverse should be true. They're the ones that need proper training and support, since they are the ones who potentially have the most affect upon the prisoners. Their attitudes and language can have a profound influence. But the very first rule CO's are taught is never to relate on a personal level with inmates. If they treat the prisoners as human beings they are ridiculed by the other COs and called "reverend" or "social worker."

"The administration intentionally runs things that way because it is more labour efficient to encourage the prisoners to fight amongst themselves," Brother Tim insists. "The easiest way to control sixty people in a small, locked down space is to have a "Bull" working with you. That way you only need one or two COs and all they have to say to the Bull or his home boys is, 'I want that floor mopped,' and it gets done. The Bull decides who does it, and in return for making the CO's job easier the Bull gets special privileges. He gets to move around the prison, or maybe suggested cell doors can be left open after lock down. It's also a convenient way for some CO's to make a little extra income. Who do you think smuggles the drugs and contraband into the prisons?

"And being forced to live in such an unfair, explosive, contained environment teaches prisoners that violence solves all problems, even if their angry rages are often only a defensive bluff, noise to hide their fear. Because if prisoners don't push back with extreme vengeance against the smallest insult, they risk enslavement for the rest of their sentences."

One ex-con at The Door is Open summed up prison culture rather succinctly: "In jail everybody watches everybody else all the time because they don't have nothing else to do and they gossip and bicker and fight and it's such petty, stupid shit, it's ridiculous. Like somebody stealing somebody's underwear, and then someone else gets stabbed for it."

"But what else can a person brutally conditioned like this do," Brother Tim asks, "but re-offend when he finally gets out? Prisoners are always worse, not better, after their prison experiences. They have been programmed to overreact.

"Every prisoner upon sentencing is examined once by a psychologist and is prescribed a dim sum banquet of programs to complete before their release: Substance Abuse, Communication, Anger and Emotions Management, Rational Emotive Behaviour, and on the list goes. They think up new ones every year," Brother Tim explained. "But the effectiveness of such rehabilitation programs is diluted when ex-convicts are released to skid row addresses and welfare dependency, because all the programs ignore the harsh truth that nearly all Canadian prisoners are poor, and poor people are much more likely to commit crimes just to survive, or cope. The simple, hard truth of it all is that suffering is bad for human beings. Suffering does not lead to salvation, it just leads to despair and bitterness."

Brother Tim observes: "Prisons intentionally cut prisoners off from any real community, and so it is only natural for convicts to turn in on themselves, and become preoccupied with their own problems, grievances, and criminal plans. The prison environment does not nurture self-examination or teach self-discipline. It makes prisoners passive and lazy and mean, instead. And without any real opportunities for growth and change, prisoners remain in a state of arrested development, in a peculiar sort of suspended psychic animation.

"Ex-convicts have forgotten how to shop, cook, look for work, and are expected to survive on a welfare cheque that pays the rent and not much else. And prison culture can become so ingrained that ex-cons occasionally stand in front of drop-in centre doors, forgetting that they no longer have to wait for guards to unlock them. Or they tremble at the sight of someone in uniform, even when it is only a meter maid, or an ambulance attendant. They can't see beyond the fence anymore."

DIARY EXCERPTS:

One guy at the drop-in centre told me how he got out of prison and then was hospitalized on the psychiatric ward of Vancouver General Hospital two days later because he had a nervous breakdown at the counter of the Main Street McDonalds. He had become frustrated by the increased prices and the large, unfamiliar menu and his own inability to choose. So he pushed a cash register at the counter server who kept cheerfully repeating: "Can I help you? Can I help you? Can I help you?"

One of my friends is a thirty-two-year-old schoolteacher. He volunteers for "Man-2-Man, Woman-2-Woman" (M2W2), a low-key, interdenominational group that visits prisoners. He goes every Monday evening to the Fraser Regional Correctional Centre and any prisoner who wants to talk to someone is welcome to meet him or one of his friends in the visitors' room.

"Mostly they're just very lonely people," he told me. "And at first they usually just come to the visitors' room to unload a lot of garbage on you. But week after week, as they start to get comfortable with you, they begin to use you as a sounding board for their expectations of their post-prison lives.

"Sometimes I'm a guy's only regular visitor. And, really, they just need to talk to someone with no jail or crime experience, someone outside the correctional system, someone outside their bad history, so they can try and imagine another kind of life for themselves."

⁕   ⁕   ⁕

One legacy of poverty is fear of losing things. Sometimes people will fight, even to the death, to protect their meagre possessions. Tonight at the drop-in centre I watched a wiry, middle-aged alcoholic pick the pockets of his best friend after he'd passed out. I wasn't the only one who witnessed the theft.

"What the hell do you think you're doing?" One tough-looking man hissed.

"That's low, man," several other people muttered.

"Fuck off, and mind your own business," the thief spat back. "You're just pissed because you didn't get to him first."

Which was probably true.

But then his buddy regained consciousness, saw the crumpled $5 bill in his friend's hand and immediately guessed what had happened. He let out a rage-filled bellow and charged after his pal, who was already running away. Cornered in the kitchen, the thief turned and started swinging both his arms like windmills.

"Come on," he shouted. "Come on, and try me!"

He appeared willing to challenge all comers, yet I could also see the terror in his eyes. He had a coyote mentality—fantastically courageous, and a coward at the same time. He'll run, but when cornered, he'll fight. In a heartbeat both men were rolling around on the floor, biting and scratching each other.

But fifteen minutes later, after we broke up their fight and Brother Tim and I had bandaged their wounds in separate corners, they were best buddies again. They left with their arms around each other's shoulders, on their way to buy another bottle of ginseng wine with the disputed $5. Drunks in a rush to go somewhere else to get drunker.

"I don't get it," I said to Brother Tim as we watched them leave. "They wanted to rob and kill each other a few minutes ago."

"They're friends of convenience," Brother Tim suggested. "And that's important. All human beings need someone to talk to."

And slowly I've glimpsed a little of what he was talking about, and noticed that plain loneliness is the reason why many homeless and very poor people are attracted to cold, urban neighbourhoods. When you're lonely and broke, the bright lights and noisy excitement of a big city can provide company for your misery, and the many random acts of bizarre behaviour and violence on skid row sidewalks become welcome distractions—live theatre and spectator sports. Prostitutes frequently fight with johns and pimps, and many Hastings Street pubs host bloody brawls, every day. The most common downtown eastside sounds are angry voices and the sirens of panic vehicles rushing to some new emergency down the block.

An old man who I caught trying to steal my jacket indignantly told me: "What goes around, never comes around, so why should I be nice to you, just because you're stupid enough to be nice to me?"

CHAPTER NINE

25¢ Sex

"IT'S HARD to get laid when you don't have any money." I've heard more than one guy at the drop-in centre say this. They are not exaggerating. Very few women pass through their lives. Non-working ladies don't lounge around, drinking stale tea and napping in the soup kitchens with all the bored, horny alcoholics. It's simply not safe.

Healthy sexual intimacy demands a price, emotionally and financially, that the typical soup kitchen patron cannot afford to pay. Consequently, most of the sex available to them is brief, impersonal, homosexual liaisons like the kind you can get in the 25¢, X-rated movie booths in the back of pornographic book and video stores, or in the shadowy seats of XXX-rated movie theatres. Most Canadian skid row neighbourhoods are cluttered with the garish neon signs of sex merchants like that, so they don't have to go far.

I was curious about the "25¢ sex" scene the guys at the drop-in centre sometimes talked about, so I went to one of the many pornographic bookstores along Granville Street and bought $2 worth of tokens (the minimum according to the sign taped to the cash register). I passed through the gold tinsel curtains at the back of the store and entered a large, dim, dirty room. There were a couple dozen booths the same size and shape as those stooped, small, automatic photo stalls you find in old shopping malls. But instead of canvas curtains these booths had thin, plywood doors with cheap latches; and instead of a camera lens, there were small video screens beside the coin boxes and a knob to change channels. Periodic orange cardboard signs taped to the black walls proclaimed: "Only one person allowed in a booth at a time." I looked a little more closely and was amazed to realize that many of the small, low cubicles were indeed shared.

A few shadowy men stood outside of empty booths, smoking cigarettes, staking out their territories. They smiled at me as I strolled by them. One of them mimicked rude sexual gestures, trying to entice me into his booth. As I detoured towards the red "Fire Exit" lamp that marked the dark horizons of the room, more ghostly faces eerily popped out of the booths and shadows and tried to flirt with me.

I returned to the same store another day and browsed the stacks of very graphic magazines while counting the men going in and out of the 25¢ sex room. In just fifteen minutes during the middle of a Tuesday afternoon, I watched eleven men enter, and eight different ones leave. That is a pretty good turnover of business, even if it is only at $2 a diddle. But the most surprising thing I noticed was that at least half of the customers were dressed in suits—taking a cheap, steamy break between downtown meetings or sales calls, I guess.

I had thought that there were gay bathhouses for this sort of thing, but when I suggested this to some of my buddies at the drop-in centre they replied: "Bathhouses charge membership fees and require photo identification." And besides, they reminded me, 25¢ sex is not even considered homosexual sex by many of the soup kitchen crew—its just the only sex available.

You see similar brisk business in the XXX-rated movie theatres. Many skid row guys hang around day and night, loitering in the shadowy seats until they get their $6 admission's worth, or just because they have no place better to go, or its raining. When I went to the Venus Theatre on Main Street, no sooner had I sat down when a young guy a few rows ahead turned in his seat and impishly showed me that he was playing with himself. And then I heard a deep voice in

my right ear as a shadowy man sat down in a seat in the row behind
mine and whispered, "Come here often?"

"No," I nervously replied.

"It's not a bad way to spend an afternoon."

"I guess not."

"Is it ok if I sit beside you?"

"No thanks," I said, and got up and climbed one of the twin wind-
ing staircases up to the balcony only to discover that is where the real
action happens. The balcony is large and broad and it was so dark that
at first the place seemed empty. Then my eyes began to adjust and I
noticed huddled pairs of men sitting together along the gloomy rows
of seats and stairs, and cigarette heaters glowing from a couple of dark
doorways against the back wall. A muscular transvestite wearing a private girls school uniform several sizes too small was smoking a smelly
joint in his seat in the top row.

As I stood on the staircase and looked around at the twenty or so
shadowy men stalking each other I noticed the elegant wrought-iron
work on the railings, and the ornate terracotta friezes on the walls,
recalling the magnificent building's salad days when The Imperial was
one of the nicest theatres in town. When it was built in 1912 it alter-
nated vaudeville acts and movies. Jack Benny and the Marx Brothers
performed on its stage. In the 1920s it became home for an important
Chinese Opera Society that produced classical Chinese plays and
imported the best opera companies from China for lengthy engage-
ments.

If a building can have a soul, I bet The Imperial's wishing it could
make a back-over flip through its own asshole and disappear.

& & &

It was much the same scene at the "fruit loop," the alias of some of the
long, meandering paths near Stanley Park's Lost Lagoon. Some of the
25¢ sex guys at the drop-in centre had told me that it was a convenient

place to get laid. I didn't have to walk very far along the crushed stone path before I saw men disappear behind bushes in pairs, and then come out a few frantic moments later, from opposite directions. Intimate strangers joined for gasping, brief beats of time.

I recognized some of the guys sitting on benches as semi-regulars of the drop-in centre—hungry hobos looking for sexual kicks, or just planning to roll a "fairy" in the bushes and take his wallet while his pants are conveniently down around his ankles. I guess the middle-class men I saw wandering the fruit loop with me don't mind the occasional robbery at knife-point. At least they seldom report it to the police, which makes them perfect victims for lazy muggers.

On my way home that night I cruised through "boystown." It's a block south of the cluster of high-priced female streetwalkers on Richards Street, and runs along Drake and Davie Streets at the edge of the famously gay West End.

One third of Vancouver's prostitutes are male, and as I drove around the blocks of boystown I noticed that all the boys for sale seemed young—possibly twenty, but just as probably fourteen. And I noticed that the competition in boystown seemed to be much more fierce than it was with the female streetwalkers around the corner. Later, when I asked a few young hustlers at the drop-in centre what their usual rates were, they confessed that because there were so many out for "free" sex, the amount they got paid was an ever-shifting thing that was determined by the time of day, the day of the week, the john's franticness for sex, their own desperation for money, and the weather. Consequently, their fees were always different, ranging from $20 to $100 for different dates on the same night.

   ℇ ℇ ℇ

One of my friends is a guppy (gay urban professional) named "Ed." For three years, he's done volunteer work for AIDS Vancouver. They assign him people with severe HIV-related conditions and he's supposed to befriend them and help out when he can with drives to the hospital, housecleaning, companionship, and other small acts of kindness.

When I suggested that his was a noble cause, helping young men die with dignity, Ed replied: "It's rewarding, but it's not always easy. A lot of street hustlers leech onto the program, and it takes awhile before they are weeded out." And then he complained about being robbed by his first assignment.

"The guy was always trying to borrow money from me," Ed explained. "And when I invited him over to a dinner party at my apartment with some other friends, he stole my spare keys from a kitchen cupboard and came back the next afternoon to rob me. Luckily I came home from work early that day because I had a dentist appointment and I caught him loading the elevator with my television, VCR, and stereo."

And I suddenly realized that Ed must be talking about "Perry," a friend of mine from the drop-in centre. Perry had described being caught red-handed, exactly like that, and then bragged that he only had to serve three weeks of a nine-month sentence because all the HIV cellblocks were overbooked.

"Was that guy you're talking about tall and thin with a bony chest and a small pink mole on the side of his nose?" I asked Ed.

"Yes, but how do you know him?" He replied, surprised.

Perry was a volunteer at The Door Is Open when I first started. He quit a few months later (after nearly three years' service) when welfare discontinued giving a $50 monthly bonus for volunteer work, but he still hangs out at the drop-in centre a few nights a week.

The first night I met him, Perry told me: "I used to be a prostitute in boystown when I was young and beautiful, and I made scads. Now parolees screw me for $10 because they can't get a woman to service them for that little."

Perry constantly laments his lost and wasted youth—and the fact that his sad career was over before he was thirty. It seems no one lasts long in such a competitive, fickle market where youth is a badge, and

beauty is a treasure. Perry isn't old but he already looks like a carica-
ture of youth, an impersonation, because he tries to dress and look like
a teenager. For Perry, incipient middle age is a kind of death, and just
as irreconcilable.

A little while ago I came out onto the rooftop of a Gastown parking garage and was surprised to see Perry dozing in the flatbed of a
pick-up truck parked near my car.

"Perry?" I whispered, because if he truly was sleeping, I didn't
want to wake him.

"Well, well, lookie who's here," he said, opening his eyes and rec-
ognizing me.

"Need a ride?" I asked.

"No. I'm just waiting for an old boyfriend."

"Is this his truck?"

"Yes, he's going to lend me some money."

"Now that's the kind of friend I need to find."

"He's not really a friend," Perry sighed. "I just promise not to tell
his wife that he's a fairy, and he lends me more money."

Perry got up out of the flatbed and bummed a cigarette off me. I sat
on the hood of my car and Perry leaned over the rooftop railings. I was
expecting him to spit onto some poor pedestrian's head, but then he
said: "When I look down like this, it's almost as if the world is waiting
for me to jump."

And I was horrified to realize that with only a slight shift of weight
Perry's life could be over.

"Don't rush things, Perry," I nervously suggested. "Your AIDS will
take you there soon enough, and suicide makes for bad karma."

After a long, broody silence, he said, "I'm hungry, will you buy me
french fries and a milk shake at the Ovaltine Café?"

"Sure, let's go."

As we got into my car I marvelled at how people can only think
about death for brief moments, before the life force takes hold again,
and they get hungry.

DIARY EXCERPTS:

Every afternoon a stooped, old man comes into the drop-in centre and one of us goes to get "Victor's" pillow from the staff room. He is a lucid eighty-three years old and because he's too stubborn to have hip replacement surgery or fall over dead, he hobbles everywhere on spindly crutches.

I always give him several sandwiches whenever there are extras with the hope that they might save him the agony of having to make the soup kitchen rounds the next day. Tonight as I was walking home I saw Victor hobbling along ahead of me; just as I had nearly caught up to him I saw him give all the sandwiches I had given him earlier to Lil the bag lady.

I wasn't surprised. One of the few truths I've gleaned from all my experiences at The Door Is Open is that the very poorest of our society are often the most generous. I've also noticed that the vast majority of skid row charity volunteers and employees are only slightly more financially stable than the patrons they are trying to help.

℞   ℞   ℞

Why don't people know more swear words? I'm tired of hearing the same ones again and again.

℞   ℞   ℞

I often hear people saying that Canada is too rich a country to have REAL poverty like the Third World poor suffer, and I guess that's true. You don't see people starving to death in the ditches in Canada. But I don't think you can really compare human poverty across the board like that. Poverty means different things in different cultures. The many afflictions of Third World poverty are indeed horrible to endure, but the poor in those places are seldom as totally rejected as they are in the skid rows of the affluent western world. Here poverty is demoralizing and dispiriting and humiliating. The Third World poor are protected from complete despair because they are never excluded by their cultures. It is only where a sense of the universal frailty of life has been lost and is no longer held to be a respected, central understanding, that people can presume that poverty can never happen to them. Skid row lives are difficult to understand for people who have never been afflicted by poverty, illness, addiction, or love.

CHAPTER TEN

Us and Them

O N THE boarded-over windows of a bankrupt store I saw a sign written in English, Vietnamese, Chinese, and Spanish:

"This Area is being videotaped for the Vancouver Police.
All recordings of criminal activity will be
Given to the police for prosecution.
Information will also be given to Canadian Immigration."

Someone had written over it in crimson spray paint, "I see you too!" and, "When do we get to put a video camera inside your living room?"

I looked up and saw a basketball-sized video surveillance camera on top of a tripod suspended from a third storey ledge across the street. And then I looked around and noticed that everyone in view seemed to be oblivious to the camera: A couple of glassy-eyed, pre-pubescent Honduran boys were indifferently selling crack to motorists pulling up at the curb.

The worst part about living in poverty is being ignored, even in your own neighbourhood. They film a lot in the downtown eastside because directors like the gritty look of the disintegrating urban landscape; but they never hire any of the locals as extras. Not because they are unreliable, but because, ironically, the casting people think they look inauthentic.

More absurdly, the City of Vancouver enforces special moviemaking bylaws regarding eating in plain sight of passers-by when filming in the downtown eastside. City Council feels it is cruel to eat catered hot food in front of poor, hungry people, so craft services dutifully build enormous tents. But apparently it is all right for downtown eastside residents to *smell* the food cooking.

℈ ℈ ℈

The hardest part of the work at the drop-in centre is watching some people spiral downwards into the black pit of mental illness. Skid row charities often seem to be filled with nothing but the blank stares of lonely, softly mumbling men and women with no place else to go.

The mentally ill who are heavily medicated are the saddest type of people living on skid row. They are easily recognizable, and many people cruelly take advantage of them. They walk around like zombies, suffering that peculiar kind of loneliness that can only be felt by someone living in a pharmaceutical cage. Their medication causes confusion, chronic drowsiness, tics, and bizarre facial contortions. The unmedicated are more dangerous and unpredictable, but also more human and interesting.

When I first started volunteering at the drop-in centre I was prone to quick, empirical judgements. I labelled every mentally ill patron as "Manic," "Depressive," or "Psychotic," because hospital workers used to be trained that way. Now I can no longer tell the difference. Where does their psychiatric condition leave off and the cruel costs of poverty and physical deprivation kick in? Homelessness can drive you insane nearly as quickly as insanity can make you homeless.

At the drop-in centre I have gotten to know many homeless, mentally ill people. They often tell me (and anyone else who will bother to patiently listen) their bizarre hard-luck stories, and I have learned to stop analyzing whether what they tell me is true or not. It is the truth for them—and while the names, facts, and details of their narratives cannot all be "real," their pain clearly is.

I've also learned that many of them aren't crazy, although much of their behaviour is.

&ebreve;   &ebreve;   &ebreve;

A few years ago, I was riding home from work on a No. 7 Nanaimo bus and I saw a man make a graceful dive from the rooftop of a four-storey parking garage in Gastown. The heavy splat of his body upon the sidewalk shook the bus. Some passengers screamed and the woman sitting beside me bent over and puked on her shoes when she saw his brains ooze from his cracked open skull. I told her not to look, but she couldn't help herself.

Suicide rates among the poor are many times higher than the national average, and those rates don't include all the stubborn skid row alcoholics in the process of drinking themselves to death, or the desperate junkies who never really know if the fix they're about to inject is the one that is too pure and might kill them. Nor do they include all the lonely, depressed people who buoy themselves up with thoughts of suicide and continue to live what they believe to be a temporary existence; because knowing that they'll probably end it all soon perversely gives them the strength to get through another hard day.

In the short time that I've volunteered at The Door Is Open, six regulars (that I know about) have committed suicide, and I don't think any of those suicides were really mentally disturbed. They were just tired of waiting around for a better tomorrow. They were defeated long before they died, because they had let themselves become conditioned to believe that if you're poor, it's because you're lazy, or ignorant, or did something bad. After years of living in harsh poverty, they probably figured, "What have I got to lose?" as they stepped into the abyss.

&ebreve;   &ebreve;   &ebreve;

A little while ago I asked Brother Tim what he thought the average person could do to help the poor. I was expecting him to list acts of mercy like giving alms, feeding the hungry, clothing the naked, sheltering the homeless, visiting the sick, ransoming the prisoner, and burying the dead. Mother Teresa's patented answer.

Instead he replied: "Throwing more money at the problems of poverty doesn't seem to help much. Skid row people won't get anywhere unless they are helped to become physically, emotionally, and financially stable.

"The best place to start," Brother Tim suggested, "is taking them away from the skid row environment, and then working on their alcoholism, or aggression, or depression, or whatever the hell their problems are. The next step should be helping them find decent jobs once they get straight enough to be able to succeed at it."

At that point someone rushed into the drop-in centre and shouted: "No prayer meeting at Harbour Lights tonight!" And Brother Tim and I watched in astonishment as nearly everyone rushed off to get a free "Sally Anne" meal, which was instantly more valuable because they wouldn't have to pay for it with the usual prayers and hymns.

"You know, I've seen you hand out hundreds of the Sisters' sandwiches," Brother Tim slyly said to me as we watched them go. "But I wonder if you've ever eaten one?"

"No," I confessed.

"Me neither," he chuckled. "I wonder why not?"

And we both shrugged and unwrapped some sandwiches and bit into them.

"They're not too bad," I observed.

We sat there quietly chewing and staring at the big empty room in front of us wondering what the hell to do next.

℞   ℞   ℞

When I first started volunteering at The Door Is Open I was a very lonely, recently separated man. I still don't know why I wanted to do it, except that maybe everyone has to answer a few calls in their life, and it had been quite awhile since my last one. I sure as hell didn't expect the place to change me, but as hanging around the drop-in centre became a habit, I noticed that like many of the regulars I seemed to be steadily retreating into myself, making my life more quiet and calm, so I could hear some of those faint, rarely-listened-to voices whispering inside my head as well.

Some nights when I look around the place, nearly every face seems to be angry, or fixated on horrible periods of their history that has cast hypnotic spells over them. In the beginning I think the most jarring thing about my volunteer experiences was learning that despite all the pain I was feeling, I didn't really have any right to complain or feel bitter. I have never been despised, and my problems are not as uprooting or long-suffered or mutilating as many of those I've heard of at The Door Is Open. I gradually stopped whining about how lousy my life was, and began paying more attention to the good things going on around me.

And I began to notice some other similarities between myself and the regulars at the drop-in centre. Many of them drink or do drugs to escape their misery and loneliness, and Vic pointed out that I read a book a day for probably the same reasons. So I stopped reading so much and learned to appreciate my solitude and stop thinking of it as loneliness. I let myself become more open to talking with strangers (and my neighbours) and I began to notice that I was attracting all sorts of unusual people and events that had important, timely things to teach me.

I learned that where your thinking is, there also are all your experiences. And I learned that all the things you have done, the loves you have loved, the suffering and small afflictions you have survived, make up the indelible parts of your spirit.

DIARY EXCERPTS:

☙ ☙ ☙

The boyfriend of a co-worker is a Vancouver police officer. When we first met at an office Christmas party, I asked him what precinct he worked out of. He replied: "Scuzzville, you know, Zone 3, the downtown eastside."

When I told him I volunteered at The Door Is Open his response was an incredulous: "Why on earth would you want to help those dweebs?"

But such "us" and "them" polarity is not exclusive to the police, or even one-sided.

A couple of months ago, I was sitting in the back of a No. 14 Hastings bus when one of the regulars from the drop-in centre appeared directly in front of me. He was drunk and wobbly, his knuckles white with effort as they gripped the stanchion between us. The other commuters around me flinched and looked down into their paperbacks and newspapers, trying to avoid attracting this rough-looking Native's attention.

"Hey, man," the 120-proof warrior slurred at me.

I smiled and said, "What can I do for you, man?"

"How far you riding?"

"Did you want my seat?"

"No, but I think it would be decent if you offered it to that lady," he said, indicating an old, stooped Chinese lady a little down the aisle behind him who was struggling with her tottering inner balance and several heavy shopping bags.

"O, I am sorry," I mumbled, jumping up and motioning the old woman into my seat.

"That's more like it, man," he slurred. "If it weren't for the elders none of us would be here."

"I am sorry," I apologized again. "I was daydreaming and never saw her."

"Yea, you white boys are like that," he said, turning his back on me.

Even after three and a half years at the drop-in centre, I still don't "belong" to his community. I hang out at The Door Is Open because I want to make my life more meaningful, not his, and he knows it.

But the experience has changed me. I'm a different person now. Sometimes people I work with at the hospital are shocked to hear that a prostitute regularly drops by my kitchen for coffee or a free meal, or that a crusty old man who lives in a hand-carved cave on the steep embankment of the Grandview Railway Cut hoses off his dog in our backyard every few weeks and my children comb the burrs and knots from the big Labrador retriever's hair with a special brush they keep beneath the steps for that purpose.

My co-workers ask me if I'm not worried about the negative influences of down and out people upon my young children. I tell them that it's good for my kids to see that bad things don't just happen to bad people, and that life's dangers are everywhere. It's just like how I teach them to look both ways when they cross every street, and to have a deep-rooted, self-preserving fear of the bone-crunching, murderous potential of all vehicular traffic.

EPILOGUE

RECENTLY I WAS riding on a No. 20 bus, on my way to see a movie with my kids at the new twelve-theatre Cineplex downtown, bored with my life, thinking about all the uphill miles of drudgery to sleepwalk through before I could rest: The dishes, the laundry, the vacuuming, the cooking, the feeding frenzy around the supper table, the repetitive bedtime stories. I barked at my three little maniacs about swinging from the stop request bell rope because they were starting to piss off the bus driver, and then I sulkily stared out of the window at the downtown eastside sidewalks rolling by. I glimpsed a couple of teenage girls smoking crack from a smoky glass tube in the doorway of a boarded-up store, and then I saw a drunk down on his hands and knees, coughing like a gorilla trying to spit up a fur ball.

The neighbourhood looked meaner and more dangerous than usual. I was glad that we were going to a matinee and wouldn't be travelling back this way after dark. And then it occurred to me that it wasn't that long ago that I used to walk by here a couple of nights a week, alone, and with a sense of impunity.

Just then, my youngest tumbled off his seat and rolled down the centre aisle like a squealing hedgehog and as I picked him up and soothed him and searched his tiny hands and face for fresh scrapes and bruises, I began feeling nostalgic for those former times when I enjoyed regularly scheduled time off just for myself. What had happened to me since then? When exactly had my free will been hijacked?

I guess I was feeling a little sorry for myself because my wife and I had just had an argument. I felt unappreciated, enchained by love, tied to one spot, unable to travel, or change jobs, never an hour off for myself from the monotonous distractions of my children, with nothing likely ahead for me but years more of this exhausting perplexity.

Then I recalled something that happened with the counsellor I saw during the early, painful days of our long-ago separation. She was talking about what I could do about my deep depression. She asked me: What did I want from my life? What did I think would make me happy? I was dumfounded by her questions, and completely mortified by my own speechlessness, which seemed to be eerily similar to how some of the alcoholics down at the drop-in centre get when someone asks them their name and they can't remember.

But in the middle of my blank despair, there in the counsellor's office, just like how a sudden cool breeze can startle you awake when a window is thrown open in a stuffy room, I remembered recently seeing a melon-bellied pregnant woman walking blissfully along the beaches at Spanish Banks in the mucky commingling of surf and sand, hand-in-hand with her husband, with two small children dancing around their legs like puppies. I had been writing my sad thoughts on the sand with a stick, wishing that my depression could be washed away by the tide as easily, when I looked up and saw that contented-looking family.

I remembered feeling so jealous that I nearly fainted, and I had to sit motionless on the sand for several minutes. I told my counsellor about it and exclaimed: "That's what I want my life to be like. I want to find a woman who will love me and I want to have at least two more kids with her. I want my life to be like that happy family I saw on the beach."

My counsellor sagely reminded me that I knew nothing at all about how happy or miserable that family was, since they were complete strangers to me. But I didn't care, because for the first time in a long while parts of my life came into focus. I suddenly knew what I have really wanted all along, and that the bohemia I had been playing around with as a "separated" man was nothing but a hollow drum.

And so here I am today, six years (and two more children) later, riding on a smelly city bus, batting my pig-headed kids off the bell rope, every moment of my life consumed by their ever-shifting whims, remembering that conversation with a stranger I once paid to listen to me rationalize about why I had to live my life exactly like I did, despite how miserable it made me. And right about then my busy world paused just long enough for me to finally realize that with three young kids to raise my life is very LOUD with meaning right now, and I'm usually far too overwhelmed to be depressed. Seemingly all my prayers from back then have been answered, and ironically it has been with the same woman that I had hated and blamed for ruining my life when I was wishing for the very life that I am leading now.

And looking back I have no idea how my wife and I ever reconciled? How we managed to turn our separate predicaments into common achievements, or learned to accept our own portions of responsibility for our difficult marriage, because in the beginning we only started spending time together again because we both were trying to understand why our marriage had been such a failure, and we wanted to explain to each other (and ourselves) why we had behaved as badly as we did.

But I guess our unlikely reconciliation was probably just about the changes we both went through during our seventeen months apart. All those hard personal lessons. And it was about all the startling shifts and countermoves of communication styles we both made as we tried to rebalance the teeter-totter of our relationship—the accidental chain of small reactions caused by both our minor changes in behaviour, changing how we reacted with each other. Somehow we began to understand each other's feelings and started resolving our problems more amicably, and slowly shed our doubting like heavy weather clothing.

☙ ☙ ☙

The bus driver cheered when we stood up to get off at the stop near Carrall Street. As soon as I got my mob safely onto the sidewalk, a weaselly-looking teenager asked me for my bus transfers, or some spare change, and my generous middle-kid gave him the loonie he'd been carrying in his pocket for three days.

As we walked along the sidewalk towards Abbott Street I could see the stadium-like architecture of Tinseltown down the block. Its sheer, massive weight and its sharp, unusual angles and diagonals, its absurd multiplication of everything, produced a bewildering, wearying spectacle: A big, architectural bully completely out of context among the crumbling brick fronts of the SRO Hotels across the street. A couple of yellow-jacketed security guards were strategically spaced along the broad sidewalk outside the mall, and a police cruiser was idling at the curb beside the McDonalds restaurant. A pair of cops were questioning a rough-looking man, and I remembered that the last time I had walked down this block of Pender Street the site was a big empty pit half-filled with rain water. The time before that it was a block of narrow old logger's hotels with small bacon and egg cafés and corner stores spilling out onto the broad sidewalk.

As we entered the mall, my kids counted the number of security guards we saw before we reached the third-floor cinemas. They counted fourteen.

☙ ☙ ☙

A bit later, sitting in my balcony seat in the large, dark theatre, I was unable to follow the stupid Disney cartoon that seemed to mesmerize my children. So I used the time to think. I remembered dropping my Wednesday evening shifts at The Door Is Open after the birth of our second kid, and that I stopped volunteering completely after the birth of our third son. But I often miss the place and occasionally drop by, even though nearly all the volunteers I worked with have drifted away too. There is always someone on the porch who remembers me, and wants to morbidly reminisce about all the guys that had dropped dead since I used to hang around there.

Sitting in the dark theatre, looking back, I recalled that when I first started volunteering I was a bitter man, looking for something to do that wasn't too self-destructive on the two nights a week I had off from child-rearing. Then I began learning my lessons—like that it is what cannot be said that is most important, and that humans are at their best when they're out of their depth, and don't know what they are doing, and that every baby arrives in this world with a loaf of bread under its arms.

I just let all my former experiences from The Door Is Open rush over my mental movie screen like that, in out-of-sequence rushes and loops of repeating images. And then I remembered an important event.

It happened at a funeral in St. Paul's chapel for a twenty-four-year-old prostitute who had overdosed in her Gastown hotel room. The small chapel was half full, and very quiet. There were a couple of fresh flower arrangements in front of the cheap, closed coffin. Most of the congregation were other prostitutes dressed in their working clothes, and a few pimps. One woman apologized to Brother Tim for having nothing black to wear, except for lingerie and a leather mini-skirt.

The funeral service seemed very long to me. But really it must have been rather short, since there were no expressions of grief from the congregation. Father Mel (the Pigeon Park Pastor) described to us in his sermon a woman that was kind, patient, forbearing, Christian. In other words, fictional, since he had never actually met her, and none of her friends had much specific information to offer except that she might have been born in Montreal and she liked to get high. The real woman, whoever she had been, had suffered and now she was dead, and that was all that really mattered. That was all Father Mel should have said, I felt.

But everyone else seemed to enjoy the wordy sermon. When the service was over Brother Tim served some doughnuts and coffee, and many of the working girls told Father Mel that when their time came they hoped to receive such a lovely eulogy.

Then one of the mingling girls asked Brother Tim, "Why is the coffin closed? She OD'd, didn't she? She wasn't run over by a car or shot in the face or nothing, was she?"

"I never asked how she died," Brother Tim explained. "That's how the casket arrived. You can open it if you like."

And when she asked to borrow someone's knife to cut the plastic seal, three vicious looking weapons were immediately handed up to the altar.

"Why didn't they put any make-up on her?" Someone complained when the casket was opened.

"They didn't even comb her hair," someone else bitched.

I looked down at the small, frail body and saw what they meant. No effort had been made to prepare her for viewing. The woman in the coffin just looked cold and dead, with not even the slightest impression of what her power had been, or could have been.

But then something human happened. One by one, the roomful of working girls gathered around the coffin and emptied their small purses upon the corpse. They applied their own make-up to their dead friend's face, and braided her hair with the ribbons from their own hair, and someone made an ingenious skirt of scarves. And slowly, as they worked and gossiped, the corpse was transformed before us—not because the cosmetics made her look much better, but because the loving attention of so many other women helped us to understand that the dead prostitute had really mattered, and her short life had been a significant thing.

More than anything else I ever witnessed at The Door Is Open, that event changed me. And when some of the women began to softly sing "Heartbreak Hotel" I could not imagine a more appropriate hymn for that sublime skid row funeral:

Heartbreak Hotel
Words & music by Mae Boren Axton, Tommy Durden & Elvis Presley

Now since my baby left me
I've found a new place to dwell,
down at the end of Lonely Street
at Heartbreak Hotel.

I'm so lonely,
I'm so lonely,
I'm so lonely that I could die;

and tho' it's always crowded,
you can still find some room
for broken-hearted lovers
to cry there in the gloom

and be so lonely,
oh, so lonely,
oh, so lonely, they could die.

The bell hop's tears flowing,
the desk clerk's dressed in black . . .
They've been so long on Lonely Street,
they never will go back . . .

and they're so lonely . . .
Oh, they're so lonely . . .
they're so lonely . . .
they pray to die.

So, if your baby leaves
and you have a tale to tell,

just take a walk down Lonely Street . . .
to Heartbreak Hotel,

where you'll be so lonely . . .
and I'll be so lonely . . .
we'll be so lonely . . .
that we could die.

"Rendak's shirt, Mother." Then she hastened to explain, lest her mother get the wrong idea about how she came to be wearing it.

They stood there in the dim entryway, lit only by the lantern Venta left them. Mirian provided an abbreviated version of her homecoming. Kellic returned near the end of the tale and waited beside their astonished mother.

"Kellic," Odonya asked. "Have you heard this?"

"Something of it."

"Now, what is with that face? Aren't you happy to see your sister?"

"Quite happy," he said with funereal dignity. "She's found a new salvage drop for us, since this one went so badly."

"Has she?"

"But she won't tell me where. She says that she's sworn to secrecy."

"Kellic," Mirian began.

"Sworn to whom?" Odonya asked.

"Lady Galanor. Mirian's going to manage things for a while." Kellic took the cane from where it was leaning against the side of the wall. "If you'll excuse me."

"Where are you going?" Odonya demanded.

"I have a few errands before a late dinner."

"No you don't." Odonya's voice was stern. "You haven't seen your sister in seven years. You're sharing a meal with her."

"I've waited seven years," Kellic said as he opened the door. "I can wait a little longer." He slammed it behind him.

Odonya sighed in disgust. "He's rushing off to that woman again."

"A girlfriend?"

"One he won't introduce me to. Well, come on then. It'll just be the two of us. Have you eaten?"

"No." She was famished, and she could already smell sizzling pork.

"You have something proper to change into?"

"Thank you."

"Death's harder on the ones left behind," she said sagely.

The sailors and salvage crew dispersed in groups, heading home in the horse-drawn carts family and friends had brought for them. Kellic had a carriage waiting for the Galanors. He offered to escort them home himself, but they demurred, and Alderra called out to Mirian that she hoped she'd be in touch soon.

Kellic stood at the end of the drive, smiling, hand raised in farewell until the carriage and carts rolled away.

Once again his eyes swept over Mirian. "Couldn't you at least have borrowed some shoes?"

"Couldn't you at least have handed over your cane? The jewels in that would have been a fine gift to the families of those dead sailors."

"I have to maintain appearances." Kellic started up the drive, punching the cane into the ground every other step, as if he actually required its use.

"Does that include potions to alter your appearance?"

His stride lagged but didn't stop. He looked over his shoulder. "Sometimes it does. Some of us have to stay and manage things."

His sharp tone was so different from what she remembered. What had happened to him? She held back from asking as she followed.

A cart came rattling down the road. She turned to see it was pulled by a swayback horse. Two men sat with the driver on the rickety bench.

"Are you coming?" Kellic called from up the drive.

The cart drew closer, slowed. The two men on the bench beside the driver were silhouetted by the sky and sea behind them, and appeared to be in conversation.

Finally the driver reined in his horse, and his head turned her way. "Pardon me, miss. I'm looking for the Raas family estate. Is this it?"

"It is."

"Oh, good."

He snapped the reins and brought the horse up the steep drive and on toward the house. Mirian stood in the grass to one side as the cart rolled up. As it came closer, she recognized her sea chest in the back. Both of the passengers stared at her, wide-eyed. "A spirit!" said the nearer. "That's her! The one who dived over the side!"

At some other time, Mirian might have had a little fun with them, but she reassured them she was flesh and blood, then tipped them a few coppers. They were still a little wary of her even after she had them carry the chest through the stout oaken door in the manor wall and onto the porch, but they promised to convey her thanks to Captain Akimba.

Kellic watched the whole thing, arms crossed.

"You should probably have had them carry it into the house for you, don't you think?"

"I can manage."

"I'll do it, then." Frowning, Kellic handed his cane off to her and bent low. He grunted in surprise as he lifted the chest.

Mirian pushed the door open and was immediately greeted with a familiar and comforting mix of scents, a blend of old wood and cooking spices and worn leather, a trace of her mother's perfume and her father's pipe smoke and a hundred other things.

"Do you carry this wherever you go?" Kellic's voice was strained.

"Not everywhere."

He moved ahead of her. "Where's this salvage drop you're taking the Galanors?"

"That's a secret."

"Don't joke, Mirian."

"I'm not joking. It must remain an absolute secret until departure time."

"I run the business now, Mirian." Kellic halted. He turned to face her as they heard the pad of slippered feet in the rooms beyond. A lantern light bobbed as someone approached the down the hallway.

"Lady Galanor has asked me to lead the expedition, Kelli And she's sworn me to secrecy."

"I see." His tone was sharp. "So you'll simply take over, then?

"Just this drop, Kellic. Then it's yours to run. Into the grou again, if you wish."

She wished she'd held back from the last. It had slipped ou and with a lantern suddenly shining on the both of them and t glad cry of two old servants who saw her, there was no chance apologize. Looking at the hardened expression on her brothe face, she wasn't sure it would've done any good if she had.

Old, round-cheeked Venta squealed like a little girl and call out for Mirian's mother.

"I'll just take this back to your room." Kellic stiffly shoulder past.

Venta's husband, stooped with age, was grinning as well. Th Mirian saw her mother.

Tall, slim, garbed in an orange wrap belted in brown, she w as elegant as ever. She stared at Mirian from the courtyard archw as if she were looking at a ghost.

Odonya Raas had been just out of her teens when Leova married her, and in her early forties she was still a handson woman, with the slim build typical of Bas'o people. Her dai face was reminiscent of Mirian's in many ways, though rounde softer. He full lips opened in wordless wonder, and then sl beckoned her daughter into her arms. The women embrace fiercely.

Venta excused herself, saying that she'd cook something, bi her precise words were lost in flood from Mirian's mother.

"Let me look at you!" Her mother held her at arm's length. "B my ancestors! Your hair's so wet. You'll ruin it if you keep it lik that. And what is it you've come home in, child?"

"Ivrian carried my sea chest back to my room."

"Get yourself dry then, girl, and we'll eat."

It was strange to join Mother at the long dining room table, and Mirian was all too conscious of the two empty chairs, one at the head where her father should have sat, the other across from her where a younger, smiling Kellic should have been.

Her mother kept conversation light, asking her further about the attack, and her explorations, and her Bas'o cousins, whom Mirian had seen far more recently.

Afterward, they retired to the slatted wooden chairs in the courtyard. A low fire burned in the small stone pit at its center, for Odonya Raas felt the evening's chill.

Both women fell silent. Mirian was wishing she'd handled Kellic better. What had turned her gracious younger brother into the miserly would-be lordling who'd met her at the docks? She felt her fists balling in anger as she remembered the casual way he'd dismissed assistance to the families of the dead sailors, all while holding his expensive cane.

She wanted to ask her mother about him, and any number of things, but after the meal it was much simpler to sit in silence with her and admire the stars.

Mirian found her gaze drifting to the other doors that opened onto the courtyard: the one that led to the room she'd called her own for eighteen years, and where she'd just changed out of Rendak's shirt and into a yellow dress. The door in the corner led to her father's office and the second-story watchtower rising above the overgrown acacias and the home's slanted roof.

Her mother's eyes followed the path of Mirian's gaze. "I used to sit up there every evening, when you were out with Leo." She had told her the same story a hundred times, but this time the ending was different. "I still watched, most days. But you know, the day he died, I was in the market. I didn't find out until I walked in and Rendak was waiting on the porch."

"I'm so sorry, Mother."

Odonya sighed and faced her daughter. "There was no need to keep things secret from Kellic, was there? This is his business."

"Not for much longer, to hear tell of it."

Odonya's eyebrows climbed her forehead. "And who told of it?"

"Lady Galanor. She's ready to pull up stakes."

"Kellic can't be blamed if the pickings are slim, any more than your father could. You think you can do better?"

"A leader leads from the front."

"So you're taking over Kellic's business."

Her mother's tone clawed at her patience. "I'm saving it. Not taking it over. I'll run just this one job. Afterward I'll turn everything back over to him." She held off commenting about how well she thought him suited for the post. Maybe she wasn't seeing him at his best.

Odonya looked at her sidelong. "You must have something very big planned."

"It may be," Mirian said.

Odonya let out a long sigh, then shook her head. "You want to salvage with the lizardfolk, don't you?"

"How did you know?" Mirian asked in astonishment.

"I know what Lady Galanor wants. Don't do it."

Mirian's exasperation grew. "Why not? You might have mentioned you'd borrowed money on both the house and the ship in *one* of your letters. I could have sent money."

"It would take a fortune at this point. Have you gone and gotten yourself a diamond mine in the Bandu Hills?"

Mirian ignored the jibe. "So it's true?"

"It's true." Her mother's chin rose defiantly.

"And how do you expect to survive without a house?"

Odonya indicated the homestead with a sharp jerk of her arm "None of this is worth your death. Rendak says a sea devil shark killed your father when he was scrounging the Chelish fleet wreck, but Leo knew how to handle them. It wasn't the sea devils. It was folk who knew he was going to work for Lady Galanor."

Mirian stilled. She started to repeat what Rendak had told her, but Odonya pressed on.

"There're spies out there who know very well that Lady Galanor's trying to find funds for Sargava. They don't care who they kill to stop her. You sign on with 'Alderra,' and it's your death warrant."

"I've already shaken on it."

Her mother's eyes might have been coals, so bright did they seem to burn. "You stupid child! You let that woman run you!"

"She didn't 'run me'! What choice did I have if I'm to save this place?" Her mother didn't answer, so Mirian pressed on. "What are you planning to do, Mother? Go back to selling carvings on the beach?"

Odonya raised her head and looked away. In profile, she looked every inch the Bas'o warrior woman she had never been, for she'd been raised by a Mulaa aunt who recognized her artistic talents at an early age. It was that aunt who'd taken her to the beach the same day Leovan happened by her display of wood carvings. Love at first sight, Father had called it in his oft-repeated rendition of the moment.

"Mother, look at me."

Odonya's chin rose higher.

Mirian's tongue grew sharp to draw her out. "You could dress Kellic up in bright Mulaa robes and have him carry the goods—"

Odonya bared her teeth. "Do you mock your own blood?"

"Kellic wouldn't survive anywhere but here. And neither will you. And you know it!"

"There's where you're wrong. I'm sick of this place and what it's done to me. What it's done to Kellic. What it did to your father." She put a hand up to her face to wipe moisture from the corner of her eyes. Her voice was still fierce. "This city ate him away from the inside, Mirian."

"He would have given his life to protect his family's holdings."

"He did. Is that what you mean to do?"

"I'll manage things."

"No. There's enough money left for an apartment in the city, at least for a few years. Kellic will have to adjust."

"And what about our servants, and our sailors, and Rendak and Gombe and Tokello? What will they do if you give up? This family has a responsibility to them!"

"They can find other work."

"Can they? Who will they salvage for, Mother?"

She saw her mother's jaw tightening.

Mirian swung her legs off the reclined chair and sat on its edge, sandaled feet on the tiles. "It was you who taught me to stand by my obligations. This homestead has been in Raas hands for over two hundred years. We owe it to those who fought and suffered and died to build this place. They're buried out back of the stables. Would some stranger tend their graves?" She halted for a moment, watching her mother's expression for signs of change. She saw none, even though she knew her mother's people placed as much or more importance on gravesites as colonials. "And we have an obligation to the living who depend upon us for their livelihood."

Her mother's response sounded almost petulant. "Says the woman who wandered away for seven years."

Mirian spoke quickly, for she sensed her mother readying to interrupt. "Six and a half. I can handle myself in the wilds. I can handle myself below the waves. And I'm the one who stopped that pirate attack."

Odonya's gaze was still stern, but there was a hint of steely pride in the set of her lip.

"I'm going," Mirian said.

Her mother was silent for a long moment. "Stubborn," she said at last. "Just like your father."

"No. Not just like."

"No." Her mother reached slowly out for her hand, squeezed it tight before releasing and climbing to her feet with a sigh. "Come on, then."

"Where are we going?"

"I thought you needed to know about the dive. I know damned well your father didn't tell Lady Galanor about it, or she would have someone else running down those lizardfolk."

Mirian stood, watching as her mother stepped into the house and returned with a lit candle. She used it to light a rusty lantern hung on one of the vine-wrapped pillars supporting the court-yard's overhang.

"Come, child."

Her mother strode across the tiled courtyard to open the weathered teak door to Leovan's office. She replaced the keychain about her neck and held up the lantern.

The room was ordered and neat—shipshape, her father would have said. The sweet bouquet of his pipe tobacco still lingered, along with the comforting smell of old paper. Rolls of parchment and charts were organized on long shelves behind glass panels. The bookshelves were liberally sprinkled with knickknacks, many of which Mirian recognized as her mother's carvings, but there were other odds and ends besides—a framed oil painting of her great-great-grandmother Mellient on the wall across from the desk hung beside a lovingly detailed chart of Desperation Bay. Hand-drawn, she knew, by Mellient and her husband.

Her father's heroes. Not just because they were bold and daring, but, she now understood, because they were rebellious. Her great-great-grandfather was said to have been at least a quarter native, of the seafaring Ijo people. And that, to hear tell, had raised more than a few eyebrows among the neighbors.

Odonya closed the door behind her and stepped past the old desk, imported all the way from a Chelish port when Mirian's remote ancestor, a fourth son of a minor noble, departed to claim land for himself. Mirian's gaze lingered for only a moment on the heavy furniture, recalling childhood days spent pressed up against its cool black side, drawing in her sketchbook while her father scanned charts or consulted family journals.

There was a treasure trove of information stored in the volumes that lined the bookshelves, provided one could decipher the family code and had the sailing knowledge to make use of it. Mirian used the same code in her Pathfinder journal.

Mirian gazed up at Mellient's portrait again, the plain woman with the copper-tinged black locks and the high-bridged nose who'd been so important to her family ancestry. Cracks had long since begun to show in the paint.

Mirian hadn't realized how different the painting of Mellient truly was until she'd seen other portraits from the same period. Those early Chelish colonists had been so determined to retain their cultural heritage that they had already ossified into an imitation of dignity. Their grim faces in the Hall of Councils had frightened her as a little girl.

Great-great-grandmother Mellient had insisted the painter show her smiling, and that she be depicted with the tan most colonists developed rather than the phony lily-white used in painting aristocratic skin tones of the time. As a little girl, Mirian had been disappointed Mellient wasn't more lovely, but she now recognized a strength of character in her appearance that was its own kind of beauty.

Odonya had been watching her. "Pay attention, child. You'd think you were half in love with her the way your father was." Odonya gently pressed a dark finger to the glassed image next to the painting. A long peninsula extended east above Desperation Bay, northwest of all Sargava's coastal settlements. This was a nautical chart, so the only topographical feature indicated on this portion of the map was the wide mouth of the Oubinga River.

"There you go, the Kaava Lands. More than four hundred miles of dense jungle. It's said everything living inside there wants to kill you or eat you. Probably both. And that goes for any people, apart from the Ijo. That's your destination. Still interested?"

"I thought this was a salvage dive."

"It is. The Karshnaar lizardfolk mean to march in to their ancestral ground near some place called the Pool of Stars to retrieve lost chronicles of their people."

Mirian had never heard of the Pool of Stars or the Karshnaar clan. The only lizardfolk in the Kaava Lands she'd heard of lived along the Little Vanji River and were known as the Vanizhar. She'd spoken with a Pathfinder who'd interviewed one of their elders at length.

"Why do the Karshnaar need salvagers?" Mirian asked.

"The clan's very small and needs assistance if they're to get in and out of the Kaava alive. And they came to your father because they'd heard he could dive. The old Karshnaar city is built into cenotes. Blue holes."

Mirian had heard both terms, natural clear-water sinkholes that formed in limestone. She'd dived in one south of Kalabuto. "Are these lizardfolk aquatic?"

"No, but the city is linked up with a cavern system. To navigate through the city, you have to hold your breath for as long as the Karshnaar, which is a good long time, I'm told. Or be a salvager."

"You seem to know a lot about the Karshnaar." Mirian was a little surprised. Usually her mother kept apart from her father's clients.

"I met them," Odonya said. "One was a female named Kalina. I quite liked her."

"Alderra said they promised gemstones in return."

"Baskets of them. They were certain the majority of the gems lay hidden in secret chambers."

"And why aren't the Karshnaar clan still on their ancestral land?"

"You sound like your father. He asked them the same question."

"And they said?"

"Some other clan drove them out."

"The Vanizhar?"

"It may be. I don't recall. Whoever they were long since abandoned the city."

"If it's such an excellent site, there may be something else living there."

"Of course there is. The jungle never stops growing, and you can guarantee that some things have crawled into such a fine set of hidey-holes for protection, and that other things have crawled in after to hunt them. If you go there, you'll be in the middle of the food chain."

Her mother could be blunt when she meant to drive home a point.

"And what is this Pool of Stars?"

Odonya shook her head. "That I can't answer. A landmark the Karshnaar need to reach before they find their city."

"Do you know where the city is?"

"No. The lizardfolk trusted your father, but not that far."

"Where are the Karshnaar now?"

Her mother pointed to the top of one of the glass-fronted cupboards, lifting the lantern so Mirian could see the warped end of a harpoon propped beside a frowning wooden mask and a cracked, cobalt-blue planter.

"They're hiding on the cabinet?" Mirian joked.

Her mother's lips turned down in irritation. "Look there, at that mask. Kalina noted it."

She considered the mask and its drooping eyelids, its exaggerated mouth.

"The Karshnaar lands are in the Laughing Jungles, west of the Undaru River." Odonya pointed at the face. "Near the edge of their territory, right outside the jungle, is a huge boulder with that face. You find that, you'll find their hunting land. And likely a whole mess of trouble."

Mirian didn't tell her mother she was used to trouble. "It looks like I have a long ride in the morning."

"By yourself?"

"I'll take Rendak and Gombe."

"You'll not stay longer?"

Mirian shook her head. "We're short on time."

"You're just like Leo."

Mirian didn't think that was true, but she held her tongue as she hugged her mother.

The older woman insisted she take the lantern. "I don't think there are any candles in your bedroom. The sheets should be fresh. I had Venta change them."

She bade her mother a good sleep as Odonya was locking the door to her father's study.

"Be careful," her mother called after, then added hastily, "I know you will, but it's a mother's duty to say such things. And you find time to pay respects to your father. He did love you."

Mirian bore the lantern's pool of light away. For the briefest instant, she remembered what it had been like as a young girl, to hear the swish of her mother's skirt, the creak of her sandal, as she slipped away after singing her a Bas'o lullaby each night.

And then her mother walked away, and Mirian was once more in the present, standing before the door of a room in which she hadn't slept in almost seven years. Somewhere, out back of the wall, her father lay at his final rest. As she put her hand to the doorknob, Mirian wondered whether she would have the strength to visit his grave come morning.

She would have to see. In many ways, she preferred the thought of a long journey into the brush searching for lizardfolk.

5

The Way through Darkness

Sylena

"I love this place, but I do tire of the heat." Sylena looked away from her own image in the mirror to meet the reflected gaze of the man who'd entered her bedchamber. She paused with the kohl pencil beneath her left eye. "If I had my way, I would go naked most of the day."

"I'm sure the folk of Sargava would be both delighted and scandalized," Atok replied.

She smiled at him in satisfaction, shifted forward on the mirrored dressing table, and returned to her work. With her perfect complexion, huge black eyes, and sharp features, Sylena knew she was a beauty, but she never tired of compliments. She wore only a black, shoulderless, thigh-length slip that hugged her petite curves. She understood the effect it could have upon a man, and planned to use it shortly.

Night always fell fast in Sargava, and this evening it had come faster because of the mist. She'd had to cast a light spell on the mirror to finish touching up her appearance, for the candlelight was sucked up by the dark woodwork of the ancient inn's "noble's suite." What she wouldn't give for one of the lovely houses of the aristocrats, with their fine, wide courtyards and shady trees. Instead, she must play the part of a merchant's daughter and live in this moldering room.

"What news?" Sylena asked. She knew Atok would not have returned so swiftly without good reason.

"The 'news,' mistress, is unlikely to please you."

She'd been watching from her room's private balcony when the *Daughter of the Mist* sailed back in to the harbor. "I'm already displeased, Atok. I want specifics. Clearly Edrek and his privateers missed them. Did the salvagers recover anything valuable?"

"They don't seem to have recovered anything at all," Atok said. The gillman's eyebrows were severely arched, leaving him with a perpetual look of amused disdain. Sylena didn't typically find the bald attractive, and the flaps along the gillman's thick neck that enabled him to breathe underwater should have disgusted her, but there had always been something strangely magnetic about her bodyguard. He frowned minutely. "Edrek has been slain."

She sighed. Edrek had been a useful operative.

"Kellic's sister killed him with a magic wand."

She paused in her work and turned in her chair. "Kellic's sister? No one told me she was on the salvage ship."

"She wasn't supposed to be. Apparently she was on her way home to pay respects to her dear father, saw the salvage ship under attack, and dove off to fight them. She surprised Edrek mid-ambush, then she and Lady Galanor led the counterattack that drove the pirates back to their ship. There was some talk that she'd sabotaged the ship from below before she attacked above."

Sylena eyed Atok carefully, trying to decide whether he were developing a sense of humor. The account verged on the preposterous.

"Either Edrek chose his pirates poorly," she said finally, "or Kellic's sister is quite formidable."

"Both, I think. I'm sure the stories passing through the tavern are exaggerated, but she's said to have thrown herself into the fray with a wand in one hand and a cutlass in the other."

"And Alderra Galanor survived."

"Yes."

Her frown deepened. "Is there any word about what Lady Galanor plans next?"

"I'm afraid I heard nothing but talk of the adventure itself. All else is wild speculation."

"Such as?" she growled.

"Forgive me, mistress. I didn't wish to report speculation without indicating—"

"*What*," she said sharply, "did you hear?"

"That Mirian Raas will take over the salvaging operation and use her powers to find riches. They say she spent years mastering the tribal magics of her mother's people and is now a sorceress of great repute."

"Is it true?"

"It's well known that Mirian Raas is a scholar affiliated with the Pathfinder Society. Apparently she used a wand, probably identical to the one Leovan used. That may be all this talk of magic is."

"But you cannot say for sure that she is *not* a practitioner?"

"No, mistress."

"Then go find out."

"As you will." He bowed his head.

She returned to contemplating the mirror, noticing that crow's feet showed near her eyes when she frowned. She was painstaking about the measures she took to preserve the appearance of youth. Sargava's sun was a constant threat to her skin, but she had found, more and more, that the place's climate agreed with her, at least in the mornings and evenings.

Atok hesitated at the door. "You are expecting company, mistress. Do you need me in attendance?"

"Kellic Raas is no danger to me." In fact, the youth was one of her limited pleasures. She had the protections afforded by both her necklace and her ring, should she ever require them.

"Don't you think he'll have all the answers you require?"

"Do you grow lazy, Atok?"

"No, mistress."

"Perhaps you need a little nap," she said with mock sympathy.

"No, mistress."

"The boy is credulous. He'll repeat whatever he's been told by his sister and the salvagers, but he won't know much else. Seek the truth from other sources."

Atok bowed formally. "It is kind of you to clarify. I will do my best."

"See that you do better than Edrek."

"Of that," he said curtly, "you can rest assured."

He shut the door behind him. She heard his footsteps receding through the outer room.

She hadn't expected the assignment to drag on for as long as it had. Kellic was a pretty boy, and she'd turned him into a fine lover, but she was long past her patience for the backward Sargavan culture. To many, the *only* reason to reconquer Sargava was to punish the nation for its insubordination. Her sister, she knew, hoped the place would be abandoned to die of rot. But then, Rajana wasn't a people person.

Sylena understood the land's potential. When Cheliax reconquered the country, preference would be given to those who had worked hard to reclaim it. And there would naturally be some Sargavans who would welcome the return of Chelish rule. Lately she had begun to toy with certain ideas about her own position in that future.

She worked on her appearance for another twenty minutes before opening the balcony doors. Now, at last, the air was cool. The view of the stars over the ocean was stunning, for the mist had ebbed.

Unfortunately, she had no time to take it in. The late dinner she'd ordered would arrive in an hour, along with Kellic, and she had studying to do.

While schooled in magic, Sylena had little interest in the careful work required to master its complexities. Unlike her sister, she labored only a little now and then to keep up a handful of spells. Even the time spent with them was onerous. She dragged out a heavy leather tome and spent a boring quarter hour poring over pronunciation charts. If you put a syllable in the wrong place in the midst of a spell, you might just end up burning your hand off.

She was delighted when the inn servants announced themselves in the outer room, giving her an excuse to put the book aside. While they arranged the meal, she dressed in an off-the-shoulder red dress with a plunging neckline and a skirt slit to the upper thigh—the kind of thing Kellic likely never saw in Sargava.

He arrived punctually at half past eight, carrying a box of expensive candied nuts and a huge bouquet of tropical flowers. Sylena dismissed the hovering servants and allowed Kellic to pull the chair out for her.

The outer room of the suite was lit by a candle-heavy chandelier. She knew her age was better disguised by dimmer light, and that the candles gave her skin a golden glow.

They didn't do badly for Kellic, either—but then, he was a good-looking man, even when dressed in the high-necked collars and cravats of a century ago. Sargavan styles were *so* backward.

His were a lovely blend of the best features of two peoples. A proud nose, but not long or severe. His lips were full and sensual, his hair black but as straight as hers. Unfortunately, he must recently have downed one of his potions, for his skin was not the natural light brown that she so admired, but more of a Sargavan olive. He'd explained to her that even though everyone in Sargava knew his heritage, his changed appearance smoothed the waters when he managed business affairs. The potions were expensive, however, and he claimed to use them sparingly.

When she had suggested they meet for dinner tonight, she'd expected to be consoling him over the loss of his ship. Now she was determined to find out not just what had happened, but what his family planned.

There was only a token difficulty in getting him to talk, owing to typical tight-lipped Sargavan social niceties. Kellic, though, was too incensed to remain silent long. By the time they'd reached the dessert course he'd opened up completely.

"I just don't understand how she made such a good impression on Lady Galanor." Kellic pushed away the half-finished torte. "You should have seen what Mirian was wearing."

"Perhaps you underestimate your sister's charms."

"I'm not saying that Mirian's unattractive. I'm just saying that she lacks social grace."

Sylena smiled as though she understood. Privately, she thought the Sargavans had rather too much social grace; perhaps Alderra Galanor approved of Mirian because she was more direct. But then she knew how much Kellic idolized the Chelish nobility. In their ranks, his true skin color would be no hindrance to social mobility.

Sylena poured another glass of the strong Chelish wine she'd brought with her and handed it across the table. "It doesn't seem a situation where social grace was paramount. If Lady Galanor felt grateful to her for helping, she might have wished to overlook Mirian's manner. You say that they came to some accord?"

"I believe so." He shook his head in anger. "She means to take over from me. She says she doesn't, but she won't even tell me where the new salvage drop's going to be."

Interesting, and likely problematic. "Did she say why not?"

"She says Lady Galanor's sworn her to secrecy. Yet I'm the one who's been running things, not her! I don't even know when she intends to leave!"

Worse and worse. Sylena had thought that eliminating Leovan Raas had removed all competency from the family. Then Kellic had blathered on that his team was sure to find a famous wreck today, so she'd sent Edrek with those pirates. That had proved an expensive failure, one she'd be taken to task for by her sister.

To make matters worse, Alderra Galanor was once more allied with someone who knew what they were doing.

It was vital she learn more about Mirian Raas. "Is your sister a sorcerer, Kellic?"

"I don't think so. I suppose she might be. She's been gone a long time. Why? Do you think she tricked Lady Galanor with magic?"

He was obsessed with his perceived loss of status in front of the Galanors. "I was just curious. You said she wielded a wand against the pirates."

"A family heirloom. Like the one my father had."

"Oh?" She knew that wand well. Atok had recovered both it and a magical ring from the arm his shark had torn off Kellic's father.

"There were two sets, and father gave the other to Mirian, even though she was leaving." It was obvious from his tone whom he thought they should have gone to.

"But you wouldn't have wanted them, would you? You're a landholder, not a laborer."

Sylena studied him while he frowned, trying to decide her best course of action. It was crucial she find out what Mirian Raas planned, and that she stop her. But the best way to do that might result in the sacrifice of one of her favorite pieces. It would be a shame to have to lose Kellic. It would take a lot of work to establish herself with another nobleman, and he might not be as easily controlled.

Still, she had her orders. She smiled sadly. "Do you wish advice?"

Kellic shook his head. "Oh. No."

"I'm a businesswoman." She broadened her smile. "And we're friends, aren't we?"

"Yes, of course we are. My dearest friend." He gave her his best smile.

"Then, while I know it's not completely proper, allow me to offer a suggestion." She put a hand over his own. "I hope you don't think me too forward."

"I would naturally be grateful for any advice, Sylena, though I don't wish to impose."

"Of course not. You must learn what Mirian plans and what sort of arrangement she made with Lady Galanor. And when she leaves for that salvage trip, be sure you accompany her."

She might as well have told him to stick his hand into a sack of snakes, judging by his reaction. She had long since suspected Kellic was a coward. She didn't mind. It made him more malleable.

"Sometimes," she said, "a gentleman must take risks. A woman likes a man who does that."

Sylena had his interest now, naturally, so she took his hand as she rose and led him toward the door to her bedchamber. She saw him gulp in desire.

She liked to be appreciated. She paused with one hand on the doorknob, her lips inches from his ear. "I have a magical gift that I will give you, to help keep you safe."

"A gift?" he repeated stupidly.

"A ring. I will let you wear it if you promise to come back to me." She opened the door into the darkness. "Now fetch one of those candles from the table. The heat's been stifling, and I think I shall be far more comfortable without all this clothing. But I don't want you to lose your way in the dark."

6

The Karshnaar
Mirian

Mirian woke with the dawn, light streaming through the windows to reveal the walls she had painted long ago. On her right wall was a seascape, the earliest and least sophisticated of the paintings, though she was still pleased with the way she'd drawn some of the distant ships. Facing her was a complex jungle landscape. As she blinked and sat up, she remembered her father bringing her the small tinctures to add to the paints to create the vibrant violets on some of the flowers, the yellow-white of the urdan roots.

He'd been a good father, once. Before he'd been consumed by bitterness.

Mirian found Tokello's little niece already awake and caring for the horses. She sent her out to round up Rendak and Gombe. Then she helped Venta pack fresh fruits and bread for the day's journey. Or tried to—Venta grew tired of her "interference" and chased her away so she could get the job done faster.

Rendak and Gombe hadn't yet turned up, although little Keasha reported they'd be along presently. And that left Mirian standing in the courtyard by herself, contemplating the visit she'd been dreading.

She trudged out to the edge of the family holdings, beyond her grandmother's long-abandoned vegetable garden, past the shack with its sagging roof where she'd shared her first kiss with a raffish sailor. She smiled at the memory and made her way to the rough stone fence that surrounded the family plot.

The tropic sun had aged her grandmother's stone. After fifteen years, it was pocked and stained as though it had withstood fifty. Only her father's was new.

She stood looking down at it, reading the engraved name and thinking of his broad rugged face. So kind, when she was young. So often frowning in later years, brought down by the city's prejudices and the vagaries of the family profession. It was almost as if he had deliberately chosen trouble, to spite the establishment and give him better reason to hate it.

She knelt by the side of the stone and put her hand to it, bowing her head. "Goodbye, Father. I hope you're in a kinder land now. I wish things hadn't been so bad there between us, at the end." She wished, too, that she knew what he'd done to twist Kellic, but she didn't say that aloud. "I miss you," she added. "And Mother misses you." She would have said more, but she suddenly found it difficult to speak.

After she'd left home so many years ago, she'd spent time among her mother's people, the Bas'o. In their tongue, she asked her ancestors to welcome him into their home and asked him for forgiveness for all the worries she had given him. Then, softly, she sang the Song of Sleep. It was the same she had heard from her mother every night, save for the final stanza, which dealt specifically with final rests and long journeys.

She rose, wiping tears from her eyes. When she turned she found Gombe and Rendak waiting solemnly on the graveyard's edge, straw hats removed respectfully. Despite the fact that one was a trim, bald native and the other a tanned, burly colonial, at that moment they seemed almost like mirror images.

Before long, all three were riding under the old stone arch and headed onto the cobbled roadway. Soon they left the ridge road and reached the Diomar Wall, where khaki-uniformed native soldiers stared at them from on high.

Once she reached the main thoroughfare, Mirian might have turned north into the city, joining the long line of ox-carts laden with pineapples, lumber, sugar cane, and pelts, but her course required a southern turn onto the cobbled thoroughfare that had caused so much trouble for the baron. Miles of thatched mud huts stretched ahead of her on either side.

A small scouting patrol, distinctive in their gray-green jackets and helms, had gathered just behind the drovers, awaiting their turn through the gate. Their colonial officer eyed her stolidly as she drew closer, and she half expected a challenge. Would he question whether the animal was her property? Ask for identification? She steeled herself for the insulting inevitability of it, and was surprised when he simply looked away.

Perhaps she wasn't the only woman of Bas'o heritage who rode a fine horse south. Or perhaps he simply wasn't in the mood to harass someone this morning.

She led her men past the soldiers and moved through the long streams of natives dressed in red, blue, and yellow cloth. Some headed toward the gate, others south toward the vast pineapple fields. These, too, looked at her with guarded curiosity and some envy.

The colonials might lump all of Sargava's native peoples together, but there were as many different tribes and ethnicities among the so-called "Mwangi people" as there were among the light-skinned northern races. Not only were they not all the same; they didn't even necessarily get along. In Eleder, for instance, the Mulaa often viewed those of the more nomadic Bas'o tribe with suspicion. And even simple things like her sturdy boots, the plain bridle, and the horse itself spoke to wealth that many natives could never hope to obtain.

Such was Eleder. And yet, even with such poverty, the folk she passed laughed and joked among themselves.

When she passed from the slums and the end of the cobblestone, she arrived at the great sweep of pineapple fields, the plants in carefully staggered stages of growth, all tended by Mulaa workers in their bright robes, heads shielded by equally brilliant scarves or grass hats.

Another hour's ride took them to fields of sugarcane, scattered with stands of palm trees and tropical grasses that demarked property lines.

They rode for hours, the sun hot on their backs, before they ventured past settled lands. Even then, the Laughing Jungle was just a smear on the southern horizon.

During that long ride, Rendak and Gombe fell to asking her more about her time away: what it had been like wandering with the Bas'o tribe through the plains, whether she'd seen anything truly interesting as a Pathfinder, what she was working on now. The two had an easy camaraderie, and she soon discovered Gombe brought out a more playful side of Rendak. When she'd left, Gombe had been a raw but promising recruit, a close-mouthed newcomer. Now he and Rendak bantered with the ease of old friends.

She had a harder time with her own spirits. The rings on her fingers felt like weights, and her eyes were drawn to them like lodestones. As angry as her father had been when she declared her plans to leave Eleder, he'd refused the return of the tools he'd given her. He claimed they were her birthright, even as she protested she'd never have need for them. It tuned out she had, countless times, making her way through swampland or diving in that Kalabuto cenote. Or just the other night, to save the *Daughter* and its crew

Because of Rendak, she now knew her father had fully expected her homecoming. And the strange thing was that once she was back on the deck, feeling the roll of waves and breathing in the salt spray, she wondered whether she had chosen right all those years ago. It wasn't that she regretted getting to know her mother's side of the family or learning the secrets of the adventuring scholars who called themselves Pathfinders, but there was something invigorating about the pounding surf and the ocean breeze. She would never have admitted as much to Rendak and Gombe, but she looked forward to more time upon the waters. The thought of returning to the dusty cave she'd been exploring so far from the ocean felt like turning her back on life itself.

And yet, to return to the sea meant to return to Eleder, and all of its ugliness.

They stopped at noon to let their horses graze. She mulled over her feelings while she fanned herself with her hat. Rendak and Gombe rooted through the supplies to arrange a meal. Only when they sat down together did she fully explain her mission.

"The lizardfolk, eh?" Gombe said. "I wondered why we never ended up working with them."

"You know why," Rendak said.

The native glanced covertly at Mirian.

"I know my brother's being an ass," she said.

"It's not quite like that," Rendak said charitably. "He's just got himself so worried about what people think that he forgot who he really is."

"He used to be a nice enough lad," Gombe agreed.

As they ate in the shade of a baobab tree, she looked for the edge of the jungle just visible through the haze to the south. Lizardfolk were rare enough anymore, at least anywhere close to Eleder. She was a little surprised that a tribe managed to live so close within the Laughing Jungle and still avoid any incidents. Humans and lizardfolk had an uneasy relationship. Either this tribe had only recently come to the Laughing Jungle, or they had learned to deal better with human encroachments than others.

Rendak broke her reverie with a light touch on her arm. He pointed toward a cheetah lying in the shade of a bush only fifty yards off. The big cat watched them with bright green eyes.

"She's a beauty," Rendak said.

Gombe froze. "Pretty's fine, but I hope she's not hungry."

Rendak laughed at him. "Cheetahs don't hunt humans."

"They don't?"

"Only bald ones," Mirian said.

Both men looked at her in surprise, then chuckled.

Mirian nodded to the cheetah as she climbed to her feet. "Good hunting, sister."

The cat stared as they mounted up and rode away.

By four bells they had left the trail and moved into the clumpy jungle grass that had grown up to replace burned-out trees. A herd of native cattle grazed only a half league west. Nearer at hand was a huge boulder. On drawing closer, Mirian saw that it did, indeed, resemble a slightly rounder version of the face in her father's study, with pouting lips and immense closed eyes.

Mirian slipped down from her horse and considered the jungle. It began abruptly, sharply, seemingly as impenetrable a barrier as a cliff face. Rendak and Gombe were more than a little troubled when she informed them she'd be heading in alone.

"You brought us all this way to watch the horses?" Rendak asked.

"I'm walking onto someone else's tribal ground," Mirian reminded him. "Don't worry. I'm an old hand at this."

"Even old hands can get hurt," Gombe said.

Rendak agreed. "Why don't you leave one of us with the horses, and the other can—"

She shook her head. Lizardfolk were famously territorial. If something went wrong, she didn't want it to go wrong for anyone but her. "If I don't come out, don't come in after me."

Rendak snorted.

"That's an order. Now if you'll excuse me, gentlemen, I've got to get moving." She turned her back, heard Rendak's furtive protest die when he saw her kneeling. Praying had been a useful way to cut him off, but it was also entirely proper to ask for both Desna's blessing and her ancestors. After the proper words, she took her shoulder pack from her horse, buckled it in an X over her chest, and started forward, machete in hand.

"We'll be waiting," Gombe called.

Mirian walked just inside the tree line for almost a quarter hour before discovering a trail. In the press of the dirt nearby she detected the print of an elongated, four-toed foot. Lizardfolk.

She advanced into the jungle. It was dark beneath the canopy, but not the unalterable blackness those sensational pamphlet-writers led one to think. Bright orchids bloomed at face level, and tulu birds and parrots called to their flocks from branches above.

Mirian didn't know whether this was a trail cut by the Karshnaar or just an animal track they used for convenience. She walked for nearly half an hour, machete in hand, wondering whether she should turn back. Rendak and Gombe would be setting up camp. She could join them and head deeper into the jungle come morning.

A branch snapped behind her. She whirled.

A lizardfolk stood there, pointing a long, straight spear at her chest.

"You are not wanted here, human."

7
Weapons and Scales
Mirian

The lizardfolk's arms rippled with muscle. Its scales were the color of palm fronds, touched here and there with spots of brown or lighter green, as a human might be dusted with freckles. Its long neck was adorned with a necklace of turquoise stones, identical to the belt that held up its loincloth. The frill that stretched from the back of its head and ran down its spine was fully erect, a sign she'd been told by fellow Pathfinders meant aggression, although the pointed spear was already a fair indicator.

"These are the lands of the Karshnaar," it continued in a rasping voice. "Leave." Was its deep voice a sign of masculinity?

Mirian hoped she sounded calmer than she felt. "I come seeking Kalina."

Her challenger's head tilted a minute degree. "For what reason?"

"I am the daughter of Leovan Raas. The man Kalina spoke with about salvaging."

"Salvaging," the lizardfolk repeated, awkwardly. "I do not know that word. But the Raas man is completed, and his hatchling sent us away."

Hatchling? She wondered how her brother would react to that description. "I'm his other hatchling. Can we continue this talk with lowered blades?"

"You enter our land without ceremony."

"I ask your pardon. I wasn't sure where your territory began." Again she wondered how this tribe had existed so close to human lands without coming into conflict before, especially if they challenged all human visitors.

"Jekka!" The higher-pitched voice rang through the jungle behind Mirian.

The lizardfolk with the spear hissed. Its long, slim red tongue flicked out to taste the air. Its snout was longer and slimmer than the lizardfolk Mirian had seen before.

Mirian stepped to the side as another lizardfolk came trotting up. The new one was slightly smaller and wore a kind of armored disk that nearly obscured its torso, as well as a tanned loincloth that matched the other's, held up by a similar belt decorated with stones of polished turquoise. In one hand it carried a distinctive axe with a blade almost the length of Mirian's machete.

The two creatures exchanged a string of vocalizations that sounded something like low-pitched bird calls. Mirian studied them and the way the skin that wasn't a true lip pulled back to reveal sharp teeth as they spoke. She longed to break into her pack and sketch one or both of them, but settled for memorizing their features.

The eyes in both faces were not cold and blank like a snake's, but alive with curiosity. Their snouts projected like a hound's muzzle rather than a bird's beak. Some colonials called the lizardfolk "frill-backs," but the frills on the Karshnaar were small, stretching only from the base of their spines to the backs of their heads.

At the conclusion of their talk, the sentry lowered its spear, its head half turned so it could speak to both Mirian and the newcomer.

The sentry's frill had begun to droop, the way a dog's hackles lowered. It stepped aside, its amber eyes boring into Mirian's own as its companion stepped forward.

"I am Kalina," the second creature said. "You have come to our lands to speak with me?"

So the new one was female. Mirian curtsied with a pluck at the sides of her pants. "I have. I am Mirian, daughter of Leovan Raas."

Kalina's head cocked to one side, birdlike. Her own coloring had none of her companion's freckling. Was that, too, a sexual characteristic? "Your markings are different," she said. "More like your mother's."

"I take after her."

Kalina blinked large golden eyes. "Your mother was kind to us."

"She is a kind woman."

"But you are a warrior. I see it. You are not like your brother. Speak, daughter of Leovan Raas."

"I want to work with you. As my father planned."

"It is too late for that," the sentry said.

Kalina's head whipped swiftly around on the snaky neck, and her voice was sharp. "It is not too late, Jekka."

"Am I, chief warrior, to take orders about safety from the chief hunter?" The sentry then lapsed into its clicking chirping language, and Kalina responded in the same.

After a few sharp exchanges, Kalina brandished her axe-like weapon, and for a moment Mirian feared the two would come to blows.

But the chief warrior pulled its spear to one side, and the blade snicked away so that the weapon seemed nothing more than a grayish quarterstaff ornamented with intricate markings and sigils.

"Wait," Kalina said. She was still looking at the sentry as she spoke, but Mirian assumed the instructions were intended for her.

Kalina disappeared around a bend in the trail and was quickly lost behind intervening foliage.

Jekka stood statue-still. No, Mirian reflected, lizard-still, blinking seldom, turned sideways to her.

Mirian was left wondering how dangerous her situation was. She rested her hand on the hilt of her cutlass. Thinking about the speed she'd seen demonstrated by both lizardfolk, she flexed the hand that still held her machete. She wished that she'd undone the hook and eye clasp on the side holster where she kept her wand. She had one shot left.

"Planning tricks, human?" Jekka asked.

"I plan no tricks."

Its tongue flicked out. "You lie."

This one was certainly going out of its way to make things difficult. "What makes you think I lie?"

"And you waste air with stupid questions."

Mirian took a slow breath. She had learned diplomacy and patience on her sojourns in the wilds. "Pretend that I'm stupid, and tell me why you think I'm lying."

The dark green head turned to regard her directly. "My blade is sheathed. I do not offer battle posture. My frill is down. I do not signal danger."

"I don't know what your stance means, or when you might threaten me again. My people explain their actions so there will be no misunderstandings."

Its tongue flicked out, and she saw it was forked. "That has not been my experience."

"That's fair enough," she admitted. "The *honorable* among my people practice such methods. I want trust between us."

"If you wish trust between the two of us," the sentry said, "your wait will be long."

"You tell me you don't plan to attack, but say I cannot trust you."

It growled deep in his throat. "You wish to pretend hatchling ignorance? I will give clarity. You are welcome upon our land. You will be offered no hostility unless you present it. My brother, records keeper of my people, will speak to you. And then you will leave. At no time before or after will I attack. Unless you give me a reason."

She'd expected any number of challenges today, up to and including pursuit by Chelish spies, or the absence of the lizardfolk. She'd never thought she'd have to try to win over an antagonistic sentry.

"What is your name, warrior?"

"I am Jekka Eran Sulotai sar Karshnaar."

"Your Taldane is excellent."

It seemed uninterested in the compliment. "An elder nest mate taught us your speech. She thought it would aid our dealing with humans."

"Has it?"

"It showed me your words were as untrustworthy as your actions."

"Do not," a new voice interjected from farther down the trail, "give heed to my brother Jekka."

Another of the lizardfolk stepped out of the trees, one with a longer snout, though the creature was shorter in stature. It wore a beige robe with the hood thrown back. At its waist was a belt adorned with the same turquoise stones the others used to support their loincloths. It raised a long-fingered hand. "I welcome you to our lands, daughter of Leovan Raas. I am Heltan. Do you speak for your tribe?"

Mirian thought for a moment. Did "tribe" mean her family or her nation? "I speak for my family."

Heltan's head moved back and forth, rapidly. "Do you revive the agreement I made with your Leovan?"

"That is what I mean to do."

Kalina came up behind Heltan and stood at its shoulder.

"That is fine!" The lizardfolk sounded truly pleased. "How soon do you wish to leave?"

After the difficulties with Jekka the sentry, Mirian hadn't expected the rest of the negotiations to be so simple. "As soon as possible," she said. "It may take a few days to ready the ship, however."

"We may sleep in your courtyard, as before?" Mirian considered her answer for only a moment. "Yes." Mother hadn't mentioned that particular arrangement. Likely the lizardfolk wouldn't have felt safe in the beds her father would have offered, and they wouldn't have been welcome anywhere else inside the city. "Just so I'm clear on the agreement, we're to help you find your city, and then you're to give our family the jewels of your people?"

"We have little need of them," Heltan replied.

"We value other things," Jekka added.

All to the better. "Well then, when shall I expect you at my homestead?"

"We can leave as soon as Jekka gathers his gear," Heltan said.

So the angry one was coming as well. Mirian looked over to him. "Did you come last time?"

"I was there. I am chief warrior," he added, as though the matter were obvious.

How safe was her mother with Jekka around? She looked to the other lizardfolk for reassurance, found their expressions inscrutable, save that Heltan all but shook with excitement.

"I guess you'd best grab your gear," she said to Jekka. As he wandered down the trail she asked Heltan, "Will he be a problem?"

"Jekka is brave," Heltan said.

"He seems angry."

"He is disappointed." Heltan's head tilted first left and then right. "I do not know the words to explain. But now it will be better."

"Do not worry, daughter of the Leovan," Kalina told her. "If he does not know your ways, you can teach him."

Somehow Mirian doubted working with Jekka would be that simple.

8

Off to the Shining Sea
Ivrian

*As I scanned the faces of the lizardfolk, I wondered at their
seeming. I knew with dread certainty that beneath that
placid façade lurked a volcano of primitive savagery and
violence, one ready to destroy any who aroused the fires of
the ancient hate that burned beneath.*
—From *The Daughter of the Mist*

There was no warning. His mother simply appeared in his
doorway that evening and said, "It's time."

Ivrian pretended calm as he laid down the pen. He considered
the paper where he'd been scribbling possible titles for the epic
he'd write, then rose and straightened his shirt.

In the five days since their return from the ill-fated salvage
expedition, Ivrian had learned everything possible about the Raas
family, particularly Mirian. Half native or not, she would make
for the ideal heroine to feature in a new series of leaflets. She was
good-looking, and if he sank some money into the booklets to hire
a good artist, she'd be gorgeous, which always drew in the male
readership, especially if there were another picture or two of her
on the inner pages.

He was so certain the leaflets would sell that he was even considering the use of his real name on the byline. Stories about a sexy
salvager might have appeal beyond the colony. What he wouldn't
give to have them gathered into some kind of book, like those

of the great Ailson Kindler, mistress of adventure. Her novels of brave heroes battling terrible horrors were in demand throughout the Inner Sea, one of those rare instances where a popular writer was also one of the best, and he'd long dreamed of following in her footsteps. Just as Ailson had based many of her tales around her own exploits, he planned to base his around those of Mirian Raas—provided he could get her to open up about said exploits. He could write an entire series with her as the star. He'd cut her in for a percentage, of course, and he was still debating how much he should suggest as he glanced out the window at the estate's wide courtyard. The sun had dropped behind the outer wall, but its lingering glow painted the clouds with amber and gold.

Ivrian had moved to the city's center to dwell in the heart of the small theater district. When his mother had told him they'd have to depart at a moment's notice, Ivrian hadn't understood at first that it meant he'd have to abandon his quarters downtown. Spies, Mother had explained, might be watching their every move.

True or not, the notion that he might be the subject of espionage appealed to Ivrian's sense of the dramatic. Besides, his old rooms at the estate were far more spacious, and Cook babied him with his favorite dishes and desserts every night.

He remained fully cognizant of his mother's hope that he'd follow her footsteps as a government troubleshooter, not to mention the inevitable family duties. Despite that, he'd actually enjoyed his mother's company in the last few days as they hosted a steady stream of specialists including tailors, bootmakers, and even wizards to outfit them for the adventure that lay ahead.

Ivrian grabbed a pack made from waterproof sealskin identical to the one his mother was already shouldering. Their traveling gear had been moved to Mirian's ship days ago so that when the Galanors left home they'd carry no luggage. They'd ridden out several times together in the last few days, hoping to lull any watchers into a false sense of security. If their watchers thought the Galanors were simply out for another jaunt, they might not pay close enough attention until it was too late.

"Coming?" his mother shouted.

"Yes, Mother."

He caught up to her on the central stairs. Together they hurried outside, down the stone steps, and past the carefully squared shrubberies to board the closed carriage.

The vehicle rolled forward as soon as his mother knocked on the panel behind the driver.

With the curtains closed, his mother, sitting across from him, was little more than a dark suggestion of herself, but there was no mistaking the excitement in her voice. "Are you ready for this?"

"Very much so," Ivrian said.

She laughed.

Ivrian felt a little guilty. His mother seemed certain that this expedition was going to change the direction of Ivrian's life. "Mother." He cleared his throat. "I want you to know how much I appreciate this. All of this exposure will make wonderful background for my writing."

"I thought you'd say that." His mother sounded pleased.

"I'm still not interested in working with the government. Permanently, I mean." He didn't add that he also had no intention of marrying or carrying on the family name or any of that. His mother surely knew his feelings on those subjects hadn't changed. He'd been perfectly clear about it before he moved out.

She was so silent that Ivrian was afraid he'd hurt her feelings.

"Son," Alderra said at last, "it's just a pleasure to be spending time with you."

That made him feel even worse, and he couldn't decide if she was still playing master manipulator or if she really meant what she was saying. Fortunately, another line of conversation presented itself.

"We're going north," Ivrian noted.

His mother sounded faintly amused. "Yes."

"The *Daughter* is berthed to the south."

"We're not sailing on the *Daughter*."

Ivrian was puzzled for only a moment. "We *are* still sailing, aren't we?"

"Yes." His mother drew out the word as though hoping to lead Ivrian to a conclusion.

"You think the *Daughter* is being watched."

"I can almost guarantee it." Alderra Galanor sounded a little smug. "And any of them would have noted a surreptitious effort to load the ship with foodstuffs and gear over the last week, and careful tending of the vessel itself. I'd hoped they'd assume we thought we were being clever."

The carriage came to a halt along the north quays. Alderra must have paid in advance, for the carriage left the moment the two climbed down.

The sun had finished its low fade below the horizon during their journey. Now there was only a dim line of light in the west.

The tall masts of ships stood black against the lighter darkness of the night sky and the wealth of stars. Waves lapped against the old stone pylons that held up the wharf as they started down its length.

Lights burned here and there along the ships creaking at their anchors, for there were sailors keeping watch aboard.

Alderra made immediately for a two-master. Ivrian followed her up the gangplank.

Waiting with a directional lantern was none other than burly Captain Rendak. He flashed the light toward but not at them, presumably so they wouldn't be blinded.

"M'lady." Rendak bobbed his head slightly.

"Is everyone aboard?" Ivrian's mother asked.

"Everyone but Mirian and the guides."

Ivrian's gaze swept over the ship and saw it was not as abandoned as he'd assumed. It might have looked silent and empty as the other ships, but it was peopled with men and women who sat against the rail or stretched out along the planks.

One lean fellow came strutting across the weather deck and stopped before them, a brimmed hat cocked rakishly over his head. He swept it off with a formal bow.

"Lady Galanor," he whispered.

Alderra swept a hand to her son. "Ivrian, this is Captain Akimba of the *Red Leopard*. He comes highly recommended."

"A pleasure," Ivrian said.

"The pleasure is mine," the dim shape whispered. Ivrian had little sense of the fellow save that he had a broad native accent and wore a calf-length coat. Ivrian envied him that choice, for the wind off the water was chill.

"Although," Akimba said, "I'd naturally feel a little better if I knew precisely where we were headed."

"Ah," Alderra Galanor said mischievously. "Where's your sense of adventure?"

Akimba grunted noncommittally. "Do you wish to be shown your quarters?"

"I think we'll wait here. Thank you."

Akimba replaced his hat and stepped over to Rendak.

Ivrian leaned close to his mother's ear. "Why aren't we taking a government ship?"

"They're spread thin as is. The government can't afford to have a navy ship wait offshore for a week or more. So I've hired the *Red Leopard*. It's swift, and Mirian thinks highly of her captain's judgment. We should be able to outrun any ship afloat, especially with as little cargo as we're carrying."

There was a clatter of wheels along the road. Ivrian turned as he felt Captain Akimba and Rendak tense. A few of the sailors muttered among themselves, and a stern voice from near the wheelhouse ordered them to shut their damn mouths. He recognized the voice as belonging to Chilton, the handsome sailor who'd become a steady presence in the household the last few days.

A covered carriage rolled into view, passing a final row of taverns and warehouses before rolling to a stop at the end of their quay. The paneled door opened, and a slim figure dropped to the ground. Though she was garbed in an ankle-length coat, her hair hidden by a tricorne hat, there was no mistaking the wide-hipped figure for a man. Behind her came a man similarly garbed, and Ivrian heard a whispered discussion between them, though he could make out no words.

"Who's that fellow with Mirian?" he asked.

"Kellic Raas, I expect." His mother didn't sound pleased.

Ivrian was about to ask where their guides were when three more figures slipped out of the carriage. Each wore a hooded robe. One carried a strange axe with a very long blade, and another held a staff.

Ivrian's attention was momentarily diverted by a sudden expostulation from Kellic, who'd drawn up beside Mirian. He was gesticulating in protest as they reached the end of the gangway. Ivrian smirked. So Kellic didn't approve of the ship.

And then Ivrian's eye traveled back to the three robed figures and he saw for the first time that something trailed along the ground in back of their robes. Were those *tails*? His hair rose along the back of his neck.

"What are those things?"

"Lizardfolk," his mother answered quietly, then moved forward to join Akimba and Rendak as Mirian climbed the gangplank to the ship.

Ivrian lingered just behind so that he might overhear. Mirian kept her hat brim low and brusquely returned their greetings, verifying with Rendak that the team and gear were aboard and stowed, and with Akimba that the ship was ready.

Ivrian watched Kellic. Mirian's brother removed his hat and stood frowning, his gaze taking in the ship as if he disliked every single thing he saw. He'd sour his looks if he kept up that attitude. What was he so angry about?

Akimba cleared his throat as Mirian and her brother made way for the three robed figures, and Ivrian heard not just mutters but entire conversations, curses, and whispered prayers as sailors caught sight of them. More than one voice could be heard talking about "frillbacks" and how they were bad luck or untrustworthy.

"Belay that!" Akimba snapped. A dark figure moved out from the wheelhouse to mouth warnings to the little clusters of crew. Chilton. Now the sailor's presence in the house as a "maritime advisor" seemed far less a pretense for his mother to spend quality time with a good-looking younger man. He must have been the go-between for finalizing arrangements like this.

Ivrian's attention was quickly pulled back to the nearer figures. "It's time to set sail," Mirian told the captain.

"I'm at your service." Akimba bowed his head. "But I lack a course. Or destination."

"North by northwest for now. Once we're out of the harbor we can talk at length."

Akimba's posture stiffened, but he nodded acknowledgment. "As soon as we're under way, I expect to see you in the cabin."

"Of course, Captain."

Akimba turned and began calling orders in a stage whisper. Instantly his men were up and moving, some scattering across the deck, some scampering up the lines.

Mirian waved the lizardfolk closer, but they remained rooted to the spot. Two sailors stepped widely around them before hauling in the gangplank.

Mirian said, "Step forward, you three. I'd like to introduce you."

Ivrian paid a little too much attention to the lizardfolk's movements and their look for their strange, savage names to sink in. The only one he remembered was Kalina. There was something ominous about the one with the staff.

The one without a weapon proved the most talkative, and civilized, for he bowed his head to Ivrian's mother in a birdlike motion. As he moved, Ivrian caught a glimpse of wide-set eyes behind a lipless, muzzle-like mouth.

"We'd best clear the deck," Mirian said. "Rendak, why don't you show everyone below?"

"Of course."

"I'm not going below," Kellic said crossly.

"Follow me, if you wish," Rendak said with a sweeping arm gesture. He led the way aft toward a door beside the stairs to the quarterdeck. Beyond it was a gangway, more ladder than stairs.

Ivrian's mother was the first behind him, and Ivrian after, which meant that the most savage-seeming of the lizardfolk, the one with the staff, came immediately behind.

But Alderra Galanor seemed not at all troubled. She said, conversationally: "We really won't be aboard very long. There's just one overnight."

"The site's that close?" Ivrian asked.

"That close."

Beyond the short gangway was a warren of narrow doors. Rendak indicated one, immediately on the left. "There you are, Lady. And, uh, Lord. The rest of you, follow me."

Ivrian wouldn't technically be a lord until, Shelyn forbid, his mother's death, but he didn't correct Rendak.

Ivrian watched the salvager lead the lizardfolk into the darkness and wondered whether Rendak was still to be addressed as "captain." Probably not, given that Akimba commanded the ship and Mirian seemed in charge of the salvagers.

His mother opened the door to their cabin and shone her lantern into the tiny space.

There was barely enough room to slide in sideways. Ivrian spied their storage chests under the bottom bunk and a small porthole beside the top berth. His mother hung the lantern on a hook high on the bunk's post.

"I call lower bunk," his mother declared sprightly. "A perk of age." She grinned. "I'm going topside. I need to be in on this meeting."

"Can I come with you?"

"No, son. This information is on a need-to-know basis. And you don't need to know, yet."

"Oh." Ivrian was a little disappointed.

His mother squeezed his shoulder. "I'll tell you all about it later. For now, settle in and get a good night's sleep. It'll be your last one on a mattress for weeks. I'll try not to wake you when I return." She raised a hand in farewell before stepping out, closing the door behind her.

Ivrian reexamined the cramped surroundings. He could hear the pad of feet on the decks above and occasional low voices, but he had no idea what was happening up there or how he'd describe it in his account. He doubted readers would be interested in seeing a cabin described in any great detail. What would he do, go on about the shades of wood grain or the precise size of the porthole?

Fortunately, he'd been on enough trips he could fake the steps of this departure. Easy enough to imagine the rattle of lines as the sails swung down, the muscled sailors straining to heave up the anchor, the billow of the sails as they swung to meet the wind.

He patted the upper berth. There was very little mattress, but at least it was stuffed with clean-smelling straw. There were two blankets, both of which felt superfluous in the stifling cabin, so he folded one into a pillow and then took off his pack.

He set it on his mother's bunk. Constructed of sealskin, the pack was clearly new. What wasn't immediately obvious was that it also bore a powerful enchantment. His mother had personally invested in five of the packs, one for each professional salvager and each Galanor. Every pack opened onto far more internal space than was apparent from the outside—a sorcerous trick. And no matter how much weight was added to one, they'd never feel heavier than five pounds. Ideally suited, his mother had said with a smile, for transporting a fortune in gems.

Right now, all that Ivrian's pack held was his portable writing desk, which he withdrew and contemplated with pleasure. Nonmagical, it was still a small marvel, complete with hinged top to double the workspace size and a wealth of small drawers that held his inkwell, quills, sharpeners, and paper. While nowhere near the expense of the magical haversacks, it had still seemed an extravagance, and he'd been delighted when his mother presented it to him.

There didn't look to be enough room to sit upright on the top bunk, so he climbed onto his mother's, rested the desk in his lap, and began to record his impressions of everything that had happened that evening. He was distracted as he felt the ship surge forward like a great beast let free from its leash.

Ivrian couldn't help grinning with a sense of exhilaration as the ship rose and fell over the wave swells. They were underway.

Once his notes were complete, he packed up the writing gear, his fingers lingering lovingly on the dark polished mahogany of the desk before restoring it to the haversack. He then stared out the porthole for a while. Mostly he saw endless waves under a velvet, star-shot sky, but under the silver moon he beheld the jagged outline of the Lizard Kings: a weathered series of huge reptilian heads carved out of a line of reefs northeast of Smuggler's Shiv. They reared out of the waves as though behemoths stood sentinel along the deep ocean beds. He'd glimpsed them only once before, and had been a little disappointed, for most had been softened by wind, wave, and rain. By night they were more fearsome, and it gave him a satisfying thrill imagining what they must have looked like in ancient times.

With the Kings receding, he reached into one of the haversack's side pockets and carefully removed his second treasure—an autographed copy of Ailson Kindler's best work, the outstanding *In the Council of Corpses*.

It was a first run of the first edition, with the misnumbered second folio, which made it even more valuable. He'd leave it on the ship rather than taking it into the jungle, of course. Now that he realized how little they'd actually be on board, he felt silly having brought it. Still, it was always a pleasure to soak in Kindler's prose. He'd give a lot to write with such luscious, evocative phrases. Every time he tried, though, it sounded too forced, as though he were a child jumping and waving his arms to get attention.

He read the familiar pages for a good hour or more before fatigue crept in. Mother still hadn't returned to tell him about the meeting. He resolved not to worry about it. There was always the morning. Besides, she had told him it was vital to catch sleep when one could while on an expedition, and he was more and more beginning to sense she knew her business.

He restored his treasure to the sealskin, dragged the heavy chest out from under the bunk to store his pack and shoes, unbuttoned his shirt, and climbed into the bunk. Already he was thinking of the strange coast that lay ahead. His mother had said something about an inland trek and a secret pool, so he fell to sleep with visions of an ancient city built of emerald blocks, choked in greenery and gleaming with golden idols shaped like lizardfolk.

So soundly did he sleep that he never heard his mother return, nor the rising winds and lash of rain and the shouts of sailors.

He didn't wake at all until the ship slammed into the reef.

9

Landfall
Mirian

Mirian woke in the darkness to the sound of the weather bell. The vessel rocked madly, and the decks creaked and trembled under the press of rain. Thunder rumbled, and a sheet of lightning outside the porthole blinded her.

She threw off her coverlet and sank down on one knee to yank her sea chest out from under her bunk.

The *Leopard* rolled forward to aft, which meant it remained under a modicum of control. Akimba was a seasoned captain with a hand-picked crew—these sailors knew the way of the seas and would do their best to keep their ship afloat.

But the gods didn't always care about the fates of individual men and women. Mirian took the key from about her neck and threw open the chest, guiding herself by the frequent slashes of lightning.

Within lay most of her gear, well ordered so that she might have found what she sought without light, if need be. There were changes of clothes, her survival pack, a satchel stocked with tiny vials filled with antidotes for jungle poisons, fine tools, and a watertight pouch of eel hide where she kept her Pathfinder journal, ink, and pens.

It likewise held her equipment belt and sword belt, both of which she buckled into place. She then threw on a light, hooded rain cape given to her by a Bas'o aunt, restored the chest, and hurried from the cabin.

Beyond the door, the storm was a monster that tore at the sky with lightning fingers and shrieked at those who dared ride the waves.

The sails were reefed, of course. Canvas raised in these winds would not only be useless; it'd be shredded.

The rain lashed her as she crossed the plunging deck. The ship rode down a valley of water and crashed into a wave higher than the ship itself. Water foamed over the prow, but the *Leopard* rose and the ocean ran back out of the scuppers.

Mirian found Akimba at the wheel. The lantern beside him had burned out, and no one had troubled to relight it.

He caught her eye as she steadied herself on the post where the weather bell hung.

"It's not safe up here!" He shouted over the storm.

"I can handle myself," Mirian shouted back. "How bad is it?"

"We're taking a lot of water."

"I'll get my people to help."

Akimba shook his head. "Plenty of hands for the pumps."

She steadied herself as the *Red Leopard* climbed a smaller wave, then rushed down another. Beyond the occasional flash of lightning rolled black sea and storm clouds in every direction.

Akimba motioned her close. As she leaned in, he spoke into her ear. "Might put guards on your fr— lizardfolk. The crew thinks this is their fault."

Mirian frowned.

"They say frillbacks are unlucky."

She steadied herself as they hit another rough wave, one that left the deck ankle deep in water before the *Leopard* bore on and spray flung from her sides.

"You know the time?" she asked. "Or our course?"

"Coming on half past five bells. The wind was with us until the storm hit. We're still north by northwest, and veering north."

"We weren't that far south of the Kaava!"

"That's what I'm afraid of. I'll handle it," Akimba added. "Now get below. See to your people."

Mirian clapped his shoulder before she left him.

Rather than a lantern, she took a glow stone from her pouch and whispered it to light as she started down the gangway. The stone was small and flat, one of several her father had recovered from a wreck a few years ago, after her own departure. By its light she saw not only the gangway, but her brother, braced miserably against it.

Kellic had put on the same gentleman's dining pants, boots, and blue short-sleeved shirt he'd been wearing last night, as though he were headed for an evening on the town. His pallor now had less to do with any potion and much more to do with seasickness. Judging from his misaligned shirt buttons, he'd dressed in the dark.

"Mirian," he said with a groan. "What's going on?"

"A storm. You'd best get back to your cabin."

He shook his head. He'd been defiant ever since she'd returned from the jungle with the lizardfolk, and increasingly ill-tempered when she refused to divulge her plans. It had driven a further wedge between them. How could she persuade him she trusted him when it was so clear that she didn't? All she could repeat was that she'd been sworn to secrecy by Lady Galanor, which hadn't impressed Kellic.

"Go on," she said. "Look at you. You're going to throw up any second."

"Where are you going?"

"To check on our team."

"That's what Tokello said."

Her brother and the healer shared the final passenger cabin. Every other passenger but the Galanors were in the vast and mostly empty cargo hold.

"Come on, then." If nothing else, maybe the healer could give him something to settle his stomach.

They maneuvered through the warren of little side doors and then sternward into the cargo bay below the weather deck.

Were this a normal voyage, the lower decks would be crammed not just with hammocks but with supplies and cargo. Owing to the nearness of their destination and its purpose, barrels and chests were at a minimum, leaving ample space.

She stepped around the gangway to the lower deck where she even now heard the steady clank and cursing of the crew working the bilge pumps. Most ships leaked, and when a ship was tossed like theirs, it leaked all the more. Probably a quarter of the crew was working below, taking turns on the hand cranks.

She walked easily over the wildly rocking planks, passing between close-hung hammocks where sailors turned fitfully. Another glow stone was a yellow beacon by the door that led to the forecastle, and it was there her own team was stationed, on the starboard side along with all three of the lizardfolk. The Karshnaar hammocks hung empty. Kalina lay curled against the bulkhead, her long, inhuman foot clawed securely into ropes that lashed a barrel to the bulkhead.

Heltan sat beside her, still and quiet. It was only after they'd supplied them with beds and canopies for the courtyard that she'd understood Heltan and Kalina were mated, for they slept together. They also tended to linger near one another, occasionally touching fingertips.

Jekka watched Mirian approach, his eyes seeming to glow with malevolence. He studied her the way her old gray cat had watched her father's blue-crested parrot, as though he held back from killing only because there were too many witnesses. She'd heard almost nothing from him from the time they'd arrived at her home.

Heltan turned his head to face her as she walked up. "Salvager Mirian," he said, "and Salvager Kellic. Good early morning to you."

Heltan was always formal and polite; he had invented titles for them based upon their occupation, apparently a lizardfolk custom.

"Chronicler Heltan," she said.

Gombe lay in the nearest hammock, snoring fitfully. Rendak had one of their chests open and was rooting through it. Tokello crouched beside him. She looked a little pale herself, and seemed to be whispering under her breath. A prayer to Gozreh, Mirian realized, muttered over and over.

She put a hand to the woman's massive shoulder. "You feeling all right, Tokello?"

"I hate the damned storms," she whispered, then rolled her eyes heavenward. "No offense, Gozreh. I know we all have days when we need to let it out, and your purpose is mysterious. Far be it from me to question—"

The rest of the healer's words were drowned out by another huge crash of thunder.

"Do you have anything to settle Kellic's stomach?" Mirian asked her. "He's feeling a little ill."

"I'm fine," Kellic said.

"Are you sure?"

"I'm fine," her brother insisted.

The ship rolled and Tokello steadied herself. "I have something that will settle him, but it will also put him under. And if Gozreh keeps working his way, we may have to swim. May he see fit not to do that," she said with a further flash of holy signs.

Kellic blanched further.

"I don't think it will come to that." Mirian tried to steady the healer with a calming hand. She moved on to Rendak, Kellic lingering at her rear like an ill-tempered shadow.

"I'm readying the gear," the mate said to her unanswered question.

"Why?" Kellic asked. "We can't even see the coast, let alone drop anchor."

"In case the ship goes down," Mirian whispered.

Kellic's eyes bugged. He looked more frightened than ever, which was a little exasperating. He wore the water-breathing ring recovered from their father's corpse. Rendak and Gombe had air bottles. Tokello didn't even have one of those, because the things were damned expensive and she never went overboard in any case. The emergency plan had always been to band together underwater to pass the bottles back and forth, but it would be hard going in the depths of the sea, at night.

Just because you could breathe water didn't mean you wouldn't exhaust yourself getting to shore, provided you could find it.

And providing there wasn't something down there hunting you.

Mirian stepped over to check on the lizardfolk. Jekka stared. Kalina slept. Heltan bowed his head in acknowledgment.

"Has there been any trouble here?" she asked. Akimba's warning aside, no one seemed to be bothering them

"No," Heltan answered. "You come to check the safety of your clan and allies. That is wise."

"They are not her clan," Jekka corrected softly. "They are slaves."

Mirian stiffened. "They work for me."

"She twists meaning, like all of them," Jekka told his brother.

She supposed he could have spoken in his own language, but Jekka was astonishingly like a human tough trying to provoke reaction.

And Heltan spoke swiftly, just as would a human diplomat eager to keep the peace. "Perhaps my brother has confusion. He says they who serve you are slaves. I think they are lesser clan."

"They're neither. They choose to work for my family, and can come and go as they please. My family pays them," she added, "so that they can afford food, shelter, and goods of their own."

"An interesting idea," Heltan said.

Rendak crossed to stand beside her. He was a few inches shorter than Mirian herself, and in the loose-fitting pants and tight shirt there was no missing that he was built of corded muscle, even if his belly was shielded by a layer of fat.

"What she means," he said, "is that Tokello and I have chosen to stay with the Raas family for almost ten years. There was no finer salvager than Leovan Raas, Pharasma preserve his soul, and his daughter's forged in the same mold."

Mirian couldn't help noticing that he made no mention of Kellic, and she held off glancing over to check if her brother listened.

"It is always about coins," Jekka said softly to his brother. He then considered the humans once more. "Our loyalty is to blood, not metal."

Rendak was amiable and quick-thinking, but he could also be a little temperamental. "Now wait just a moment."

The ship rocked and dipped. They heard the wash of water over the decks and every one of them looked up to the joists. But the ship rose once more, and the wave washed away.

Rendak resumed as if there'd been no interruption. "Leo paid for my services. But he earned my loyalty because he was a good leader. Like Mirian." Then, belatedly, "And her brother."

Jekka's hostility was faintly tempered now with curiosity. "What happens to your loyalty without the metal she pays?"

"I've served the family in lean times, too," Rendak said. He didn't mention this was one of them.

"In our cities," Mirian explained, "people need money to eat, and to buy clothes. Different clans specialize in providing different things. And our blood ties are smaller than yours."

Jekka's teeth showed at that; Heltan put a hand to his brother's shoulder.

Mirian pretended she hadn't noticed. "When my clan takes in metal, we share it out with those we trust so that they can buy food, and clothes, and whatever else they need."

"Such as Crown's End whiskey," Heltan suggested. The lizard-folk had a great fondness for the alcohol, although it didn't actually seem to have any effect upon him.

Rendak laughed, and a little of the tension left his shoulders.

Heltan cocked his head at him and then let out a soft, coughing noise.

"Yes," Mirian agreed.

"You see, Jekka" Heltan said. "It is as I told you." He turned back to Mirian. "Unlike me, Jekka has kept from humans."

"Most of them," Jekka said darkly.

Heltan spoke quickly, forcing cheer into his voice. Probably he hoped no one would pry further as to Jekka's meaning. "Our clan has specialists as well."

"You probably have other clan members at home who make your clothes, or bake your breads," Mirian suggested. "And perhaps you barter with other lizardfolk for some—"

"No," Jekka said curtly. "Brother, rouse me when the storm ends. The chatter of humans tires me." He closed his eyes and leaned against the barrel.

Heltan looked up, his expression unreadable. "It was interesting to speak with you, Mirian Raas. And you also, Filian Rendak." He added after a moment: "Is Filian a title?"

Rendak chuckled. "No. That's just my name. Like Mirian's."

"So Mirian is not title of clan leader?"

"It is my personal name," she said.

"Forgive me, then. When Rendak used it, I assumed it was a title used in deference. I do not mean to take liberties."

"It's fine, Heltan. Rendak knows me well enough to use my personal name in casual situations."

"So your personal name can be used by those outside your family in certain situations?"

"Yes."

"How does one judge when that is permissible?"

"Brother," Jekka said softly, his lids closed, "now you weary me *and* the humans."

Once more Heltan made that soft coughing sound, and when Mirian raised her hand in farewell he returned the gesture. She stepped over to the chest with Rendak.

"Is everything in order?" she asked.

"Aye."

Gombe snorted in his sleep, shifted, and resumed snoring.

Rendak rolled his eyes at his friend. "Gombe can sleep through a rutting earthquake. And lizardfolk staring spears at him. Gods, I could feel Jekka's eyes on my back the whole time I was sorting through the chest, as if he was wondering where to stick me. Or how good I'd taste."

"I don't think he was wondering that," Mirian replied, though she thought he might have been contemplating the former. "It's hard to guess what they're thinking."

"Damned right it is."

"We're going to be working with them for days," Mirian reminded him. "Weeks, maybe."

"So you said. You really think we can trust them?"

"They're probably wondering the same thing."

Rendak nodded, pushed his dark hair back over his forehead. "Look, I'm all for us getting along smooth as Taldan glass. But I'm not planning on eating them, so it'd be real nice if I knew none of them were—"

The ship slammed to a halt with a smash of broken timber. Mirian was thrown into Gombe's hammock, stubbing her foot on the open supply chest. She grabbed the rope from which Gombe's hammock dangled. Gombe's grunt of surprise was followed by screams below, shouts above, and panicked exclamations from sailors starting awake. Loudest of all was Kellic as he lost his footing and tumbled away under four swaying hammocks.

The ship canted almost twenty-five degrees to port, and Mirian heard water rushing in.

A reef? The shore? A sandbar? There was no way to know what they'd hit, and no time to curse. Every moment counted. "Up!" Mirian shouted, biting her teeth against the pain in her foot. Gombe lurched out of his hammock. Kellic's glow stone had tumbled down the deck after her brother and lay shining near him. By its light she saw him pulling himself upright. "Kellic! Are you all right?"

"I think so," he called back. He said something more, but his voice was drowned out by the sailors, cursing as they struggled from their hammocks and scrambled for the gangway aft. None came their way, likely because the door to the forecastle had a lock on it and only a ship's officer would have a key.

She hoped Akimba was still alive up there. She hoped that there were enough boats, and that they could get everyone into them. She thought fleetingly of Lady Galanor and her son. Right now they'd have to manage on their own. She had her hands full taking care of her people here. She'd warned Alderra this trip was likely to be dangerous.

Gombe and Rendak were quickly slipping on their packs, one padded side pocket of which held an air bottle. Tokello held a glow stone for them to see by. She no longer looked nervous, merely disappointed, as if things had gone just as badly as she'd expected. At another time her expression might have made Mirian laugh. She put a comforting hand on the healer's wide shoulder and felt the hard muscle beneath the woman's robe. "We'll get all of us out of here alive," she said.

"If Gozreh wills it," Tokello managed, and she bent her head, mumbling a prayer.

Mirian had already prayed to both Desna and her ancestors before turning in last night; she hoped they'd still be watching now and would understand there was little time for such niceties. She unsheathed her wand as she walked on across the slanted deck past the lizardfolk, who were up and gathering their gear. They watched as she steadied herself beside the door to the forecastle.

Beyond the door lay the forward cargo compartment and a hatch to the deck. Assuming they got past that, there was still a storm and an ocean trying to kill them, and Gozreh alone knew how they'd fare even with salvaging gear if they were out in the deeps.

One thing at a time. She tried the door, ensuring it was as locked as it looked, then pointed her wand and muttered the single word.

Nothing happened, apart from the ship settling another five degrees further to port. Was it her imagination, or was the sound of water rushing in getting louder? And there were people screaming for help below.

Focus, Mirian. She had to get her people to safety first. Before leaving Eleder she'd tracked down a wizard to recharge the weapon to its full capacity. She spoke again, and this time the bolt of acid appeared along the end of the white wand and sped toward the lock. She was almost too close, for it spattered, and the sizzling sound it made against the lock was an uncomfortable reminder of what it could do to flesh.

She heard a hiss behind her and turned to see the lizardfolk staring at her. All three stood in a row, perched like birds to lean at an impossibly steady angle. It was damnably eerie. And water was starting to come up through the planks along the port side, just inches behind her brother, who'd foolishly left the glow stone in the water as he climbed his way up beside Mirian.

A nacreous hole outlined in green had formed where the lock in the door used to be, reeking of burning wood and metal. The top of the handle remained splattered—the bottom portion was pitted and smoking. She gritted teeth, set hand to the thing and stepped away, so that as the door fell open toward her the damaged portions swung past her torso.

In the dim space beyond Mirian perceived a jumble of casks and chests, although most of the gear within remained securely tied. From starboard there was a feeble light source. Gray light poured through the grating that led to the deck.

She then turned and waved on her people. "Go! Go!

Rendak, Gombe, and Kellic needed no urging and quickly hurried through. Tokello came after, still muttering a prayer.

"Hop to it," Rendak said to Gombe. "We've got to force that hatch open."

She looked back at the lizardfolk and found them staring.

"What are you waiting for?" she demanded. "Go!"

The Karshnaar clan raced nimbly ahead of her. The water, meanwhile, had climbed a third of the way up the deck.

She heard one of the men grunt, and the sound of creaking hinges, and then Gombe's deep voice called: "We're out!"

Only then, with her own people free, did she turn back and fire three times into the deck below, creating a hole.

"There's a way up here," she called down. "But the edge is hot, so protect your hands!"

She couldn't tell if anyone heard, but as the ship lurched ominously she started after her team. Mirian pulled herself over the canted doorway, then clambered easily up the stair steps of supplies lashed to the shelves in the forecastle. The square of lighter darkness that shone above brought in crisp, cool air, and salt spray. She recognized Gombe's silhouette as he reached down to offer a hand. He sounded relieved. "You decide to go sightseeing, ma'am?"

From somewhere beyond, a trilling threnody whistled through the air, and she saw Gombe react violently, withdrawing his hand to clap it over his ears.

Mirian scrambled past him.

In one sweep she took in a flurry of information. The storm had mostly spent its strength and rolled eastward, a line of night shot through with lightning. The horizon brightened beneath it, enough to show a shadowy coastline to the north, no more than a half mile out

The *Red Leopard* lay broken on a string of jagged fanlike reefs that stretched out from the shore, now hidden, now exposed as the choppy waters slammed in and out.

The ship's two boats were over the side, along with a good portion of the sailors. The one to port was overturned, and people scrambled to hold on to its side or throw themselves across it. The first mate was in charge of the other, on the starboard side, and was tossing a rope back to the ship, up to where Alderra braced along the rail. The ship had listed far to port.

Mirian's gaze snapped back toward the cabin, searching for sign of the captain, and that's when she saw the trio of bird-winged figures gliding past the men clustered at the rail. The figures sang, and men and women alike cast loving eyes upon them.

Harpies.

10

Flight
Ivrian

We were tossed like the toy of a titan, flung with the casual disregard of an angry child so that the ship lay broken upon treacherous, surf-pounded rocks. But the gods were not done with us yet! Out of the predawn sky flew three winged devils, singing a sweet melody of death. Harpies, determined to lead those few who survived to a watery grave. As I stepped onto the deck, I met the lovely eyes of Mirian Raas, emerging from a hatch at the prow, and we nodded at one another in resolve. We would slay the harpies and save the sailors, or die in the trying!

—From *The Daughter of the Mist*

Ivrian was tossed bodily from the bunk into the hull below the porthole. For a long moment, he wasn't entirely sure where he was or what had happened, and the lack of motion and the frantic calls of the crew only prolonged his disorientation.

He only fully awoke to what was happening when some of the words penetrated his consciousness. The men and women outside shouted about boats, and abandoning ship, and some called out for aid from Desna or Gozreh, or pleaded with Pharasma not to take them. What had happened? Was the ship sinking?

He climbed to his feet on the listing deck, astonished he wasn't more badly hurt. Only his back was a little sore. "Mother?" He reached out to the lower bunk, but his mother wasn't there. In fact, the sheets were undisturbed.

The ship slanted more on creaking timbers, and he heard the rush of water. Not just from somewhere outside, but *in his very cabin*. "I'm not going to drown," he said. "Definitely." He fought down the panic, bent down, and dragged out his chest. It was wedged tightly against his mother's, and he realized instantly that the moment he pulled it clear it would slide into him. Yet he had no other choice if he wanted his air bottle. He got the chest free, bracing it against his own body as he keyed the lock and pushed open the lid.

He ignored the cool ocean water creeping up his toes and felt around inside the chest, fumbling past his shoes. First he came to his sword belt and sword, which he grabbed, but of greater import even than the pack with all his writing materials was the enchanted air bottle, which might be all that lay between him and drowning. The blessed thing lay jammed protectively at the bottom, snug in a padded leather case. He grabbed it and slid it onto his sword belt.

The water had risen to his ankles now, and he cursed. Where was his mother? He was going to have to grab her gear for her.

He slung his pack over his shoulder, then slammed the chest shut. He was getting ready to manhandle it into place when the ship shifted again and he lost his footing. He slipped into the water and the chest slid after. He hit the hull with his rump and heard an alarming smashing sound from the leather case with the air bottle. Then the chest rumbled toward him. It struck the water with a splash and crashed into his knees.

Cursing in pain, Ivrian pushed free, climbed over, then fought his mother's chest clear even as the water climbed calf-high. He wrestled with his mother's lock, grateful the same key opened both chests. He felt inside for agonizing moments before finally realizing that neither his mother's weapon, pack, nor air bottle was within. At some point in the night she must have come in and removed them.

Cursing once more, Ivrian stepped past his mother's chest and let it slide into the water after his own. He dropped his broken air bottle after it. So much for breathing underwater. He'd have to find a boat.

The cabin was filling fast. He was waist-deep in cool water as he pulled himself along the bunk for the door. The cursed thing naturally opened inward, falling open with such speed that it banged one knee. But then he was through and into the passageway. There was no mistaking the pound of the surf rolling the ship, or the crack of further timbers. He started up the tilted gangway toward a patch of lighter blackness and fresh, salty air.

Ivrian reached the threshold in time to see Akimba cutting at the rope that tied him to the wheel.

And then he heard a warbling from somewhere above. It was strange, beguiling, enchanting. Gods, he thought, it was like a gift from Shelyn. Surely she had sent some angel down to perform for them. Smiling, Ivrian looked skyward. Nearby, the captain dropped the knife, and it went skittering down the deck. His haggard face widened in a beatific smile.

Ivrian found the source of the melody in the three winged forms hovering above the ship. He just had to get closer to them. But how? The mainmast was broken and pointed the wrong way, but it suddenly came to him that there were stairs behind the quarterdeck that led to the stern deck. He started toward them.

His mother grabbed his arm and shook him. "Snap out of it, Ivrian! Those are harpies! They're playing with their food!"

It was the pain that broke the spell, and Ivrian rubbed at the stubble on his face. He heard a horrible scream and whirled around to see that one of the harpies had dropped on the captain, planting one taloned foot on his face as the other tore his jugular. Blood fountained.

"Gods," Ivrian whispered again.

His mother whipped a knife from under her billowing blouse and tossed it in one fluid motion. It drove into the creature's back, dead between the spot where its wings met.

"Nice shot!" Ivrian cried.

The creature screeched in pain and rose in a sweep of beating wings that sent a fetid stench wafting over them. In that dawn light, he saw only her outline, but there was no missing the widening of the creature's jaw as she swooped down toward his mother.

Ivrian dashed up the ladder he'd been eyeing. Halfway up he twisted and struck at the harpy, slicing deep through one of her wings. The creature turned, lashing at Ivrian with a whip.

It missed the hand he gripped the ladder with; he gritted his teeth and leapt out, slicing. He connected with the creature's thigh, the injury spraying blood.

But the harpy wasn't finished with him. He felt the sting of her whip as he dropped away.

He struck the rain-slick timber, his feet going out from under him. He bumped past the captain lying limply in his remaining ropes and slid on toward the submerged rail visible through the steel-gray water.

Ivrian released his sword and scrabbled for purchase on the deck, and the weapon clattered beside him so that he now had two further fears: breaking himself on the rail, and cutting himself on the length of his own sword.

But the sword bounced on and plunged into the water. He braced himself for impact, feet first.

Shelyn finally smiled, for as he struck the water his feet didn't drop between the rail posts but on them. He had a surface to support himself. And as he caught his breath he perceived an overturned boat drifting nearby. A trio of sailors clung desperately to it.

One looked past him and pointed. Ivrian couldn't make out the woman's words over the pounding and warbling and screaming, but the expression on her face was clear enough.

Ivrian turned in time to see the harpy drop toward his face.

11

Farewells
Mirian

She choked back a cry of rage as Akimba sagged. Ivrian's brave slash at the harpy's wing startled her, but Mirian couldn't spare that conflict more attention, for a crowd of sailors climbed eagerly toward the rail to greet the closest harpy, charmed by her song and oblivious to the wicked blade she carried.

As the ship settled, one of the bedazzled sailors lost his balance and fell past Mirian, grinning as though he hadn't a care in the world. He smashed his head on the hatch through which she'd climbed and then twirled into the water below, vanishing from sight.

Heltan and Kalina had already started down toward the choppy water, but Jekka scrambled lizard-swift to join the line of crowding sailors.

Heltan called warning to him, but he didn't turn back. Could not, Mirian knew, just as she knew Gombe was caught by the same song.

The harpy glided in, slashing at upraised throats. One by one, the sailors slumped, alternately falling over the side or tumbling down the deck, gurgling and dripping blood.

Next in line were Gombe and Jekka.

If Mirian were a real magic-worker, the wand would be more dependable, but her chance of success with the weapon was only fair, and there were no second chances with this. She thrust the wand back in its holster, leapt up, and grabbed two ankles—one Gombe's, one Jekka's.

Precariously as both were balanced, the sudden weight took them out of the line of attack. Gombe slid with her in a heap so that they wedged against the frame of the open hatch. Jekka dropped down, missing the hatch cover by inches, and plunged into the water, his staff clumping along the canted deck in his wake.

Rendak and Tokello had their swords out, but the monster swung away from the falling bodies, the dawn revealing her malignant grin.

Heltan shouted something in his own language and dove after his brother.

Kalina was more surprising. She reached toward her round cuirass and produced a slim metallic disk a little wider than a pie pan, then sent it curling through the air after the rising harpy.

The weapon caught the creature in the shoulder blade just over the black wing and brought forth a scream of pain. The lizard woman sent a second of the weapons whirring at a another harpy. This one was in mid-dive for Ivrian, who'd ended his slide against the submerged ship rail. Kalina's second throw was even keener than the first, and sheared through the creature's neck.

The womanlike head bounced one way while the limp body dropped near Ivrian.

That, apparently, was enough for the harpies. One turned and beat wings to the northwest. The one wounded by Kalina tore the weapon from its body and tried hurling it back. The cast flew wide and the disk dropped into the choppy water. Kalina pushed off the deck in a graceful dive, parting the waters at about the same place the weapon had vanished.

The wounded harpy flew after her sister and they circled like vultures a half league out.

Mirian paused to catch her breath and take stock of the situation.

The sky had lightened further, though the coastline was still a dark silhouette to the north. She spotted a low, sickle-shaped sandbar beside the reefs, and in moments she was urging those in the water to swim there and right the overturned boat.

She could find only seven living sailors, and five were streaked with blood. It was hard to tell how severely injured they were, so she sent Tokello to the sandbar to treat them.

As the Galanors climbed over the deck to join them, Heltan dragged Jekka out of the water. The warrior had survived, but his right leg was twisted at a gruesome angle.

The ship seemed to have settled in, though it still creaked ominously. Mirian was staring at it when the *Leopard*'s strapping first mate's rowed in from the stern. Chilton had eight crew members with him, and she waved him close.

The man made a handsome spectacle as he braced himself in the prow and formed a speaking trumpet from his hands. "Where's Captain Akimba?"

"He didn't make it," Mirian answered grimly.

At that moment, Kalina rose from the waves with one of her silver disks and dropped it beside her mate. Her appearance brought an audible gasp from the nearby sailors. She ignored them, turned, and dove back in.

Chilton called to Mirian. "We've got to load up and get out of here."

"Take the crew to shore, then come back. My people will salvage supplies."

This met with some debate aboard the boat, which the mate silenced before calling to her again: "Ma'am, you'll be killed."

"We're salvagers," she answered. "This is what we're experts at."

The boat rocked with another wave. "But what about those harpies? You'll be in danger from them as well."

"Go on, Chilton," Alderra urged. "Mirian knows her job."

The mate still looked troubled. "We can watch for ourselves," Mirian assured him. "We need food, and maps, and a compass or three. By the time you have a camp up on the shore we should have everything ready. Leave us the one boat, and take the rest of the sailors."

There were mutters about not boarding a boat with any frill-backs, but Chilton called back, saying he'd row back with a few people once they were settled.

"I'll head in with them to help pick a good site," Kellic suggested.

Mirian didn't want to criticize her brother in front of the sailors, so she kept silent as he splashed out waist-deep and clambered on board. All but two of the sailors on the sandbar went with him.

Earlier, Kellic had sworn he meant to prove his worth to the salvage team. His chances of that were sunk even further than the *Red Leopard*.

"We'll come back for you," Chilton called. "Good luck!"

Mirian waved a farewell, and soon the vessel was rowing out, heavily laden. She thought she caught Kellic looking back at her, but turned away in time to see Kalina resurface. She'd nearly forgotten the lizard woman was below. Her people truly must be able to hold their breath for a long time.

Kalina exchanged a few hooting chirps with her mate as she stepped onto the sand, then turned to Mirian. "Why doesn't your healer mend Jekka?"

Mirian looked to Tokello, who was watching the receding boat. "Tokello, we have wounded still." She pointed to the lizard man lying beside Heltan.

The big woman frowned, stepped around the Galanors, and moved in close Mirian.

She spoke almost directly to Mirian's ear. "You want me to heal the frillback?"

The extent of her hostility was startling, and Mirian pulled back in surprise, studying the older woman's blocky face. "I want you to heal one of our company."

"Each time I use the magic, it drains me. You want me wasting it on a frillback when there'll be who knows what to worry about ashore?"

Mirian had no time for nonsense. "He's one of our guides, and without them, our ship and family are on the chopping block." Her voice snapped like a whip. "And it's a gods-damned order, not a request!"

Tokello grumbled, but stepped away and knelt by Jekka. She set her meaty hands to the wounded lizard man's leg.

Jekka's mouth opened spasmodically in a hiss, his eyes widening further, but as the healer chanted, the warrior's leg straightened, and a dark brown patch among the green scales faded completely away. Tokello rose, wiping sweat from her brow, then frowned at Mirian.

Mirian was disappointed to discover such prejudice in a woman she'd always admired, but she had more important things to worry about. She glanced over the rest of her team. Rendak and Gombe waited with the Galanors. Ivrian, she thought, had proven more able than she'd expected. More useful than her own brother, at least.

"How far off course do you think we are?" Alderra asked. She looked a little disheveled, but capable and determined, her long silvery hair clubbed in a ponytail.

"I'll have a better idea when we reach the shore," Mirian answered. "Right now, though, this is a job for experts. I want you two to stay with the sailors and—"

"We can help," Alderra objected. "We have air bottles.""

"We only have one, actually," Ivrian added. "Mine broke when I lost my balance."

"It doesn't matter," Mirian said. "You two aren't trained. Stay close. We can hand things down to you."

Heltan had come up beside Alderra. "We, also, can assist. And I thank you for having your priest heal my brother's wounds."

"We're working together now," Mirian said.

Kalina emerged again from the choppy water, this time bearing Jekka's staff. The lizard man visibly brightened before formally bowing his head. So thankfulness was not unknown to him. He and Kalina stepped up to stand on either side of Heltan.

"You were pretty formidable with those weapons of yours," Mirian told Kalina.

The lizard woman regarded her with luminous eyes. The dawn painted her in reds and golds. "We call them *gwangas*." Kalina sounded a little breathless. "Usually I hunt for meat," she added, "but I do not think those bird women would be good to eat."

"No," Mirian agreed. "Kalina, I want you to stand watch. You're the only one besides me with a distance weapon. Heltan, Jekka, pull those bodies out of the water."

"Ah, yes," Heltan agreed. "To keep predators off."

"Yes," Mirian agreed, although she had actually been thinking of burial.

"You two," she motioned to the remaining sailors, "stand here with Lady Galanor, and we'll hand goods down to you."

The elder of the two, a sun-browned woman with a bulbous nose, knuckled her forehead in a casual salute. "We'll help any way we can, ma'am. We're glad you're not leavin' the bodies for them monsters."

"No." Mirian's voice softened as her mind turned back to poor Akimba. "We won't."

Her gaze tracked to where the boat closed toward the shore. Gods willing, the sailors would face no challenges once they put onto the beach. All she could see with the rising sun was white sand and palm, but there was no telling what lurked within the jungle. Along with the standard predators could be any number of angry tribes, human and otherwise. Maybe, if their luck had turned, there'd be an Ijo fishing village close by.

"All right, you lot," she said to her salvaging party, "come with me."

She started up the slanting deck, using rails, barrels, and broken lines for leverage. "First priority's looking for survivors, then finding the rest of our gear. Be careful in the hold. The ship seems wedged pretty tightly but—"

"This ain't my first dance, Mirian," Rendak said, not unkindly. "We'll get it out. And then the ship's stores?"

He was right, of course. She felt a little foolish, but decided against apology. "Right."

The salvaging job proved one of the simpler she'd managed. As the storm dispersed, the waters smoothed, which meant the ship remained safely against the rocks. There were no survivors left aboard. Charts, weapons, and a great deal of food stores were recovered easily enough, and the shoal was soon crowded to overflowing.

They'd also found one of the ship's cats, which had clung ferociously to Gombe's shoulder and badly gashed his arm as he handed the feline down to the sailors. The ship's rats were out and swimming in a line for the shore, sensing the route by sight, scent, or some sense unknown to Mirian.

Heltan's assignment had proved the most challenging, and when Mirian popped out of the forecastle hatch to hand the last case of charts to the waiting sailors, she saw him resting a few feet from a pile of sodden bodies. The lizardfolk's white robe was stained red.

"What happened?" Mirian asked.

"A wave pushed him against a reef," Kalina answered. "He is but surface-hurt. The rest of the bodies are lost to the sea god. There are sharks now." She pointed.

Fins circled only a hundred yards out, and two sharks wrestled with a lumpy, pale object in the water. Better not to think about what that had been.

Mirian made a last trip with Rendak up to the captain's body. As she bore his front half she couldn't help reflecting that he and all of his crew would be alive even now if she hadn't sought his services.

"You," she said quietly, "were a good man." She would have liked to have known Akimba better, in gentler circumstances, and she was somber as she handed him down to his waiting sailors.

When the ship's boat returned, pulled by weary sailors, they loaded it with weapons and the dead. The other was weighed down with casks of salt pork, fresh water, and themselves.

Almost everyone on the shore seemed inclined to laze on the sand, thinking their survival had been enough work for the day, but Mirian and Chilton organized them into work parties. Watches had to be set, food had to be prepared, bodies had to be buried, and temporary shelters of canvas rigged.

The sailors approached all of these duties a little less grudgingly after they'd breakfasted on some salt pork and meal cakes.

"Any idea where we are?" Mirian asked Chilton.

The big mate shook his head. "The captain tried to hold us on course, but I'd need landmarks to know for sure."

"That's what we'll find, then." She spent some time going over the peninsular map with Rendak and the rest of her team, Ivrian watching over their shoulder.

That reef that had keeled their ship was almost surely the Manta's Spine, but she'd been in the wilds long enough to know that not verifying locations could be very dangerous. She sent Rendak and Chilton east along the shore while she and Gombe journeyed west. She'd hoped Kellic would volunteer for something, but he seemed set on losing every possible chance to make a good impression.

The tropical sun blazed down as they walked, and Mirian was glad they'd been able to recover footgear, for the shoreline beyond their landing point was rocky.

The jungle steamed in the morning, and a cacophony of sound rolled out at her as she advanced. She did not fear the jungle, but she treated it with wary respect. There was good reason to stay clear of it this morning, for once they were a few paces within they'd have no chance of seeing any landmarks through the vegetation.

She and Gombe walked forty-five minutes southeast before spotting the broad mouth of a river. Seabirds hovered over the water, diving now and then for fish.

There could be no mistake about their location, for there was only one true river in all the Kaava Lands—the Oubinga. Mirian chuckled a little and looked at the expanse of fronds directly to the north, otherwise completely identical to all the others they had passed.

"Captain Akimba got us close enough for spitting, storm or no storm," she told Gombe. "This is just about where we need to be."

"You still mean to go in?"

"I don't see why not. Chilton can find a fishing village and Lady Galanor can get word back to Eleder. By the time we come out of the jungle there'll be a ship waiting to take us home."

Gombe stretched a hand up to rub his nose, then nodded thoughtfully. "That sounds just like what your father would say. Why not? We've got everything we need to do it."

She really wished people would stop telling her how she was doing just what her father would have done.

Upon their return they discovered Rendak had experienced even better luck. He and Chilton had found a small Ijo village just a half hour east. The Ijo had coexisted peacefully with the colonists for centuries. The sailors could make their way there, and back to Sargava, safely.

While Chilton had his surviving crew ready their gear, Mirian gathered her expedition.

Once apprised of the situation, Heltan eagerly bobbed his head. "If that is the Oubinga, I can find us the Pool of Stars."

Kellic ceased playing with a silver cuff link. "Wait. You mean you want to go in? Still?"

"Everything we need survived intact," Mirian said. "Lady Galanor can go with the sailors and send another ship to pick us up."

"I'm going with you," Alderra said. "I thought I'd made that clear. I can send a letter with Chilton to deliver to the Minister of Defense. They'll take care of us."

"I thought you might insist on coming." Mirian's gaze drifted to Ivrian.

"Don't even suggest staying behind, ma'am." Lady Galanor's son shook his head. Of all of them, he was the only one who looked well rested. "I know what I'm in for."

"I don't think you do." She cleared her throat and glanced at Alderra, wondering why she was so set on taking the boy with her. Did she really think he was up to this? Her attempt to season him would likely kill him.

Rendak spoke up then. "What Mirian's being too polite to say, m'lady, is that we'll have our hands full enough just keeping ourselves alive, and we don't want to take anyone in who can't hold his own weight. Now I know you're brave, lad, and I know you can use a sword, but it takes more than that to survive in the jungle. No one here will think less of you if you go with the sailors."

But Ivrian was already shaking his head, adamant. "I'm a fast study." He all but bounced on the balls of his feet, so eager was he to get moving.

The elder Galanor didn't interject her own opinion; she simply observed. If anything, Mirian thought, she looked amused and a little proud.

"All right then," Rendak conceded. "Just so you know if you fail to heed us, it might be your final lesson."

"Social station's got nothing to do with survival in the jungle," Mirian continued. "You two need to do what we say, when we say it, if you want to come out alive. Understood?"

"Indeed it is," Alderra said at last. "You're the expert, and my son and I both know it."

Mirian still didn't think that either of them quite grasped what they were getting themselves into, but they were adults.

"Very well. Lady Galanor, you'd best get that letter written so Chilton can deliver it. The rest of us will start gearing up."

She started to move out from under the canopy of sailcloth with the others, but her brother plucked at her sleeve. His voice was low. "Mirian."

She stopped, turned.

He had trouble meeting her eyes. "Do you remember your murals?"

What a stupid question. Mirian had loved her bedroom, and painting it with assistance from her father and mother remained one of her happiest childhood memories.

"I used to stare at your murals for hours," Kellic said. "I'd sneak in when you weren't there and pretend I could vanish into that jungle wall, into a land of adventure, or go diving into that seascape." He finally found the courage to face her. "But I'm not as brave as I thought. I'm not an explorer like you and father."

She nodded, slowly. At least he was being honest. "I was starting to guess."

"I realized that I'm just not cut out for this." He was fiddling with a small ring on his right hand, set with a ruby. "The whole time the ship was sinking, and all morning, I just kept thinking about Sylena, and how if I died I'd never see her again. And now I think about walking into that jungle and I just can't do it. I don't want to be anywhere without her."

So maybe it wasn't that he was a coward. He was in love.

"Look." His dark eyes bored into her own. "You've got a gift for this, it's clear. Why don't you stay and run the ship? I'm sorry I was so rude before. I was trying to take care of things, and I should have realized we really needed someone on the ship. Someone like you."

She shook her head. "I don't want to stay, Kellic. I'm leading this one expedition for you and mother. Then I'm gone."

He seemed not to have heard her. "I could manage the business side, and you could lead the salvagers."

This was neither the time nor the place. She realized he wasn't really looking to discuss the future in detail; he just wanted to explain his actions. "Kellic, it's fine. If you want to go, go. We can talk about the rest of this later."

He nodded quickly. "All right."

He suddenly seemed very young, and she felt a surge of affection for him. She put a hand on his shoulder. "You really love this woman?"

"I do."

"Well then, introduce her to Mother. And then get to proposing."

He nodded. "It'll be a little easier to do when you come back. With money, I mean. No one wants to marry a half-breed, let alone one without any money."

She shook her head. "No one who dislikes you for your race deserves you, Kellic."

Kellic fidgeted with his hands. Mirian wondered where he'd picked up this particular habit, then realized he was removing their father's ring.

He pinched the black band between his thumb and forefinger and extended it to her. "Here. Let Lady Galanor borrow it."

"That's generous of you."

"Good luck," Kellic said, and then he embraced her. It was tentative at first, but he pressed himself to her with honest affection.

A little bewildered by the moment, Mirian returned the hug.

"I'm sorry," he finished as he stepped away.

As he smiled awkwardly, she thought of the little boy whose hand she used to hold as she walked him down the jetty to see their father. Maybe a little bit of that loving, loyal person was still there. "It's all right, Kellic. You have a safe trip."

"And you, too. May Desna guide and protect you."

Rendak accepted the news about Kellic with little reaction, then turned down the ring, saying he was too used to the air bottle. "Give it to the little lordship."

"What about Tokello?"

"Tokello can take care of herself. Lady Galanor's got an air bottle. But a prancy fellow like Ivrian will need any extra edge he can get to improve his odds."

Ivrian brightened visibly when presented with the ring and told its properties.

"It's wonderful," he said. "Thank you! I'll take very good care of it."

"You're welcome." She turned from him, trying not to wonder why her own brother hadn't shown some of the same spirit. She addressed the group. "All right, you lot! Let's not keep the jungle waiting."

12

A Verdant World
Ivrian

Only days before, I had thought those reptiles savage, primordial, feckless beings. But as we advanced into the jungle, we learned to depend upon one another. It was either work to one goal or die in the trying, for death's shadow loomed behind every jungle fern, shone in the gleaming eyes of poisonous vipers and the coiled roots of vampire vines. It glistened on the surface of the blood-red berries of the jurap bush, which produced so virulent a poison that merely brushing against one with open skin could send a man into convulsions.

—From *The Daughter of the Mist*

Mirian's team wouldn't permit Ivrian to carry any essential gear, probably worrying that he'd wander into a sinkhole and lose a shovel or cook pot or something. He didn't understand their lack of faith. Hadn't he proven himself against the pirates and the harpies?

He didn't complain, though. Complaining had never gotten him anything. Instead he waited, knowing there'd be more chances to prove himself.

While he'd studied a great deal of information about jungle travel, there were many surprises: how cool and dark it was under the canopy; how loud it could be, what with bird calls and chattering monkeys and other strange sounds echoing around them;

how frequently they had to stop and apply the oily pulp gathered from fever grass to keep off small biting insects.

The writer in him was always at work. When he slipped and caught himself on a tree trunk a hand's span from a snake, he tried to remember that stark feeling of terror so he could later set it down. When his right heel began to ache, he amused himself by trying to choose the best adjectives to describe the pain.

Most of the time, Mirian kept them walking single file. Occasionally they had to halt as the vanguard cleared a path with machetes. As they advanced deeper and deeper into the jungle, though, the canopy thickened and heavy undergrowth grew less common.

As they walked, Jekka or Kalina was always in the front, usually with Mirian. Heltan kept to the middle of the pack with Tokello and Ivrian. Rendak and Gombe usually brought up the rear, though one of them occasionally traded out with Kalina or, as the day wore on and the salvagers' faith in his mother grew, Alderra Galanor.

The middle was obviously reserved for noncombatants, and as a reprieve for those who weren't patrolling. While it irked Ivrian to be so casually placed here, his position of relative security meant he was better able to watch the expedition at work.

He was bone-weary by midafternoon, and very pleased when they stopped for a breather upon a boulder-strewn hillock. He imitated the others in searching carefully before he sat to make sure there wasn't anything on the rocks inclined to bite him. He found nothing but moss and a few black ants.

Mirian put Heltan and Gombe on first watch before sitting down with one of the maps. Just half a day through the jungle and the paper was creased and sagging. All the humans looked to be sagging a bit as well. Their exposed skin was beaded with sweat, which eventually washed away the fever grass paste.

Ivrian studied Mirian's profile, trying to decide if he should describe her as "striking" or "beautiful." She must have sensed his attention, for she looked up suddenly and met his gaze. He glanced away, staring at the back of Gombe's head and then down, as if he'd been slowly surveying the camp and had just happened to look her direction. From the corner of his eye he saw her fold the paper, take a swig from her canteen, cap it, and join Rendak and his mother, who were pointing into the jungle and talking in hushed tones.

That left him alone with the two lizardfolk sprawled on the hill beside him.

"Do you plan to court her?" Kalina asked.

He was surprised to find her staring directly at him. She was shorter than the two male lizardfolk by several inches, and her color was duller. He thought that her eyes might be a touch larger and brighter, too.

"Court her?" Ivrian asked.

"Do I use the wrong word?" Kalina crawled closer and crouched beside him. "I do not know how you humans do it. I assume you sing a song or build a home."

Ivrian grinned. "Well, yes, that's sort of how it's done. But I don't plan to court Miss Raas."

"Why not? She has vigor and—how do you say it? The wiles."

"She's in charge, for one thing."

The lizard woman cocked her head. Her color brightened.

"She's my leader. I'm lower in status." He decided not to add that this demotion was only temporary. "Plus, she's not impressed by me."

"But you stare and stare. Do you think of impressing her with a song?"

"Is that how your people do it?"

"Heltan sang his love. He is a fine one for words, and knows the whole history of our clan. But tell me of your song."

Apparently he'd met a romantic lizard woman. "Um, I'm not a musician. I'm a writer, and I was thinking of how to describe her when I write about our journey."

"Oh!" Kalina's head bobbed. "Will you describe me?"

"I will."

"What words will you use?" She sounded eager as a child offered sweets.

"I'll say that you are a fierce hunter, very brave, and extremely inquisitive." At her uncomprehending stare he decided to use simpler words. "Er—that you ask good questions."

"These things are true. You should say them."

"Also," he said, "I'll tell people how you're nice, and that you befriended me."

"Is that true?"

"You've said more to me than anyone else in the last four hours. That seems kind to me."

"Is that how humans know if they are friends?"

He laughed, a little sadly. "Sometimes. I would be your friend, though, if you wished it."

Her mouth opened, and she produced a dry coughing sound. "How strange to have a human friend."

"You can have no human friends," Jekka said. He had risen to one knee. "Their hearts bleed, but they carry no feeling. It is only coins they want."

"You know that about all humans?" Kalina asked.

Jekka nodded toward the other side of the hill, where Mirian's head was just visible. "She saved me because she needs guides. To find money. And him—" He pointed a finger at Ivrian. "He sells stories for money."

Kalina's eyes widened. "Is this true? You trade stories for money?"

"I do." Normally he said this proudly, or with carefully modulated modesty, but the confusion he felt was present in his voice.

The crest along Kalina's neck and head fluttered as she stood. She cocked her head at him and walked away.

Utterly confused, Ivrian found himself in the uncomfortable position of seeking an explanation from Jekka, who supported himself with his staff as he stood. The lizard man's eyes were brooding pools.

"What did I say?"

"Stories are sacred. For the teaching of young and the sharing of truths. For lessening sorrow and remembering past—and evils done," he added. "Kalina's sister was our clan's storyteller. She would have sooner died than trade her tales for gold."

"It's different for humans."

"Yes." Jekka lifted his staff and walked away.

As they started back up, Ivrian felt even lonelier than before.

A few hours later they halted along the banks of a river. He was about to ask if it were the Oubinga again, but his mother was already asking the same question of Mirian.

She shook her head.

"This is a tributary," Heltan answered. "We are still days from the Pool of Stars."

That, Ivrian knew, was a landmark (rivermark?) they sought, a place where the Oubinga broadened almost into a lake. He'd heard Mirian talking about it with the lizardfolk earlier.

Mirian, Rendak, and Kalina walked cautiously along the muddy bank, studying the murky waters. They consulted briefly, and then Kalina whipped out one of her metal disks and sent it spinning into the lower treetops.

Nearby birds erupted from the greenery with frightened squawks and spilled into the sky above the river.

It wasn't until a brown monkey thudded into the ground that Ivrian saw the disk embedded in its chest. The mammal's brethren shrilled in alarm and scrambled, setting branches swaying, but they weren't swift enough to avoid Kalina's second disk, which brought down another monkey larger than the first.

Ivrian was impressed with both the speed and lethality of the lizard woman. Mirian and Rendak went forward with her and stood looking at the corpses.

"Kalina is an excellent shot," Ivrian told Heltan.

"She is a fine hunter," the lizard man agreed.

"Are we going to eat the monkeys?" Ivrian asked.

"Fish," Heltan said. "The fish who rend. I don't know your human name for them. The monkeys are for those fish."

"He means the piranha," Tokello said.

"Why are we feeding the piranha?"

"To distract them." The healer herself seemed distracted, uncertain whether to be concerned about the jungle behind them or the dark river before them, for her gaze shifted warily between the two. "The fish can shred an animal to bone in a dozen heart-beats. At least that's a quick way to die in the jungle."

"You mean there are worse ways?" Ivrian asked.

Her laugh was without humor. "You don't know the half of it. There're bugs out here that can bite you so gently you'll never notice, and then you'll waste away for weeks. And then there're the boggards. If you're lucky they'll kill you before they start eating."

"The writer Ivrian looks troubled," Heltan observed. "Perhaps you should give him fewer details."

"I wish I knew fewer of them myself," Tokello said, stepping away.

"If it makes you feel any better," Heltan said, "the root salve should protect you from the bugs."

"What protects me from the fish?"

"The monkeys," Heltan said, as if it were obvious.

Ivrian didn't fully comprehend the plan until Gombe wandered over with an explanation. "Rendak's going to toss those monkeys upriver. The moment the water froths, we start across."

Ivrian finally understood. "Wait—are you sure this will work?"

"Probably," Gombe said. Then he grinned. "If it doesn't, you won't care for long."

Heltan broke into a coughing laugh, one he traded with Jekka.

Ivrian crowded near the shore with the rest of them. They were rejoined by Kalina, who'd cleaned her weapons and was returning them to her chest holster. Mirian had wandered upstream with Rendak and now watched the thick jungle behind him.

Gombe lifted a hand to Rendak, signaling readiness, and Rendak heaved one of the monkeys farther upriver. The corpse hit with a splash of droplets that seemed bright and clean when separated from the dark river. By the time the second body struck, the water was alive with foam. It didn't take much imagination on Ivrian's part to picture small silvery bodies tearing those monkeys into bloody hunks.

"Go, go!" Gombe urged, and Ivrian stepped into the surprisingly cool water, ankle-deep in muck, then onto a firmer river bottom. He was knee-deep, thigh-deep—and then abruptly there was nothing at all beneath him, and he was left behind as the lizardfolk swam ahead with undulating grace.

Ivrian was a decent swimmer, but he didn't usually try to move through the water while carrying a pack of gear. He dropped like a stone, hit the floor of the river with both feet, and pushed up enough to gasp at the air. He held his breath, marveling a little at the green glowing fins that had formed from wrist to elbow and extended from his feet. He paddled frantically, gurgled for help. He felt a firm hand grasp him, pull his head above the surface. He found his mother looking at him in disgust, locks of wet silver hair straying over her forehead. "You've got a ring that allows you to breathe water."

He reddened even as Alderra Galanor dragged him with her, kicking for the shore.

In another moment he was once more on solid footing, then staggering up into the shallows, scared witless that he'd soon feel the brush of those horrid teeth. He knew piranha could reduce flesh to bone in seconds. He was just walking onto the muddy bank when Rendak and Mirian emerged from the water and turned to consider the river.

His mother stepped close. "You're embarrassing yourself, and you're embarrassing me. What's gotten into you?"

"Sorry."

"You're better than this. Get your head out of your ass or you'll get yourself killed. And maybe whoever's trying to save you, too."

"Sorry," he mumbled again.

His mother stepped away to consult with Heltan, who was soon pointing one green finger northwest. Gombe sidled over, scratching his broad dark nose. Ivrian braced himself for another joke at his expense.

"It's not easy getting used to the tools," the salvager said. "You should have seen me the first time I went down with an air bottle. I didn't have the tube down far enough, and I sucked in half the ocean! I nearly drowned." He ears seemed to waggle as he shook his head. "You just have to stay calm."

Ivrian nodded.

"That's really the secret," Gombe went on. "Keep your wits, and keep looking. But don't be like Tokello. She wears herself out every day because she's so damned nervous something's going to snatch her. She looks over her shoulder so much she's going to strain her neck."

"Thanks."

Gombe grinned. "Hey, next time you sit down for a seafood meal, think back on this. Kind of puts the whole 'fish dinner' thing in a different light, doesn't it?"

"I suppose it does," Ivrian said. Gombe whopped him on the shoulder and trotted on.

Normally someone of Gombe's station wouldn't have dared touch him, but that didn't bother Ivrian. He watched the salvager join the others, reflecting that people often proved different than one expected.

"Stop daydreaming, lad," Rendak said as he passed him. "Time to get back to it."

They resumed their trek. Late in the afternoon, Jekka came rushing back from the front and ordered everyone to halt. Ivrian was walking with Heltan and his mother, and both went statue-still. He was about to risk a whispered question when he felt the ground shake beneath him.

Earthquake?

No. It was too regular.

Something vast and terrible was striding through the jungle. Monkeys in the canopy screeched warnings as the treetops swayed. Birds scattered. Smaller animals bolted through the undergrowth.

Greenery obscured the stomping monster from his sight. Curious as he was to glimpse the thing, he was grateful when its tread receded.

Just as Ivrian was about to ask what the monster was, the entire jungle echoed with a bone-rattling roar.

He decided then that he'd stay quiet for just a little longer. This, he thought, must be what the rabbit feels when the hound is loosed.

They remained still while a second, more distant roar shook the jungle.

"What was that?" Ivrian whispered at last.

"A thunder walker." Jekka sounded surprised. "Have you never heard of it?"

"A dinosaur," his mother said.

"What would we have done if it came after us?" Ivrian asked

"Scattered," Gombe said from behind him. "And prayed."

As evening drew on toward night, they climbed into the canopy to hang their hammocks, but not before there was some extended—and alarming—discussion among the salvagers and lizardfolk about scouting for giant spiders. Apparently the site they'd chosen was safe, for they were soon perched on sturdy branches dozens of feet above the jungle floor.

Dinner consisted of preserved rations and water, and was followed by an application of more fever grass paste. Ivrian tried to rig his hammock and was embarrassed to have to call over to Rendak, who was assisting Tokello with hers. The salvager raised a hand. "In a moment."

But it was Kalina who swung down from a higher limb, landing dexterously along his branch.

"What do you need help with, Writer Galanor?"

He gestured to the tangle of netting and ropes. He'd made a thorough mess of things, mostly because he was too nervous about falling while he secured the ropes. Sixty feet looked a lot farther from above than it did from below.

Kalina set to work, undoing knots and spreading lines, scrambling back and forth along the heavy tree limb while Ivrian watched. The lizardfolk might not be civilized, but they knew how to rig a hammock.

He spoke quickly, for it was the first chance he'd had to try fence-mending with her. "Kalina, I think you may have misunderstood about me. I think stories are sacred, too. But my people can't hunt for food in the cities. We have to find other ways to eat."

She manipulated the ropes, her back to him.

"And I tell stories. That's what I'm good at. Or, at least, that's what I'm okay at. I'm trying to be better. I suppose I'm really an apprentice at everything I'm doing."

She finished at last and turned to him. "Your ways are different. Heltan has reminded me of that, and of how important your moneys are to you."

"It's true."

"Jekka says that you have no god but metal."

He thought about that for a moment. "I suppose there's a lot of truth to that as well. What is your god?"

"Our god is Gozreh." Her voice took on a reverence. "The two-part god. He breathes the wind that brings rain, and she makes the seas that give us fish. He gives us speed and cunning, and she shows us the resilience of the river."

Once again, Jekka joined the conversation uninvited. His voice drifted down from above. "Our god looks the other way while our people die."

Ivrian looked up and saw the lizard man's face peering down at him from a hammock the color of dried leaves.

"I used to think that he slept," Jekka continued, "or that he had other needs, or that he worked in ways unknown to us. But I think Gozreh is lazy or forgetful, or that he prefers humans." This gloom-filled pronouncement delivered, Jekka withdrew his head.

"Is he always like that?" Ivrian asked.

Kalina's tongue flicked out delicately before she answered. "His mate and younglings died last year. He has never been the same."

"I'm sorry to hear that." He honestly was, although it was difficult to imagine Jekka's animosity might not simply be borne of unreasoning hatred.

"Have you had younglings, Writer Galanor?" Kalina asked.

"Me? No. And please, call me Ivrian."

"Ivrian. That is right. You have no younglings, but you are thinking of mating." She stared at him with unblinking eyes.

"No, no. I'm not interested in women. For mating, I mean."

There was a rustle to their left, and he saw Mirian climbing her way over. "How is everything here?" she asked. "Shipshape?"

"It is fine now," Kalina said. "We were just discussing the making of younglings."

Ivrian blushed. "I'm not really interested in younglings." That wasn't quite true. Ivrian liked children. "I mean, I don't need them of my own blood." And that wasn't quite true either, because his mother had hinted, sometimes not so subtly, that he was going to have to marry and produce an heir, no matter his personal preferences.

"Some among my people take pleasure with the same sex. Is that how it is with you?"

"Sort of." He wasn't entirely comfortable talking openly about sexuality in front of Mirian Raas, who still lingered.

"Some people," Mirian said, "find talk of such matters a private thing."

"Oh. I did not know." The lizard woman's gaze swung to Mirian. "Do you have younglings, Salvager Mirian?"

Ivrian half expected Mirian to explain that this, too, was private, but she only smiled. "No. Do you?"

"Not yet. But Heltan and I hope. We must have others to whom we can teach the songs of our people."

"What of your folk back home?" Mirian asked.

Kalina's tone was flat. "There are no folk back home."

"I don't understand," Ivrian said.

"This is my clan." Kalina pointed to the row of hammocks slung above. "This is all that's left."

"Only you three?" He'd had no idea.

Kalina nodded. "Only three here. But maybe more elsewhere. The city we seek—the place our clan comes from—was but an outpost. There may yet be others of our larger clan, out there in the far green, if we can find record of where their cities are. Heltan says that the books of the city will tell us."

Mirian slid closer on the branch and bowed her head in a gesture reminiscent of those nods given by the lizardfolk. "I'm truly sorry, Kalina."

"You are kind-souled. Like your mother."

"Kalina," Ivrian said, "I hope this isn't too forward, but can't you breed with other clans?"

"You do not understand. We are—how do you say? Learned. The Karshnaar are ages old. When your folk still hunted with flint and stone, we had mastered steel. We sailed the waves in great black ships and gave names to the stars. We were many. Now, we are only three."

"I have but two in my clan," Ivrian said. "My mother and me."

"Ah, but you are in a human world, and you have loyal allies and means to find gold to bring you more. We Karshnaar have no allies."

"You have us," Mirian said.

"That is good." Kalina stared at them for a moment, expression unreadable. "It is time for sleeping now, Salvager Mirian and Writer Ivrian." And without any more preliminary, she scampered up the trunk.

"Your mother mentioned you were a writer," Mirian said. "I hope you're not thinking of writing about our expedition."

Ivrian felt his stomach sink. "I'm mostly a playwright," he said. "But being out here, seeing how real people have adventures, will add some verisimilitude to anything I set down on paper." As he said it, he realized it was true, but he wondered why he didn't just come out and tell her his plan. Was he as much of a coward as Kellic Raas?

"I see you've got the same hammock setup as your mother," Mirian said as she looked over Kalina's work. "Don't forget to rub some more salve on your hands and face. Something always finds its way through the net, even one as fine as this."

He nodded slowly, then exchanged a good night before sliding back to the sturdy-feeling trunk where his pack was fastened. As he opened it to extract the container of salve, he berated himself for lacking the courage to be honest. Yet soon he realized that it wasn't just cowardice that stilled his tongue, but understanding. Mirian would never let him write about her unless he proved himself first.

Well, he could do that. Doubtless there would be other chances for distinction. There would be more rivers to cross, and the next one wouldn't frighten him.

He hoped.

It proved to be loud in the jungle at night, but Ivrian woke only once, when distant screaming broke through the canopy. It went on for several long moments. It sounded human, but from what direction it came, or how far off it really was, no one could say, though they whispered of it in the darkness.

No one thought it would be a good idea to investigate.

After that, Ivrian had trouble sleeping. He grew more and more uncomfortable, feeling his throat was dry, and finally clambered out of his bag. He pushed the netting aside and carefully made his way to the tree bole to retrieve his waterskin. It was there that he heard a low mutter of conversation from farther up in the canopy. His mother's voice, he thought, but he didn't pay heed to it at first, for he was taking a long swallow of water. Probably too long a swallow, really, for only the gods knew when they'd have access to clear drinking water again.

Frowning at his own weakness, he capped the container, stowed it in his bag, and then was distracted by his mother's low laughter. What could possibly be amusing after that horrific scream?

Brushing a small black ant from his arm, Ivrian advanced softly to one tree limb over and looked up to where he could dimly make out a row of hammocks. He could see nothing, but by straining he heard a soft conversation underway between Mirian and his mother.

"Of course I'm serious," Alderra was saying. "You're a capable and intelligent woman. And you could keep a lover. You wouldn't be the first Sargavan couple to pretend a marriage."

Ivrian paled in embarrassment. Was his mother actually suggesting marrying him off to Mirian Raas? How dare she!

Mirian laughed, which wounded him a little. "I'd think you'd want a colonial woman."

"I want someone of sense, so my grandchildren have sense. And I think the two of you could be friends and allies. You know he's a brave young man."

"He's got heart, I'll give him that."

That was a compliment of sorts, at least.

"He needs a strong woman to inspire him. A passionate woman."

"A woman to turn him from men, you mean? That doesn't work."

"It can," Alderra said. "He's a boy still. Self-absorbed, wide-eyed. Someone like you, who sees how the world works, could guide him into adulthood."

Ivrian felt his nails digging into his palm. How dare his mother speak of him like that! He was most assuredly not self-absorbed! Shelyn save him—he didn't even *want* his mother's money, or her obligations!

"When I marry, I'd rather not have a project," Mirian said.

"My dear, marriage is always a project. But I'm glad to hear you're not opposed to the idea in principal."

"Then you're not listening. I don't want to battle for any man's interest. Are you interested in a daughter-in-law or a brood mare?"

"I'm not sure, but I think you've just insulted me."

"You badger me with proposals when we both need sleep, then take offense when I challenge you?"

"See," Lady Galanor said, agreeably, "you're honest and practical."

"More qualities you want bred into your line?"

"No! That was a compliment. Surely you can't fault a woman for trying to look out for her son's interest. I mean to make a man of him, one way or another."

"Boy."

It was a low-voiced warning call. Ivrian looked up to find the square shape of Tokello's face looking at him from a hammock slung along a branch to the left.

While Mirian and his mother whispered on, Tokello braced a hand on the branch and peered out of her bug netting.

"I don't think Mirian would like you listening in," the healer whispered.

"It's not her I'm angry about."

Distantly, his mother said something about "shaping the boy up."

Tokello glanced up toward the source of the noise, then looked at Ivrian with unblinking eyes. "Sometimes you hear things you shouldn't. Take me—I've heard the whole conversation. I don't want to, but I can't help it. I can't sleep through everything like Gombe."

Sure enough, the salvager's snoring sounded even over the omnipresent buzz of insects and the call of night animals.

"I don't even think that scream woke him," Tokello said.

"Mother's trying to engineer my life," Ivrian said. "She thinks I'm still a boy."

"She thinks you're *young*. And she's got the truth of it. If anyone could straighten a man out, it would be our Mirian."

The healer's double entendre seemed to have been unintentional—Ivrian was pretty sure she hadn't even noticed.

"But she's got no right," Ivrian objected.

"If she's your mother, she's got the right. It doesn't make her right, though, boy. You seem fine to me. The gods know I've seen enough snot-nosed lordlings in my day wanting old Tokello to step and fetch for them. Fah! As though a fifth-generation Mulaa healer were a porter. Two of those little blue blood bastards nearly ran down my grandchild in the street last week."

"I'm not like that."

"I know." Tokello's tone gentled. "You hold on to that, boy, and you fight for what you believe as strongly as you fought for us back on the *Daughter*, as bravely as you fought that harpy, and you'll end up all right. Now get back to your bunk and get some sleep. This night talk is foolishness."

Ivrian stared at her a moment longer, then nodded and moved carefully back to his own hammock. He didn't feel entirely settled, but the healer's words, gruff as they were, had lessened the heat of his anger.

He shook his head as he felt fatigue washing back over him. He *had* to find his own way. Maybe even strike out on his own and leave Sargava—although that, too, would take money he didn't have.

It was all so unfair.

As he drifted back to sleep he wondered briefly what it would be like to have Mirian in his life each day. The idea was too strange to consider for long.

He drifted off thinking again about a handsome but useless Varisian actor he'd wasted a month on, although when he dreamed, he found himself standing before Tokello at a white altar in the sunlight.

When the healer told him to turn and lift the veil of his bride, he did so, but found nothing there but a star-shot void full of whispering insects. As he stepped back in horror, he could hear his mother shouting to get on with it and kiss her, and he screamed as the darkness reached for him with clawed hands.

13
The Stone and the Mirror
Sylena

Sylena rarely thought of herself as fortunate, but she smiled almost gleefully as she looked up from the black stone where Kellic's distorted image was projected.

He'd survived. Even better, Kellic had decided to stay upon the shore rather than venture into the jungle, which made it all the more likely he wouldn't end up dead.

It was as though the Infernal Dukes had shown her special favor. Now the salvagers and Lady Galanor were nearly certain to get themselves killed exploring the hinterland, and she would still get a marriageable Sargavan landholder.

She had watched much of the previous night's events through the focus of the magical ring she'd given him, hearing almost everything Kellic himself had heard, which is why she'd set sail in the early morning, packing her goods in a rush and taking up residence once more in her "father's" trade ship—in actuality a Chelish warship decked out as a merchant.

Now they were two hours out from Eleder, and a weary Sylena sat at the desk in her cabin, employing the ring's sophisticated scrying magic to obtain a navigational fix on her lover's position. Beside her on a ring of gold was the monitor stone and a large map of the coastline, over which she dangled a crystal shot through with crimson flecks.

Just as the crystal settled into its position, the mirror she'd hung on the cabin wall crackled with a burst of violet energies.

Rajana. Of all the cursed luck.

Sylena scowled and raked her hair back with her fingers, then set down the crystal and smiled at the mirror.

The image was not quite a twin to her own, but there was no mistaking the family resemblance. Rajana had the same fair skin, but her eyebrows were more highly arched, her nose thinner. And there were no humor lines about her eyes because her sister almost never laughed. Certainly she seemed ill disposed toward laughing now.

Rajana's eyes took in the surroundings. "You've boarded a ship."

"Yes, of course."

"Perhaps you're already on your way to Crown's End to celebrate your success?"

"No." Sylena put on a brave smile. "I'm merely off to clear up the loose ends."

Rajana coolly appraised her. "Which loose ends are those, Sister?" Even in that emotionless tone, she managed to sound disappointed. But then Rajana was always disappointed.

Sylena forced her smile wider. "Naturally, I want to carry through the assignment so as not to displease Her Infernal Majestrix—or you."

It wasn't enough. Rajana's frown deepened. "Please, Sylena, just give me the details. I called in a number of favors to buy you that storm. Did it work or not?"

"It wrecked the ship, but Lady Galanor and the salvagers survived. They're heading into the jungle, but they'll probably die there."

Rajana slowly closed her eyes and put a hand to her head. "You're aware that our expenditures, both in capital and in favors, are going to attract attention very, very soon? Attention we will not want."

Sylena managed a gay laugh. "You're always so gloomy, Rajana! At every turn, the Sargavans grow more desperate, their task more difficult."

"They're still on the expedition!" Rajana cut in.

But Sylena went on as if she hadn't heard. "With any luck, Lady Galanor will never return from that jungle, which will mean an end to all of her schemes." She sniffed. "I don't understand why we couldn't have moved against her more obviously to begin with."

"Because Her Infernal Majestrix wishes subtlety in our dealings. Assassinating one of the baron's chief advisors is hardly subtle!" Rajana breathed out. "You still haven't explained what you're doing on the ship. Do you have a plan?"

"I intend to wait offshore to see whether any of them come out of the jungle. If they do, I'll take their treasure."

Rajana considered her. "You're certain where they'll emerge?"

"The other survivors are supposed to go in search of a ship to pick them up. I intend to be that ship."

Rajana's face remained expressionless for a long moment. "That's not a bad plan, Sister."

A rare compliment. Sylena bowed her head.

"I pray that it goes well for you," Rajana continued. "I want to wrap up this mission and return home."

"Of course."

"I hope that you haven't grown too fond of that Raas boy. I know how emotionally involved you can be."

Sylena cleared her throat. "I'm not 'emotionally involved.' I just don't know that we should kill Kellic. I may yet have a use for him."

Rajana sighed. "Use him however you want, so long as you kill him before he returns to Sargava.

"Of course."

Rajana frowned. "Report to me as soon as you have news."

"Yes, Rajana."

Her sister swept a hand across the distant mirror so that the image cleared, and Sylena confronted her own face. Only then did she flip it the tines, something she would never dare while Rajana watched.

The scrying ring was of Rajana's own design, and both sisters could use its magic to watch what its wearer did. But Rajana had little patience for listening to people talk, and it appeared that she must not have been eavesdropping when Kellic told Mirian Raas he would propose marriage to Sylena.

It was all working out so very nicely. In a half day or so, Sylena would drift up to offer assistance, then anchor offshore until she had proof Alderra Galanor and Mirian Raas were dead, or else had seen to that part herself and taken their treasure. Then she would have the gratitude of her superiors *and* a marriage proposal from someone who would be an important player in the new regime, as well as Sylena's pretty puppet.

14

The City and the Stars
Mirian

O ver the next few days, Mirian saw Ivrian handling himself with more and more confidence. Apart from crossing the stream, he'd made few newcomer blunders. She found it difficult to believe that an aristocrat—a pampered artist, for Desna's sake—could be so honestly eager to please a bunch of common folk the typical Sargavan blue blood wouldn't have been caught dead with. A few days in his company, though, assured her he wasn't acting.

She tried not to reflect too much on the difference between Ivrian and her own brother. Both were inexperienced and city-bred. Like Ivrian, Kellic had attended the finest fencing academies in Eleder. Yet it was Ivrian, not Kellic, who'd thrown himself into the fray when the *Daughter* had come under attack. Her brother couldn't even be bothered to sail on his own ship. What, she wondered, was the difference? Upbringing? Natural affinity?

That the well-mannered aesthete had more guts than her own brother, raised around salvagers, disappointed Mirian more than she wanted to admit, though it engendered no animosity toward Ivrian. Instead, she found herself thinking about her father's drunken tirades about the other colonial nobles. Was her brother a natural coward, or would he have grown into the man she thought she'd seen in her little brother if Leovan had been less focused on the other colonials, a little less lost in his own problems?

Maybe the difference was Alderra Galanor. With her for a role model, it was no wonder that Ivrian had turned out well. Alderra never complained or shirked duty, even when given the opportunity due to her age or alleged lack of experience. The latter was obviously a cover, as Mirian had quickly realized that Alderra was no stranger to the jungle, or privation. Mirian figured Alderra for a well-preserved mid-fifties, but she might have been older. She was fit enough that she had no trouble keeping pace, and she certainly showed no lack of energy in the evenings, when she would regale them with tales of her journeys to far courts.

As the days marched on, the group began to function more and more cohesively, its members growing accustomed to depending upon one another and becoming familiar with each other's strengths and weaknesses. Even Jekka changed a little. He could hardly be described as warm, but he seemed comfortable with some of his human companions. Mirian came to prefer walking point with him even over Kalina, whose attention was a little too easily distracted.

Mirian was on point with Jekka on the morning of their fourth day of travel when he pulled up short and crouched, slim tongue extended. This, she'd learned, was how lizardfolk smelled. She sank to one knee, watching him

The branches overhead stirred in the wind, and creatures far above hooted to one another. Jekka turned his head right and left, then dropped to advance in a rapid, scuttling crawl.

He vanished into the undergrowth, popping up again next to the trunk of a great tree. He rose slowly with his back to it. It was only then that he looked back to Mirian and gave a sharp nod.

She followed, head low. Her machete was sheathed at her left hip, her cutlass slung at her right. She loosed both as she came forward.

She reached the bole, wide enough for three people to link arms around. Jekka met her eyes once more and started around on the left, gray staff lifted.

Mirian circled on the right. They arrived together to find a deserted campsite and a fly-encrusted head impaled upon a sharpened stake. They crept about the site looking for spoor and sign. The tracks were not dissimilar to those made by Jekka himself, though the foot that made it was broader and the impression of the toes slimmer.

The desiccated head was human, possibly an Ijo tribesman, though it was so decayed it was hard to tell. Other, older stakes were thrust into the ground nearby, a single skull impaled upon each. Most were human, others human-sized but oddly proportioned. The collection resembled a grisly fence.

When the rest of the party came up, Ivrian pointed to the human head, his handsome face a little green. "Was he the scream we heard a few nights back?"

"Might be," Mirian said.

"Possibly." Jekka leaned closer and flicked out his tongue. Mirian couldn't help her mouth from twisting in disgust. The lizard man didn't quite touch the fly-encrusted face; the tongue quivered an inch or two away from the head, then got sucked back into Jekka's mouth. "Probably. He's about four days dead." He looked to Mirian. "This is a boggard tribe making territorial claim."

"Boggards." Gombe pronounced the name like a curse.

Heltan sounded genuinely troubled. "These should not be boggard lands."

Alderra strode up to Mirian's side, almost brushing against her. "Are we off course?"

"I don't think so. Keep your eyes open. If the frog-people are here, it means we're coming up on swampland, and they like to leave vicious little surprises in ankle-deep water."

They found the swamp a half hour on, as well as the most recent victim, his head impaled upon another spike in a line of seven. This time the others realized to their horror that the nearby fire pit was for roasting the rest of the victim. The boggards didn't let the material left over from the fence go to waste.

"Who was he?" Ivrian asked.

"No way to know," Mirian said.

Alderra answered him. "Some poor tribesman, probably. Or some unlucky chap out looking for treasure. There's said to be lost cities and pirate gold and magical fountains hidden in the jungle."

Tokello was looking more and more dour. She wiped more salve across her high forehead. "Does this mean the boggards have a big territory?"

"Boggards claim a lot more land than they can defend," Mirian said. "Because they're cowards. A tribe will put up a fence like this and refresh it every few months, hoping no one will come into their lands and hunt *them*."

"Somebody should," Jekka said with frightening intensity.

She understood his feeling. "Much as I'd like to take a few more boggards out of the world, I'd just as soon keep us out of trouble. I think we can steer a little out of the way and swing back toward the Pool of Stars. We'll veer west for about an hour, then due north, and we ought to arrive about noon."

Unfortunately, on her course they ended up in lowland after only a quarter hour and had to venture north, right past another death fence. There was no helping it: they had to cross into the lands of the boggard tribe.

Still, there was no sign of the hated things either within or without their territory, and just after noon they finally arrived at the banks of the Oubinga once more.

The Oubinga was the largest river in the whole of the Kaava Lands, its source deep in the jungle highlands, three days east of the legendary Mbaiki ruins. From records she'd studied in Eleder's Pathfinder lodge, Mirian knew it began as a stream, but here it was more than a quarter mile of muddy water flowing swift enough that they could see the current.

Mirian looked up from the river to the ribbon of blue sky unobstructed by the canopy. After so many days beneath the leaves, open sky seemed incongruously bright.

Heltan relaxed upon sighting the stretch of water. They moved quickly along its southern banks, ever on the alert for both the crocodiles that sunned on the riverside and boggards that might well be watching them from the jungle.

In another half hour they arrived at the Pool of Stars.

It was not at all what Mirian had expected. Heltan had described what she'd imagined as an inlet. What she found instead was a huge rim along either side of the river, so perfectly circular on either side that it might as well have been carved. The currents slid past the curving banks, allowing moss and detritus to collect and scum the surface.

Alderra, beside her once more, pointed to another skull fence facing the river from a few feet into the jungle. "It seems we have boggards here as well."

"At least it's the end of their territory," Gombe said.

Heltan exchanged a few words in his own language with Jekka, who seemed to start, then hissed violently. Heltan turned from his brother and knelt just short of the river's edge. He closed his eyes.

Mirian sidled over to Kalina. "Is this something I should be worried about?"

"Heltan asked Jekka if he wished to pray and give thanks. He used to be the god-speaker of our clan."

"But he's not now?"

"No," Jekka said, with an air of finality. "My brother wastes breath and delays us near a border with our enemies."

Heltan rose. "Gozreh has not abandoned us, Brother. She has helped guide us here."

Jekka growled and turned away.

Heltan caught Mirian's eyes and gestured to the river. "The Old Ones witnessed a trail of stars through the sky one evening.

The stars burned as they fell, but one touched down at the river, so hot it burned through both earth and water, and left this mark. Behold the Pool of Stars!"

Mirian put Kalina and Rendak on sentry duty while the rest set to raft-building. Many eyes watched them from the trees: the ever-present birds with bright plumage and monkeys of varied sizes, but Mirian was sure she felt other things as well. Would boggards dare attack a large, capable party outside their territory? Their natural instincts were cowardly, but if a leader meant to prove himself, or if there were a boggard war party large enough, they'd attack with no hesitation.

The more obvious threats were sunning themselves on a sandbar twenty-five yards off. If Mirian hadn't known better, she'd have assumed crocodiles were simply lazy and uninterested. As the expedition worked along the shore, a few nosed in closer to watch, though none ventured within striking range.

Building a raft in the wilderness required climbs into the canopy to chop larger limbs, trimming and shaping them into similar lengths and sizes, and finally tying them with rope and vines.

Although she trusted the sharp-eyed Karshnaar to keep watch, Mirian remained alert for the distinctive shush of spears through the air, or the slap of bare amphibian feet through the mud. But the boggards never showed. Maybe they were rounding farther east through their territory, planting more stakes.

The only bad moment was when Gombe's hand was bitten by a venomous blue tree snake. Mirian was fortunately close at hand with a dose of anti-venom. Noting how he eyed the trees nervously after that, she tasked Gombe with making spears from some of the trimmings. "In case the crocodiles get too close," she told him, which was true, but she also wanted to keep his mind focused on something other than snakes.

All in all the process took three weary hours, but she was pleased enough with the raft that she could imagine her father nodding in respect.

After all that labor, the crossing of the Oubinga proved almost anticlimactic. The most dangerous thing they encountered was a curious bull crocodile who trailed a few feet aft. About two-thirds of the way over he decided they were too big to challenge or not worth his trouble and drifted back to the sandbar.

They dragged the raft into some bushes and started north in what immediately proved hillier territory. The Karshnaar talked among themselves, then picked up the pace. Mirian knew from their previous conversations that they were now only a few hours from the ruins of their old city.

She halted the group for a quick reminder. "Now's no time to let down our guard. We're close, but that just means we're nearer the lands of enemies." She looked at Heltan. "Anything you can tell us about the lizardfolk tribe that drove you out?"

"The Vanizhar are less sophisticated, but more numerous. But as I told you, we've heard that they were driven out as well."

"I remember," Mirian replied. "But not everything you hear should be believed."

Jekka sounded sanguine as he responded. "We are used to being surrounded by enemies, Mirian. We are vigilant."

The air felt less humid as they climbed into rockier terrain. Even though they were among trees, they could look down upon the tops of the giants below and even make out the distant river. Mirian understood now how ancient lizardfolk might have observed falling meteorites.

Evening drew a dark blue mantle over the forest. Just as Mirian was readying to call a halt, they arrived suddenly at a decaying tower intricately fashioned from perfectly fitted stones, each carved with tiny lizard figures. It was stunning work: she longed to pull out her sketchbook and record the details while she still had light. But there'd be no time, for as expedition leader she had to secure the area.

Beyond the first watchtower was a vast clearing scattered with more, some completely crumbled into ruin. Every few hundred feet were wide pools filled with clear water. The place was still but for the croaking of frogs in the lush grass.

As they ventured deeper inside, a flock of parrots flew skyward with a beat of red and blue wings and startled cries.

Mirian was so busy looking for dangers that she didn't realize there were stones hidden by the layer of dirt and detritus and weeds until she was well into the plaza's middle. As she bent down to examine one, Ivrian halted beside her.

His voice was heavy with awe. "This place must be at least three miles wide. I had no idea it would be so large."

"And our lizardfolk guides say most of it lies underground." She brushed more dirt away to see that it wasn't just a path but an entire run of triangular stones, carefully set one beside the other, each carved with glyphs. Words? Letters? Or merely decorations? She'd have to ask Heltan. "I think the entire space is paved."

She wished they had time for a proper investigation. She'd have to report this site to the Pathfinder Society. It was clearly of greater import to the history of the continent than the simple cave complex she'd been exploring. Somehow, she'd steal time to sketch some of these images. All she'd managed to draw so far on the expedition were a few doodles in the dying light each evening, mostly of the Karshnaar or interesting-looking leaves and bugs near her hammock.

The lizardfolk moved swiftly through the ruins, reminding her of scurrying geckos as they advanced from place to place. Something caught Jekka's attention, and he summoned Kalina, who motioned to Mirian. She hurried over.

It was easy to see what had them worried. There were boggard tracks in the mud beside one of the wide pools.

"These are several days old," Jekka told her. "And look here." He paced to a path worn by the passage of many feet. Mirian followed it, flanked by Jekka and Kalina, all the way to the edge of the trees that formed the city's northern border.

Alderra joined her as Mirian stood frowning at the dark mass of jungle.

"A different boggard tribe," Jekka decided.

"There are no skull fences," the aristocrat pointed out. "Do you think there are boggards living in the pools or towers?"

Jekka sampled the air with his tongue. "No. We would have smelled them. They come to that pool only."

Mirian led them back to investigate as twilight swept in. A stream of bats passed overhead, wakened to hunt the nighttime insects.

By shining her glow stone into the pool, Mirian could look a good long way into the cenote, enough to tell that its sides had been carved into a perfect circle. A round side-tunnel intersected the vertical tunnel some ten feet below the surface, and a faint green glow came from somewhere deeper. "What's that light?" she asked.

Heltan had joined their group. He said, "Our people cultivated a phosphorescent fungus so there would be light beneath the water. Is it too late to dive, this night?"

"We should rest," Jekka told him.

Mirian agreed. "We have to set up camp. We'll approach it fresh in the morning." They'd pushed hard today, and it would be foolish to risk a dive right now.

She tasked Gombe and Rendak with looking over the nearest tower for a defensible sleeping arrangement. Tokello plopped herself onto bare flagstone with a weary sigh and took a pull from one of her waterskins—one that Mirian had long guessed actually contained wine, for Tokello always seemed a little happier come evenings, and Mirian was fairly sure it wasn't just because they'd stopped.

Jekka was still prowling about the site, as if on the hunt. Mirian asked Kalina to keep watch and went after him. Ivrian trailed a few feet behind.

She caught up to the lizard man. "What's wrong, Jekka?"

The warrior halted in his examination of the same boggard trail. He turned and waited for them. His voice was low. "I am puzzled, Mirian."

"Why?"

"This is good ground. There is fresh, clear water. Even a boggard is not so stupid as to miss the advantage. Yet they come only to this pit, and then they depart."

She nodded. "What's your conclusion?"

"I think there is something strong in the waters that keeps them out."

"Something strong?" Ivrian repeated.

"Something that's liable to find all of us tasty," Mirian said.

Jekka cocked his head and let out that strange coughing noise she'd learned to recognize as lizardfolk laughter.

She waited for him to recover. "But if they're frightened of it, why return?"

"The boggards worship strength," Jekka answered.

She nodded. "Any idea what it could be?"

"Anything that likes the water and is large," Jekka answered. "I think it will have sharp teeth."

"That doesn't really narrow it down," Ivrian objected.

"It gets to the essentials," Mirian countered. "There's something in there that's dangerous enough to keep out an entire tribe of boggards, and impressive enough that they come to pay their respects. If that's not a warning sign, I don't know what is. We'll have to be on our guard."

"Always," Jekka said.

15

The Tower in the Night
Ivrian

We had come at last to the deserted outpost of the lizardfolk: a vast, broken field of towers, haunted by forgotten glories and the ghosts of the scaled people who'd shaped that city from the jungle impossible centuries before. As night fell, we took shelter at the height of one of the towers, though Mirian remained troubled that stairs led deep into tunnels beneath the earth.

We could never have guessed what tragedies lay before us. For doom clutched at our expedition with skeletal hands, and some of us would feel its grasp.

— From *The Daughter of the Mist*

Ivrian didn't care much for the tower, not once they'd scaled its height and explored its depths. The crumbling stairs led down through dark chambers and into long corridors lined with that luminous green lichen. Heltan remained so eager to explore that he asked twice more if they might at least venture into the opening halls, but Mirian and Jekka vetoed the idea at the same moment.

The salvagers and the lizardfolk cleared the tower of some undesirables—centipedes as long as a man's arm, and a few spiders as wide as pineapples—then declared the upper rooms safe for sleeping. Three rounds of sentries were assigned at both the entrance to the underground and the tower's height, and Ivrian wasn't sure if he should be pleased or irritated he wasn't posted to either. Neither was Gombe, for the salvager was still a little weak from his snakebite.

Mirian advised against a cooked meal, saying there was no point attracting attention with smoke.

"The odds are good that if the boggards who made that trail live anywhere close, they already know we're here," she said. "But there's a chance they've missed us."

Jekka voiced agreement for the second time that evening. Ivrian wouldn't have said that the lizard man's attitude had become warm, precisely, but a change seemed to have occurred. It had been a day or two since he'd complained about human habits or customs, and more and more Ivrian was seeing him in consultation with Mirian.

Still, the others remained more kindly disposed. Heltan seemed to have struck up an honest friendship with Ivrian's mother, and Kalina chattered happily with any and all. Even the wary Tokello would talk with her.

After another dinner of dried rations, Ivrian copied the habit of the salvagers and laid his hammock upon the tower's third floor, one level below its height and two above that yawning door into darkness. The rough fabric was little enough mattress to pad him from the cold stone, but he made do like the others and sat hunched over his writing desk, making notes.

He was roughing out a description of his first view of the city when Kalina trotted up the stairs and crouched at his side, peering at what he did.

Without comment, she suddenly swung her axe about, blade at the ready. Ivrian's breath caught in his throat. Had he broken some taboo? Were they under attack?

Then he saw the lizard woman draw out a whetstone and set it against the blade with precise, rapid motions. The scraping, whining noise was a bit of an irritant until he realized this, too, was worth noting, and so he stopped trying to conjure metaphors for the ruins and watched Kalina work.

"I've never seen an axe like that before."

"It is a *laumahk*," she told him. "A weapon crafted by the elders and handed down to the finest hunter of each generation." Her lips parted, and she produced a soft hooting noise. It was a mournful sound. "I am by default the best, for I am the last."

"I'm sorry," he said, and he was. He leaned in closer. There was a curious gray sheen to the long blade. "What kind of metal is that?"

"Starmetal," she said. "I do not know what you humans name it. It was forged from the metal found in the crater of the Pool of Stars. Like the blades of Jekka's staff."

"It must be a very old weapon," Ivrian speculated.

"I do not know how to say the count of years in human words."

"Centuries are hundreds of years," he said, then added, "A hundred is ten tens."

"Then my *laumahk* is many centuries old. You see that it does not rust." She stopped her sharpening, and with a deft turn of the knob on the weapon's pommel she suddenly extended the haft. "It can be wielded two-handed, if I wish."

Ivrian was more interested than ever. "May I hold it?"

Kalina cocked her head to one side and showed the tip of her forked tongue. "May I see your writing desk?"

"Certainly. Everything I've written so far is just notes, though. It will sound much better once I tinker with it a bit."

"I cannot read your language," Kalina admitted. "But I want to see your writing and what lies within the compartments."

They traded places. Odd to think she wanted to see what he did even though she'd understand nothing of it.

While the lizard woman opened and closed the little panels and drawers, examining the pens and pen blades, inkbottles and paper, he gingerly touched the axe—laumahk, he corrected.

He kept his fingers away from the razor-sharp blade and instead studied the carved shapes of jungle animals along the haft, and the means Kalina had used to lengthen the weapon. The haft telescoped out nearly two additional feet.

"There used to be a point at the far end, for jabbing," Kalina told him, "but it broke off against a *k'rang*. I do not know what you humans call them. A lizard my height, with sharp claws. They hunt in packs."

"I'm not sure what we call those either," Ivrian said. "But I'm glad I haven't met one."

"Yes. They are very hungry. Show me the symbols where you write of me."

Smiling, Ivrian set the deadly weapon aside and searched his parchments until he found the first paragraph he'd written about Kalina. He explained to her which words said she was brave and which said she was Ivrian's friend, pointing to them as he read aloud.

The lizard woman hissed in what he hoped was contentment. She tilted her head and stared at the wall of the tower directly across from them. Mirian sat there, a notebook propped on her knees, working quickly with a pencil while staring at them.

"What does she do?" Kalina asked. Before Ivrian could speculate, she rose and moved quickly to Mirian's side.

The lizard woman's frill ruffled and her scales brightened to a lighter green. She let out a soft cooing noise and knelt for a closer look.

As Ivrian walked over, Mirian tilted the paper so Kalina might see what she did.

He leaned in beside the lizard woman, curious that he should feel comfortable enough to do so. He might have expected her to smell of swamp and weeds, but she was almost free of any scent. Certainly she smelled far better than Rendak and Gombe after a long day hiking.

He marveled, for Mirian's long, calloused fingers had sketched both of them, though she'd put far more detail into Kalina's portrait than his own.

"You're very good," he told her. His artist friends had always told him that hands were hard to draw, but Mirian had great facility with them, including Kalina's dexterous fingers as her image held the ink bottle for examination.

"Heltan!" Kalina called, "Jekka! Attend!"

Soon both of the male Karshnaar crowded, one to either side.

Jekka asked a question of Kalina in his own language, and she answered in the same. Then she said, "Do you see? She is a crafter."

"Do you fashion this for gold?" Jekka asked Mirian.

She shook her head. "No. I draw pictures of the places where I journey so my friends can see what I've seen."

Jekka blinked at this information.

There was no mistaking the eagerness in Kalina's voice. "Do you have other pictures?"

Mirian handed over the sketchbook, demonstrating how to move the pages. "Be careful turning them," she said. "Some are quite fragile."

All three of the lizardfolk then gathered about the book, making it hard for Ivrian to see much. He glimpsed a ruined wall carved with Mwangi faces, a trio of unfamiliar natives at work clearing foliage. This was followed by a study of an odd-looking bird with a long beak perched on a low branch.

Heltan and Kalina talked rapidly in their own language as they turned the pages. Jekka remained silent.

"I had no idea you were so talented," Ivrian said. "At artwork, I mean."

Mirian shrugged, but she couldn't completely disguise a glow of pride.

"Do you know what?" he said. "We might combine forces."

Her eyes transfixed his own, and he felt himself withering, for there was little warmth in her expression. Perhaps it hadn't been a good idea to bring up the matter. "I've been keeping a record of our journey," he said. "I *am* thinking about writing a record of our expedition—"

"I don't think so," Mirian said.

"Hear me out. I think there'd be a real market for this sort of thing."

"No," Mirian said. "These drawings are private."

That was a head-scratcher. "You shouldn't hide talent like that."

"I'm not hiding it, Ivrian. It's just not for sale."

"But—"

"I don't wish to discuss it. Now, the hour's late. Tomorrow may be the most dangerous day we've yet spent, so you'll want a good night's sleep. I suggest you get to it."

Confused, he nodded. As Mirian retrieved her notebook, he reflected that it was curious he'd won the friendship of a creature not of his own species far more easily than he'd gained that of their expedition leader.

16

The Sunken City
Mirian

They began at dawn, only to learn that the passage below the tower was blocked by a cave-in a hundred paces farther in. That disappointed Mirian more than it did Heltan.

"It is better to go in through the central pool, anyway," the lizard man said blithely. He reached out to touch a huge clod of black dirt that lay before them. "The central route through was told to me, as it was told to my ancestors. If we had gone in this way it might have taken days to orient ourselves."

Mirian grunted her disapproval. She liked the idea of a safe spot to which they could retreat, especially since she needed to leave a few members of the expedition aboveground. Tokello and the Galanors were no divers.

The tower had been an ideal base camp, but she didn't want them stationed far from where they were going in, so they'd have to find a new one.

She made the best of the situation. There was another tower, one a little less sturdy, only a hundred yards from the pool Heltan declared to be the city's central entrance. She and Rendak climbed up to explore, Jekka trailing.

If this second tower opened onto the tunnels, there was no longer any evidence, for its bottom floor had collapsed into its lower level, making further exploration impossible. Still, the upper floors were defensible once she and Rendak and Jekka had divested them of a small snake nest and cleared out enough vines and leaves to determine no other dangerous creatures laired inside.

They climbed down and she surveyed the team. The sun was visible over the tree line, which disappointed her. She had hoped to start their exploration at dawn. The longer they delayed, the more chance boggards would turn up in force. "All right, Tokello." She pointed up to the tower. "You've got the roof and a half level beneath."

The healer sighed.

"Gombe, I want you to stay with her."

"But Miss Raas," the salvager protested, "I'm feeling fine now."

"No 'buts.'" He still looked a little pale. And then there was the other matter. "I'm not leaving Tokello out here by herself. Which reminds me. Lady Galanor, Ivrian—"

"We're coming with you," Alderra said, a hint of steel in her tone.

"I thought you'd say that. I leave it to you. But let me remind you that I've no idea what lies below. It's something that keeps the boggards away. It's my recommendation you leave this to Rendak and the Karshnaar and me."

"I'm up for any challenge with you," the older woman said confidently.

"I'm sure you are. But you're not a trained diver."

"I'm a quick study, Mirian. And so's my son."

She nodded politely. "Ivrian's held up nicely, but he's not nearly as well seasoned as yourself. I think he should sit this one out."

The lady brushed back her mane of graying hair, an action somehow vain and strangely endearing at the same time. "If there *is* something under there, won't you need *more* swords?"

"Perhaps."

"If there's one thing I'm good at," Ivrian said, "it's bladework."

Mirian had to nod. She supposed Alderra had a point. And Ivrian had followed instructions to the letter. She studied him and wished again it was Kellic standing there, so filled with enthusiasm to prove himself he was practically ready to burst. She sighed. "If we have to fight underwater, you two stay well clear. Do you understand? If you try to help, you're liable to blunder in and trip us up."

"You can count on us," Ivrian said with a smile.

Definitely one of the most upbeat young men Mirian had ever met. It wasn't all naivete, either—more just curiosity.

Like a Pathfinder, she realized. She wondered if that was what her venture-captain had thought of her the first time they've met, when she and some Bas'o hunters had helped the Society track an artifact thief through Devil's Cradle.

"All right, gear up." She pointed at the Galanors. "Remember: you two follow our lead. And I mean you listen to our guides, too. If this were an army, you'd be the privates."

"Any army would be lucky to have a general so accomplished." Alderra quirked a smile and offered a salute.

Mirian had Rendak go over the use of an air bottle with Lady Galanor again while Mirian pulled Ivrian aside and explained once more how best to use the water-breathing ring. He nodded and asked no questions, which didn't reassure her. She then motioned Gombe forward and had him pass over two of the short spears he'd carved. Alderra handled hers with familiarity, and Ivrian imitated his mother.

"If you *must* fight underwater," Mirian said, "you'll have much more success with a spear than a sword. Jab, don't swing. Unless you're me." She'd already explained that her second ring let her move more easily underwater. "Don't try to do what you see me doing. It's not possible without magic."

Heltan led the way in, his brother at his side. The more scholarly of the lizard men carried a spear himself, and Jekka flipped out the spear blade of his staff. Mirian and Rendak followed them.

The water was cool and clear and tasted rich with healthy plant life. She floated a moment to let her lungs adjust.

The lizardfolk were already moving into the circular maw of a large tube that opened into the cenote, their tails and feet granting them extraordinary momentum.

Mirian would have liked to have examined the drop site in more detail, or waited to ensure the Galanors got in safely, but she had to keep the Karshnaar in sight, so she kicked after. She heard the dull sound of a splash as one or both of the Galanors plunged in behind. As prearranged, Rendak lingered to swim with them.

The lizardfolk moved on, sleek and graceful. It was odd to see Heltan without his robe. He looked much more the warrior, now, focused solely on what lay before him.

In contrast, Jekka sometimes glanced back, just like Mirian. Rendak, shirtless and barefoot, swam just behind the Galanors, who were side by side in tight-fitting short pants and blue shirts. Kalina brought up the rear. Her laumahk was strapped to her back, a spear in one green hand.

Mirian had thought they might have to rely on glow stones, but the phosphorescent fungus shone in long green lines among the fitted stones. The light source appeared to have been set up to grow in slotted channels on either side of the tunnel, but it had overflowed and eaten into the mortar.

Two hundred feet on they came to a point where two tunnels crossed. The lizardfolk surfaced in a small vaulted chamber to catch their breath. Mirian, troubled by a flash of white below them, dived.

She found another tunnel mouth running diagonal to the upper one. At the floor below the intersection, she spied a pile of bones.

Many were animal skeletons. Others were the froglike skulls of boggards. But there was no missing the distinctive look of human jaws mixed among them.

Troubled, she kicked up to join the lizardfolk, breathing out the water so she could gasp in cool, stale air and converse with them.

"Are you ready to move on?" Heltan asked, clearly excited.

"There are bones down there," she said. "A lot of them. Boggards. Lizardfolk too, I think. And humans."

Rendak surfaced beside her, then Ivrian, who didn't remember to breathe out the water before he tried to breathe in air and had to steady himself against the limestone roof as he heaved up the water in his lungs. She winced in sympathy. That was a mistake he probably wouldn't make again.

Jekka eyed her. "That makes no sense. No one who lives here would dirty the waters. I don't think even the Vanizhar would do that."

"I don't think it's the Vanizhar," Heltan said.

Ivrian's coughing rang off the stone in the tiny space, echoing loudly. If there was something here, the noise he was making would surely attract it.

"Do you have any idea what it is?" Rendak asked. "Did your people keep crocodiles as pets or something?"

"No." Jekka sounded insulted. "We do not keep crocodiles as pets."

Mirian shifted her attention to Heltan. "The water must be connected with some outside source, or it would be stagnant. Do you know how large that source is and where it originates?"

"I do not. Your reasoning is sound, though. Probably there are ancient grates so that unwanted animals could not enter the city, but water could. If one of those grates is broken, something may have gotten in."

Kalina surfaced beside her mate, patted his shoulder. The dull green light reflected brilliantly off the turquoise stones of the lizardfolk's necklaces, as though conjuring a sympathetic glow. Mirian pushed over to check on Ivrian, who was still coughing.

The elder Galanor was diving deeper to explore. "Keep an eye on her ladyship," Mirian told Rendak, who nodded, fitted his mouthpiece, and ducked under the water. She addressed the others. "All right. We know there's a predator in here. Let's stick a little closer together. Heltan, how far do we have to go?"

"Not too much farther. Follow me." Heltan ducked his head and turned into the north tunnel. Jekka followed a moment later.

"Come on, Ivrian," Mirian said. "Breathe out before you try to breathe air, or this will happen every time."

"Right," he gasped.

It was much farther than Heltan had suggested. They swam deep into the tunnels, veering now right, now left. Heltan never hesitated, though he and the other lizardfolk rose occasionally for the necessary gulps of air. Seeing that they didn't pause to converse, Mirian remained below, constantly scanning the passages. Twice they passed through cenotes that opened to the sky, which was a little reassuring. If they had to get out fast, at least they wouldn't have to retrace their way through the entire maze.

They finally arrived at a set of stairs that started in the water and led up into a soaring stone chamber. The tiny glowing, shell-like fungus grew here as well, spread out all along the sides of the wall. It cast eerie emerald light into the thick cobwebs that walled the place.

"I hate spiders," Rendak muttered.

"Stay in the water for now." Mirian stopped on the first stair above the water. Heltan paused just ahead, two down from the rim, and waited as Mirian pulled off her waterproof haversack and set it on the stair. "I don't think there's enough living down here for spiders to grow monstrous. But even little ones can be deadly poisonous. Heltan, are the books you seek close?"

"They will be close," Heltan promised.

"Then I've no good way to clear these webs." At Heltan's inquisitive head-turn, she said, "Fire would destroy both the webs and your books."

Heltan gave a little coughing laugh. "Neither flame nor water will harm a Karshnaar book."

"What do you mean?" Mirian said. "Are they stone?"

"My people wrote upon book cones formed of metal. Paper was unknown to them, but it would not have lasted down here in any case. Burn the webs if you wish."

"Oh, I wish. You'd best get back to the water for safety."

The lizard man seemed reluctant, but he retreated to Mirian's side, his scales glistening from immersion.

Setting the web ablaze proved simple. Mirian carried two wooden hafts for use as torches, along with cloth and oil, and it was the work of mere moments to prepare one, strike a spark with flint, and toss it.

The barrier transformed into a vast sheet of flame. A blast of heat rolled over their faces. Rendak cursed in astonishment.

Mirian had known what to expect. The surprise was the high-pitched scream and the skittering of something within the flames. A large shape blundered around inside.

"What *is* that?" Ivrian whispered.

"Let's hope we don't find out." Mirian pulled her wand free and loosed her sword from its scabbard.

Whatever it was never wandered out of the engulfing fire. Thankfully, the terrible noises stopped after the first minute. The inferno raged on, and when Mirian realized the entire expedition was almost hypnotized by the fiery destruction, she reminded Rendak to keep an eye out below. Shamefacedly, the salvager slipped his air bottle between his lips and dropped. Jekka went with him.

A moment later she felt the stairs themselves shift beneath her, and she started, worried she'd somehow set off a trap. But the stairs remained solid, merely shaking. Her eyes then tracked instantly to the ceiling, fearful a quake had struck and the whole city would come tumbling in upon them. But the motion ceased.

"Are earthquakes common here?" Mirian asked.

"Not that I have been told." Heltan's gold-flecked eyes never stopped watching the blaze. "The fire dies at last."

The lizard man was right. The last of the fuel had been consumed, and darkness followed in its wake, for the flame had burned all but occasional patches of the fungus.

"Time for glow stones," Mirian said. There were only six in all, and she'd left one with Tokello, so she restored her cutlass and stepped out of the water with one of the rocks, commanding it to life with a single word. She saw a tiled floor worked in bright greens and blues, scorched here and there. Off to one side lay a blackened heap.

"Kalina," she said without looking back, "get Jekka and Rendak. Forward, Heltan?"

"Forward."

They walked on, and the light from the glow stone shone on a browned pile of bones.

Heltan glanced at the skeletal remnants. "Boggards," he said.

They reached a branching corridor, one lined with archways into small chambers. Heltan hesitated only a moment before veering right.

"You're sure?"

"I am sure," Heltan said. He sounded almost as though he were.

Mirian was troubled by the darkness beyond each of the archways and the thought of what might lurk within it. Though there had apparently once been a track along both the floor and wall, just as in the underwater tunnels, other fungus had mostly taken over from the sort that glowed.

A hundred feet on they walked around the rim of another cenote entrance, veered north down a nearly identical tunnel, and discovered a second webbed hall.

Mirian had them stand back while she worked the same trick. This time there were no screams from inside, though Mirian counted no fewer than eight piles of bones. Some in this group Heltan identified as lizardfolk, but most were boggards.

"Were the spiders guardians of your people?" Ivrian asked.

"No!" Heltan turned, his voice thick with disgust. "They must have crawled in here after our enemies drove us out. We would not have allowed such horrors in a place where our hatchlings walked."

After another turn, Heltan stopped, hissing, and shone his light midway upon a wall. He had discovered a metal plate inscribed with lizardfolk faces. Beside it was a round opening of decorative red stone. Unlike nearly every other surface, the frame was completely devoid of decoration. That, apparently, marked it as special.

Jekka said something in his own language to Heltan and held up one hand, as if to motion his brother back.

Mirian stepped forward with Jekka, wand in one hand, glow stone in the other.

Mirian quickly had the sense of a large open space. The light fell upon a floor laid in alternating veins of blue and crimson marble. She couldn't imagine how much effort it had taken to maneuver such stone into these corridors. Her light then spilled onto a skeletal rib cage of approximately human size. She plied the beam farther and found an entire being lying across the marble, humanoid but topped with what was certainly a lizardfolk skull.

And then Heltan said a word behind her, and gentle amber light bloomed from the ceiling, illuminating the entirety of a vast rectangular chamber. The ceiling was tall and supported by octagonal pylons as wide around as tree trunks, each carved with the minute figures the Karshnaar artisans seemed to love. Row after row of shelving stood scattered in an almost haphazard fashion between the pillars, each stacked with black cones incised with strange glyphs and symbols.

Between and before the shelves lay bodies—dozens upon dozens of them, each picked clean to the bone, though there was no mistaking the cause of death. Spears and axes were thrust through rib cages and embedded in skulls.

To Mirian's eye it looked as though the boggards and lizard-folk had met in some great battle, though she was surprised that the victor had simply left all the bodies where they lay.

"These aren't Karshnaar, are they?" Ivrian asked.

"These must be the Vanizhar, who drove us out," Kalina replied. "And they were killed in turn."

"Stay sharp," Mirian said, mindful of all the shadows and potential hiding places. She glanced back at Heltan, who stood frozen, one hand depressing a red square sunken into the door frame.

"Rendak, I want you on watch by the door. Ivrian, stick with Kalina. Alderra, you're with Heltan. We're all to stay in sight of at least one other group at all times. Clear?"

The rest of the team replied in the affirmative.

"Heltan, how long is that light spell going to last?"

"Until we depress the panel once more." The records keeper's voice was tense with restrained excitement. He finally withdrew his hand and crept forward, eyes bright.

"Do you know where to find the books you need?" Mirian asked.

"I never knew that there would be so many . . ." He trailed off.

And there *were* so many. As a lover of knowledge and ancient secrets, Mirian understood something of Heltan's reverence for the shelves of black rock and the strange dark cones stacked concentrically upon them, even if she could not read them. She felt herself drawn toward the nearest shelves as a needle toward a lodestone, but resisted. She refused to be distracted until she was certain the area was secure.

Jekka's presence was reassuring as they walked forward together. It was strange to think how threatened she'd felt beside him only a few days earlier.

Each bookshelf stood as high as her own head, supported by intervening struts. Their perfectly smoothed black stone was chiseled with a parade of inventive images. Lizardfolk walking, running, lying down—and sitting in contemplation of book cones.

The hollow black cones themselves stood upon their wider ends, sometimes with five or six cones stacked together, sometimes only one or two. All were covered in tiny red glyphs.

"By the gods," she said. "Heltan, this is beautiful. What's recorded here?"

"The history of my people. The history of the world. Poems and songs and deeds and discoveries."

Jekka advanced past the corner of the next shelf. He stopped short with an explosive hiss, and Mirian hurried to his side.

Here was horror of a different sort. Not a monster waiting in ambush or some trap weighted to fall, nor even a macabre battle remnant. What Jekka had found instead was a makeshift oven assembled from broken pieces of stone and a vast pile of melted slag. Nearby, a long line of carefully prepared spear lengths stood propped against the wall, ready for the dusty metal points strewn on the floor beside the oven.

Each of those points had been manufactured from the melting of ancient books.

When Heltan rounded the corner, he let out a strangled cry unlike any sound she'd heard from the lizardfolk. The noise brought Kalina running, Ivrian puffing to catch up. Rendak shouted to make sure everyone was all right.

"No one's hurt," Mirian called back. She looked at the grief-stricken lizard man. Words failed her.

He chattered in his own language with his wife and brother. Kalina cooed and stroked the frill along Heltan's neck while he babbled, hands rising and falling uselessly as he contemplated the ruin.

Fully a third to a half of the books seemed to have been torn from the central shelves, many of which had been smashed to create the oven.

"How many books do you think were lost?" Ivrian asked. "Who could have done this?"

She'd momentarily forgotten the writer's own love of the written word. Of course this would affect him. "I have no idea what was destroyed," Mirian answered sadly. "There may be no way to know. This is a loss for all the world."

She turned away from the lizardfolk and scanned the rest of the area.

Alderra Galanor waited quietly to one side, like someone come to a funeral to pay respects who hadn't known the deceased especially well. Jekka stepped away. Mirian motioned to Ivrian to go with him.

As the writer followed the lizard man, Mirian moved to Heltan and addressed him. "Records Keeper Heltan. I grieve with you."

He looked up. His color had dulled almost to a gray.

"Have you lost the books you required?" Alderra's focused question, her precise diction, cut through to the heart of the matter and awakened Heltan's dignity.

The records keeper climbed to his feet and adjusted his necklace. Some of his pallor faded. "I do not yet know. It may take me a while to find what I seek."

"Perhaps now that you know where the books are," Alderra continued, "you can show us the jewels."

Heltan's head bobbed in agitation. "But I don't know for certain that the books I need haven't been destroyed, or where they are. It may take some time."

"How much time?" Alderra's tone cooled.

"We shouldn't delay down here for long," Mirian pointed out. "There are boggards above and scavengers below." Not to mention something that the boggards themselves feared in the water.

"I have no certainty how long this requires. Will require. I would like to verify the books are here first."

Alderra's age showed as lines deepened around her frown. "Perhaps you can tell us where to find the jewels for ourselves." She glanced to Mirian. "We can briefly split our forces."

"I'm not certain that's wise," Jekka said. Mirian was inclined to agree.

"I don't see a problem," Alderra insisted. "Heltan's going to be busy here for a while. How far away is this treasure vault?"

"Not so far," Heltan said. It seemed to Mirian that he had grabbed on tight to this suggestion. "I can describe the path for you."

"Lady Galanor—" Mirian began.

"We have verified that what the lizardfolk wanted is here," Alderra said without looking at her. "I want to verify that what *we* want is here."

Ivrian stepped forward with parchment, ink, and even his desk. Mirian hadn't realized he'd brought that as well. "Can you draw us a map, Heltan?"

The lizard man bobbed his head. "Yes. A map."

Mirian joined Ivrian beside the records keeper. Heltan's gray-green coloring brightened as he played with the desk's drawers and ran his hands over the dark wood. Perhaps all Karshnaar were crafters at heart. After a moment he took up the pen and dipped it into the ink that Ivrian opened for him.

Heltan called to his brother. "Jekka, you must take them. Kalina will stay and assist me. Come. Look."

Jekka approached reluctantly, leaning on his staff as he peered over Heltan's shoulder. Mirian stood on the other side while Alderra and Ivrian watched with interest.

Heltan drew with no real facility. There were vertical lines and horizontal lines that crossed them. At least they were straight.

Heltan pointed. "Here is the hallway outside. Follow it north past two cross points." He pressed a green finger against a hash mark. "At a third cross point you will arrive at a water entrance.

Take it to the lower crossway. Pass another cross point and turn south. Pass another cross point and turn east, then surface. You will arrive at the Chamber of Ancestors."

"The Chamber of Ancestors?" Ivrian repeated. "What's that?"

Heltan turned his head farther back than a human could have managed. "A repository of beautiful things made by our people."

"And you're certain that the jewels will still be there?" Alderra seemed focused keenly upon the money. As well she might, Mirian thought, given that it was her job to recover the jewels for the state. But it still made the aristocrat sound grasping.

"Yes." Heltan bobbed his head swiftly. "Now listen with care. Once you arrive, you will see a wall of Karshnaar faces. You must push in the proper sequence of stones to enter, and wait no more than a slow count of five between each depression. Anyone who fails will not live. Pay close attention."

"'Will not live,'" Ivrian repeated. "How will they die?"

"That information has not been passed down." Heltan looked seriously up at the young man. "Consider, though, that my people designed Jekka's staff. Such spring blades might hide within the walls. Or there may be some other danger. So you must pay attention. I wish neither my brother nor my human allies to perish."

Heltan then described the order of the faces, and their look. He quizzed Jekka and Mirian until he was satisfied, then handed his rudimentary map to Mirian and the desk to Ivrian.

Mirian stared at the map, committing it to memory.

"Well," Alderra said with forced pleasantness. "What are we waiting for?"

"It's a little farther off than I'd expected." Mirian was still uncertain. "Jekka and I will scout out the area. The rest of you—"

"Now hold on a moment," Alderra objected. "How are the two of you going to carry back a fortune in gems?"

Mirian shook her head. "You're staying here. This place is too open and exposed, and needs more warriors to protect it. Jekka and

I will leave most of our supplies with you so we can carry whatever we find."

"I'm afraid I must insist that I accompany you," Alderra said icily.

Mirian's gaze was cool. "Remember when you promised to obey me? We already know there are giant vermin and boggards down here."

Lady Galanor drew herself up. "Then take Rendak and Ivrian. They can help carry, and I daresay they're stronger than I am."

"Rendak's the only one of you I've got complete faith in. Sorry, but I've known him far longer. So he stays here to keep you out of trouble." She held up a hand to silence Rendak's protest and considered the younger man waiting eagerly nearby. Was he ever *not* excited?

Alderra's look was sharp. "Sargava needs these gems, Mirian. Take my son. And if you must leave Rendak, take his haversack. Fill it with gems. That's what I bought it for."

Acting general or no, Mirian knew when she heard an order, one that ultimately came down from the Baron of Sargava. "Very well. Ivrian, leave your blade and take a spear. Empty all else. We'll take any shoulder bags with us. Heltan?"

"Yes?" The lizard man turned away from the row of black cones he'd been running a finger along.

"Is there anything from this chamber your people want? You said it's full of beautiful things. Do you want any of them?"

Heltan's head tilted to the left, and he tasted the air with a minute flick of his tongue. "Salvager Mirian, I would that I could bring it all. I would that I could look upon the place with my own eyes. But I have enough sorrow lying before me already."

17

Faces in the Stone
Ivrian

Our imaginations peopled the place with a hundred dangers even as they raced ahead in contemplation of the wonders that awaited us in the Chamber of Ancestors. I did not speak to Mirian of it, but I worried that someone might have learned the Karshnaar code and plundered the tomb, almost as much as I worried that we might misremember that code and be cut in half or crushed to paste beneath some ancient trap.

—From *The Daughter of the Mist*

The corridor was in slightly better condition than the first ones, complete with short runs of shining little fungi. Certainly the green light was eerie, but it was better than nothing. Because it grew in long trenches at both head and foot level, Ivrian could easily see there weren't any monstrous spiders or centipedes waiting to drop on him. What webs he saw were of the typical variety. He still gave them a wide berth.

With his pole shifted to its spear end and pointed before him, Jekka sounded almost friendly as he spoke with Mirian.

"It is wise," he said, "to leave more warriors to guard a larger space."

"Yes," Mirian said.

They neared an intersection. "You are not more worried that we will be encumbered while carrying the treasures?"

"Not with these magical backpacks."

He'd grown a lot friendlier today, and Ivrian wondered whether that was just the natural result of his spending time with Mirian. Perhaps seeing her artwork last night had something to do with it. Whatever the cause, a calmer, less irritable Jekka was a more reassuring companion.

They advanced into the next segment of hallway. A long swath of its ceiling was cracked. Mirian flashed her light over its surface and revealed tree roots that had fought their way through the rock.

Jekka continued to prove uncharacteristically talkative. "I begin to see that a contract is a pledge that guarantees honor between humans. I suppose such contracts are necessary when there are so many different clans."

"Yes," Mirian agreed.

"Unfortunately," Ivrian added, "many humans don't honor their contracts anyway."

Jekka glanced back at him and stopped to consider Mirian, who halted and cocked an eyebrow at him.

"But you do," Jekka said.

"My clan prides itself on honoring its contracts," Mirian said. "My father risked his life to honor his."

"All for the riches?" the lizard man asked.

Mirian's smile was a little sad. "Not really. For the thrill. To go places no one had ever seen. To find secrets, to solve puzzles."

"He was a hunter, then."

"Of a kind."

"And you are like him."

"I suppose I am."

They reached another intersection, surveyed the dark corridors, moved on. What else lay down these silent halls, he wondered? How many lizardfolk had lived and died here and raised families? And how many artisans must it have taken to chisel the carvings into every surface? It was, he thought, a little *too* much. Like the homes of the extraordinarily rich, where everything was gilded, even the bathing chambers.

Jekka was talking once more. "I think you are more interested in the hunt than the riches."

"What about you?" she asked quietly. "What are you interested in?"

Jekka was suddenly brusque. "I am here to help my brother and my cousin."

"But not yourself?"

Jekka paused, just a few yards shy of the glistening pool at the center of the next intersection. His voice became solemn. "The mark of doom is upon my people, Mirian. Do you truly think there is some lost land where my clan still lives?" He didn't leave time for her to answer. "We are finished. It doesn't matter if the final blow comes from your kind, or the boggards, or even others of our own folk. All are instruments of Gozreh. He does not want us here. My mate said he must have great need for the Karshnaar in the spirit world, for he had taken so many. But I think he does not care."

"I don't know about gods," Mirian said. "But I can hope, Jekka. You and your people are brave and determined. Sometimes that's enough."

He studied her.

"Enough talk. It's time for a dive." Mirian turned to Ivrian. "Do you have the hang of this now?"

"I do."

"All right. Jekka, he can't swim as fast, so you and I will have to slow down. I don't want us spread out too far."

"Understood."

Jekka and Mirian consulted the map a final time. As Ivrian completed a second scan of the hallway behind them, he understood the depth of the change that had occurred between the two. He couldn't imagine seeing the tall woman and the slim lizard man standing so easily side by side in that seemingly long-ago age when they'd boarded the ship together.

Apparently satisfied, Mirian slipped the map into her haversack, one of two she now carried, like Ivrian, each on a shoulder. "Let's be on with it."

She pulled free her sword, stood with feet planted wide as she blew out all her air, then dropped into the water. Jekka slipped in a moment later, facing the opposite direction. Ivrian waited a moment for the waves to cease their rocking, then watched as his companions got out of the way. Mirian waved him on with one dimly glowing, fin-coated hand. He could tell from her pained expression that she was still transitioning to gill breaths.

Soon he was cold and wet along with them, sucking in the water through his own set of glowing gills. He would have thought whoever had dreamed up the kind of magic that made it possible to breathe underwater could have worked a little harder and made it comfortable.

Before he'd adjusted, both Mirian and Jekka were kicking down through a circular passage to the lower level of water tunnels and turning south. Using the fins that appeared on arms and feet wasn't as simple as Mirian made it seem. He couldn't imagine he looked as graceful as she did.

Underwater fronds were mixed in with the fungus in the lower transit hall, casting strange shadows.

Here and there he was startled to see the silvery flash of tiny fish. He hoped these weren't piranha—he'd neglected to ask what those looked like. The creatures seemed wary, which was probably a reasonable indicator they weren't inclined to eat him.

He thought he'd paid attention to Heltan's directions, so he was surprised by a couple of turns Mirian and Jekka made. Most alarming of all was a deep thrumming noise that scattered a school of those tiny fish. It sounded as though someone were beating a great underwater drum.

It was so startling that once again he forgot to empty his lungs before he surfaced, and he spent a long minute coughing water as Mirian and Jekka climbed free. He decided he'd leave that out of any account he wrote—assuming he could acquire permission to write it.

He studied the hall as he recovered. It was different from the others he'd seen. First, it was on the same level as the upper water passages, but it was filled with air. Second, the floor was covered in an inch of water. Third, there was nothing at all within the short corridor but clear red tiles. Only at the hall's far end, thirty paces on, was there any ornamentation whatsoever. Hundreds upon hundreds of small Karshnaar faces looked out on him, arranged in parallel rows from floor to ceiling.

"This," he managed weakly, "is going to be trickier than I thought."

As if placed merely to add to his apprehension, a series of bones were strewn near that decorative wall. His bare feet splashed little waves as he followed Mirian and Jekka. Seven skulls. Lizardfolk or boggards, he guessed, though he wasn't practiced enough to tell the difference. "They must not have known the pattern," he said.

Neither Mirian nor Jekka answered.

"Hey, did either of you hear that strange noise while we were underwater?"

"Yes," Jekka answered.

"Do you have any idea what it is?"

"No," the lizard man said without turning. "But I do not like it."

"What about you, Mirian?" Calling her by her first name felt unnatural, but she showed no sign that she objected.

"I'm not sure what to think, but we need to be cautious. Now stand guard behind us. Jekka and I have to concentrate."

Right, he thought. He turned, holding his spear ready. He felt a little ridiculous poised there with a shortspear, standing with legs naked to the knee, two backpacks crossing his shoulders. If I survive to describe this, he thought, I'll downplay the absurdity of my appearance.

His eyes widened involuntarily.

"I'm definitely going to survive this," he muttered to himself. "Definitely."

18
Prayers of the Karshnaar
Mirian

"It is just a matter of counting," Jekka said. It was the first time Mirian had heard him try to reassure anybody.

"So you're just as surprised as I am by the number of faces?"

"Yes."

Maybe, she thought, he was trying to reassure himself. The decoration, door, or deadly trap—whatever it was, exactly—was twenty lizard faces high and twenty across, offering them a field of four hundred visages to choose from.

"It strikes me that your brother could have been clearer."

"I am thinking the same thing. He might not have known their number."

"Fair enough."

Mirian studied the display for a moment more. "All right, here's a thought. Let's use these." She brushed fingers through a patch of the soft, shell-shaped green fungus that supplied light for the complex and came away with dully glowing fingertips. "Let's both count, and then I'll mark the ones we need. Carefully. Before we start pressing."

"Cunning," he said. "But what if a touch is enough to activate the defenses?"

"These look like they're designed to slide," Mirian said. "And your brother said to push them in. They're not going to go off if they're touched lightly." She paused. "Probably."

She glanced again at the nearest bone pile. That skull, she thought, looked as though it had been crushed, and she was distracted momentarily as she searched for where there might be a trap release hidden in the red tile. Unfortunately, the grouting was well concealed by the damnably useful fungus.

"I count seven over, three down from the right, here." Jekka pointed at a snout with a tiny horn.

Mirian counted once, twice, then nodded. With exquisite care she touched that face with one glowing finger, leaving it with a tiny stripe. It looked like war paint.

She and Jekka then spent a laborious quarter hour counting the rest of the faces. Only twice did they disagree over carved faces deep in the mix. Both times it was Jekka whose counting had been off. The first time he seemed flustered. The second time he bobbed his head low.

"I apologize," he said, frill flaring.

Mirian wasn't sure what to make of the physical movement of the frill, which was at odds with his embarrassed tone. "It's all right. The mistakes won't hurt us until we start pressing faces."

Jekka gave a short, coughing laugh and his frill dropped. It would be nice, she thought, if someone had a handbook for what lizardfolk social cues were. And even though she was in the midst of life-and-death calculations, she realized that such a write-up would be of tremendous use to other Pathfinders. She resolved to draft that paper herself.

Providing she survived what they were about to do.

"Are you ready for this, Jekka? Let's rehearse it once before we start pressing."

"Given my errors, perhaps we should rehearse twice."

She chuckled. "Among my father's people, there's a saying: third time's the charm."

Jekka tilted his head to one side. "I understand this phrase. Every action improves with practice."

"It's supposed to be about luck," Ivrian added from behind them. He had been so quiet that Mirian had almost forgotten he was there.

"I no longer believe in luck," Jekka said, "but I practice careful preparation. Let's rehearse three times. For charm."

And so they did, counting down, resting a hand in front of each of the nine marked lizard faces but not touching them. The first face to press was in the high middle, then down to waist-high on the right, then very low on the left, and so on.

It really seemed to her that they had the matter down after the first rehearsal, but they did it twice more. Afterward, Mirian stepped back, hands on hips. Something still bothered her. "You're sure that your brother has the combination right?"

Jekka seemed puzzled by the question. "My brother *thinks* he has it right."

"If your people entered the vault all the time, wouldn't the places where they touched the sculptures be worn down?"

"Oh, that's good thinking," Ivrian said behind them.

After a moment, Jekka said: "I agree with Ivrian."

"So where does that leave us?"

Jekka stared at the wall for a long time. "I do not see any areas worn more than others. I imagine two possibles."

"Yes?" Mirian asked.

"One. The vault was rarely opened, so there's little wear. Two. The material is somehow resistant."

"Three," Ivrian suggested, "they've been deteriorating at the same rate down here for so long you can't tell anymore."

Mirian thought that over. "No, you'd still be able to see something that had been rubbed a lot. I'm going to hope you're right, Jekka, and it's option one. Because there's always possibility four."

"And what is that?" the lizard man asked her.

"That Heltan's wrong, and the moment we press any of them we'll be killed."

Jekka's long dark tongue darted out in a hiss. "Then Gozreh would have played another joke upon my people. And two humans."

"If I hear *anything* going wrong," Ivrian said, "I'm diving right into this water here. I like you both and all, but—"

"Wisely reasoned," Jekka said. "The only bodies lie near the faces. Presumably someone standing back by the pool would be safe."

"You're right." Mirian nodded at the lizard man. "Get back there."

Jekka turned his head to stare at her. "What?"

"This is my risk. You don't even want the material that's in here. You contracted to guide me, and you have."

Jekka's mouth parted, and she thought to see him taste the air again, but it closed, opened, then closed once more. "I am still unclear on the boundaries of our contract, Mirian," he said, "but since you shared danger with me, I must share danger with you."

She shook her head. "No. You were just telling me that there are only three of you left. I'll be damned if I'm going to let you risk yourself to get some gems you don't care about for some people you hate. Go back by the pool."

He blinked at her a moment, fingered his staff. Once more he opened his mouth as if to speak but hesitated.

"Well, go on," she said crossly. She wanted to get this over with. "The longer we delay, the longer we're away from the others."

"You are right again. But there is a battle prayer of my people I would share."

"I thought you didn't pray."

"Then think of it as luck, because I think the gods pay attention to humans."

"Very well." She hoped her impatience wasn't obvious.

The lizard man fell silent.

More than anything else Mirian wished to start the process so she'd know whether she was going to live or die—hopefully the former. But if the latter happened, she hoped to be killed in one fast bludgeon or a good slice. If there were some sort of blade involved, could a healing potion save her?

"Are you still carrying that healing potion, Ivrian?"

"Yes."

"So if there's a trap and I get cut, you'll pour it down my throat, right?"

The youth drew himself up solemnly and bowed. "You have my word, Mirian."

Was she growing soft? She realized she had become fond of both the murderous lizard man *and* the self-involved writer.

"Well?" she asked Jekka.

"Your pardon. It took me a moment to think of a good translation." He stood tall, raised his staff, and addressed the ceiling. "'Gozreh, let it be that my comrade slides past the blows of her enemy and brings death to those who oppose her. Grant her the speed of her youth, the cunning of the k'rang, the wisdom of maturity, the luck of heroes.'"

Jekka passed one hand over her in a cryptic gesture.

She was strangely moved. "I thank you," she told him formally.

He bowed his head. "I do not believe that a Karshnaar god-speaker has ever whispered a prayer for a human before."

"What's a k'rang?" Ivrian asked.

"A swift hunting lizard that stalks on two legs. Very deadly. I don't know your human name."

"I think Kalina was talking about those a few days ago," Ivrian said.

Mirian offered a faint smile. "So I'm old and slow, eh?"

Jekka cocked his head to one side. "I do not understand."

"She's just having fun with you," Ivrian explained. "Because you wished her the speed of her youth."

"That is the wording of the prayer," Jekka explained quickly. "I meant no insult."

"It's all right, Jekka. No insult taken. Ivrian's right."

"So that was mockery?" Jekka said.

"Teasing," Ivrian said. "Not at all the same as mockery."

"Explain."

She held off sighing. She really wanted to get started. "It's something friends do. Although teasing can be cruel as well, like poking a stick at a tethered animal." She threw up her hands. "It might take a lifetime to explain our differences, and mine might be really short. But I didn't mean it as mockery, Jekka. It was a sign of good fellowship, as your prayer was to me. I thank you."

He bobbed his head once more.

"Now get back there." She thumbed over her shoulder.

"Yes. Of course." Jekka sounded troubled, but he withdrew, feet splashing through the thin film of water.

She looked back at them a final time. Jekka held tight to his weapon. Ivrian waited beside the pool as if he meant to fling himself toward her rather than jump to safety at the first sign of trouble.

"Look," she said, "there's no point in my risking myself if you two aren't ready to drop into the water. And you damned well ought to be keeping sentry anyway, Ivrian. Isn't that your job?"

He turned, reddening. Jekka's position didn't change at all.

Mirian pivoted and considered the faces one final time, running the sequence through her head. How had she gotten here, again? And how stupid was this? By all rights shouldn't Alderra or her brother be doing this?

She sighed and put a hand to the first face. She whispered a prayer to Desna and her ancestors, and pushed.

The face sank halfway in with a gentle rumbling. Mirian moved quickly to the next, down on the left, and so on. The green glow she'd rubbed on the faces was fading, but she could still see the way.

Each one sank in as she thrust carefully with her palm. So far there'd been no ominous clunk or sound of gears. She arrived at the seventh face, right in the middle, then leaned down for the eighth face, one row over on the very bottom, and then finally the ninth, two faces over from the one in the middle.

It sank in.

And nothing happened.

Mirian stood on the balls of her feet, eyes shifting over the wall. Had she missed one? Done something out of sequence?

"Maybe you should get back," Ivrian suggested.

Then the floor gave way beneath her, and she and the water and the bones all slid down into darkness.

19

The Chamber
of Ancestors
Ivrian

*Splendors lay to right and left, wonders the likes of which I'd
never seen, nor even dreamed. But as my eyes shifted from
one glittering marvel to another, I knew a sense of fore-
boding. Little did I know of the cunning, hungry thing that
had lain in wait for countless years . . .*

—From *The Daughter of the Mist*

One second Mirian was standing in front of the wall of faces.
The next she'd plunged out of sight with a little cry of surprise
and a thump as her body hit something hard. There was a splash
and rattle as the water and bones cascaded after her.

For all that he'd been told to dive the moment a trap opened,
Ivrian's first reaction was to race after Mirian. Quick as he was,
Jekka arrived ahead of him.

Maybe it wasn't a trap, Ivrian saw, even as Jekka dropped down
the newly slanted flooring. Runoff from the accumulated water in
the passage trickled after him. As Ivrian reached the edge of the
ramp, he saw Mirian picking herself up from a stone floor ten or
twelve feet below. This surely wasn't the end that had come to the
previous explorers, or else their bones wouldn't have littered the
entryway.

It might be, Ivrian thought, some other kind of trap. He
lowered himself onto the watery slide and dropped after the others,

twisting his feet at the last moment so he just missed knocking down Jekka.

He stood, grinning. "That was sort of fun."

"You should have stayed up top," Mirian grumbled, fumbling through the bags hung along her belt. The place was completely dark apart from the light drifting in from the hall above, but there was no missing her expression as she turned to address Jekka. "And it would have been nice if your brother had mentioned the *floor* was going to drop in."

"I don't think he knew."

"Funny what information was passed down and what wasn't."

Ivrian tried not to grin.

Mirian produced the glow stone. The light caught upon the reflected glow of a crystalline object: a sculpture of a lizard head, Ivrian recognized, just as the light roved on.

Once he had his own glow stone working, it became clear they were in a round room the size of a small auditorium, lined with shelving. Half of it was given over to display, the other lined with tables covered in dust-draped metal tools. He walked among the tables examining the implements. Those, surely, were pliers, and that a hammer, but he couldn't for the life of him determine what that spiral tool with the sharp edge was for.

"Was this a workshop?" Ivrian asked.

Jekka's attention was focused elsewhere. "I do not know." The lizard man strode carefully through the room, his feet near soundless on the moist floor. He peered into every dark crevice.

Ivrian felt less concern. There was an air here of safety. As he swung his glow stone about, he could imagine the ancient lizardfolk sitting at the high benches beside the tables. On the curving wall behind were raw supplies: a riot of gems and colorful minerals in sagging, time-eaten wicker baskets. On the wall opposite were finished works. He heard Mirian muttering in astonishment.

"It's everything Heltan promised," Ivrian breathed. Container after container of gemstones of every color. He followed the circle of the wall to where Mirian marveled at a sculpture in blue marble shot through with strands of gray veins. It portrayed a sinuous serpent with sharp teeth and vestigial legs that flowed out behind it.

"Do you know," Ivrian said, "my mother's been afraid all along that there wouldn't really be much here. But there's *too* much. How do we even choose?"

While Jekka patrolled the shelves, Mirian walked slowly beside other carvings. Here was a row of twelve lizardfolk heads, each seemingly carved from solid ruby.

"Look at the workmanship," she breathed. She picked one up gingerly and almost dropped it as the thing suddenly coughed at her. At that noise, all the long line of them let out the same sound: the laughter of the lizardfolk echoing through the empty chamber.

Mirian held it at arm's length, apparently concerned the strange object might do something else. But after a few moments the sound ceased, and that made by the others died out as well.

She glanced back to Jekka, who was poised as if to spring to action. "What is *this* for?"

"I do not know, Mirian." His voice was heavy with melancholy. "Perhaps my brother will. I wish he had come. He scours the dry words of my people, but here he could look upon the work of their hands and come to know them."

Ivrian said, "We should leave most of this so that, when your clan revives, your children can come to see what their ancestors were capable of."

"You are more hopeful for my kind than I am," Jekka said.

"Isn't it possible your brother's right?" Ivrian asked. "That some other branch of your people is still alive, and he's going to learn their whereabouts?"

"Anything is possible. But many things are unlikely."

"Let's stay focused on the mission," Mirian said. "I want to gather these heads and the gems that are already cut. I think that marble sea drake sculpture might be portable, if we wrap it right. A lot of these other pieces are going to be damaged, though. Too many delicate parts."

Ivrian concurred. It was hard to imagine carting some of the more intricate carvings along with them, like that beautiful tropical bird sitting in a nearby alcove. Claws, beak, and finely detailed feathers could all be broken or damaged.

"The government probably won't be as interested in art, anyway," Ivrian said. "Those are of negotiable value. The Free Captains want gold."

"Probably true. But I'm taking these little heads anyway."

Mirian wrapped each one individually in a wealth of rags she'd stuffed in her haversack. Ivrian, meanwhile, packed up the worth of several small cities in cut rubies and emeralds. Though Mirian worked with care, every now and then she'd accidentally activate one of the heads and its laugh would set his skin crawling.

Jekka wordlessly handed over his own empty pack to Mirian and continued to patrol, although Ivrian thought it more of a tour now, for it seemed the area was secure.

"Jekka," Mirian said, "is there anything here you think your brother or cousin would want?"

The lizard man paused, his back to them, still as the white marble statue of a hooded lizardfolk head he faced. "No."

"And you?" Mirian asked.

Jekka half turned, speaking to them in profile. "I wonder if one day some remnant of your folk will guide some other race to the ruins of Eleder, and a human will stand contemplating lost greatness and wondering what went wrong." He turned the rest of the way to face her and spoke with finality. "No. The memory of this place is enough."

Ivrian gaped at Jekka. The savage lizard man was a philosopher. He'd never have guessed.

They filled the haversacks to their brims. Magical as they were, each continued to weigh no more than five pounds, just as they had when mostly empty. Plentiful riches remained, but there was nothing more to transport them in.

"We'd best get moving," Mirian said. "I wish we'd asked your brother how to seal this place."

"We'll be back, though, won't we?" Ivrian asked.

"We might," Mirian said. "We have more than what we came for, though. And I imagine Heltan's going to want to cart a few of the book cones."

"Mother's letting him borrow a bag like these haversacks," Ivrian said. "It's a little heavier and harder to carry, but it will also hold a lot more."

"Huh. I wonder if it'll have room for our supplies. Why didn't she mention it before?"

"Probably so we wouldn't stuff it with our supplies," Ivrian said. He wondered how he was going to carry his writing desk. There was certainly no room for it in his haversack now.

Climbing up the thick stone ramp proved more challenging than sliding down until Jekka noticed the narrow steps carved into the stone on the ramp's right side. He led the way up, and Ivrian followed. Mirian came last. As she stepped to the narrow ledge on one side of the ramp, it was already returning to its closed position.

"How did the floor know to do that?" Ivrian wondered aloud.

Mirian shrugged. "Magic, most likely."

"Oh. Right." Ivrian was filled with giddy excitement. That room, and the treasures it carried, just about guaranteed a best-selling leaflet or two, depending on how long he stretched out the account of their adventure.

As he dropped after the others into the flooded corridor, he began to wonder, though. If he *did* tell the story, wouldn't he have to change things around a little? Especially if he wanted to preserve the rest of those treasures? Maybe he could set the lost ruin to the south, in the Laughing Jungle, or somewhere else.

His mind awash with the possibilities, it took him a moment or two to notice that faint vibration again. A thrumming. Jekka and Mirian looked to right and left as they reached a corridor. Mirian dug out her wand. He heard her talking, faintly, in the water, and swam closer to see if he could understand.

"—large." Jekka answered, and said something about moving faster, which sounded good to Ivrian, except that Jekka and Mirian immediately surged ahead and he had no way to keep up. He kicked vigorously, but he didn't have Mirian's extra ring or Jekka's powerful tail, just his legs with the magical fins. Thrash as he might, his speed didn't increase.

They reached the circular opening to the upper water tunnels. Mirian floated by the rim, waving at him impatiently to hurry.

He shouted to tell her that he was hurrying, but that's when he saw something from the corner of his eye and wasted a moment turning to look.

In the far distance, a large creature sped along that glowing green passage.

Straight toward him.

20
The Thing
in the Depths
Mirian

Mirian knew a sea drake when she saw one, even if she was stunned to find one this far inland. The blue-green water dragon's undulations stirred the seaweed flourishing on the floor of the lower tube. Its maw seemed tens of feet wide, open in a laughing expression. Its winglike fins and whipping tail produced that thrumming they'd been hearing.

She'd been chased by one of the damned things when she was a teenager. Only Rendak and her father's daring distractions had gotten her free. She and the two adults had spent the better part of six hours holed up near the beast as it alternately blasted with its electrical breath or slapped on the sunken hulk with its tail to try to panic them into flight.

She screamed at Ivrian to go, but it seemed an eternity before he was finally into the waters of the upper tunnel.

Jekka had swum up to the entrance to the dry corridors and waited, spear ready. As though a spear could stop a sea drake. It occurred to Mirian then that the ancient Karshnaar must have known of the thing, or they wouldn't have carved the creature she carried in her pack.

Mirian kicked down to the writer, grabbed him by the wrists, and added her momentum to his own, pulling him up to the rim. From below came the steady, wall-shaking drum of the sea drake.

The drake sculpture in her pack was beautiful and sinuous. As the real creature pushed into the upper passage, she got a much closer look at head than she would have preferred: the spiny back-ward-pointing ridges on its skull, the glowing yellow eyes, the great mouth full of needlelike teeth, the fanlike frill waving from its jaw. A real sea drake was lovely in the way of a well-made knife.

Mirian shoved Ivrian up into the hole and turned, wand leveled. She spoke the magic word.

Nothing happened.

The monster squeezed through the break between the two submerged tunnels, gaining speed as it got its winglike fins past.

Mirian turned back to the surface, only to have two vise-like hands grab her shoulders.

Jekka. As she leveraged herself up, coughing in agony—she'd forgotten to breathe out, damn it—he dragged her away from the pool's surface.

The drake head burst up, mouth agape, preparing its deadly electrical breath.

From the other side of the water pit, Ivrian rose and drove a spear deep into its neck.

There was no doubting the young man's courage, that was certain.

The drake gurgled in pain and dropped out of sight, slopping water over the circular rim. A moment later the floor rattled, and Mirian realized it had slammed its body into the tunnel floor.

Still vomiting water, Mirian staggered to her feet and waved for Ivrian to get over to her side of the hallway. And then she realized he was facing the right direction, and it was she and Jekka who'd come up on the wrong side.

"This way!" Ivrian shouted.

"Mirian, hurry," Jekka said.

She needed no urging.

The lizard man raced to the lip of the water and cleared it in a running leap. Mirian didn't think she could do that, particularly while she was still coughing water. Instead, she stepped onto what had probably been a wide, safe ledge of stone the ancient lizardfolk had used to bypass the water. Except that the ledge was now slick with glowing green plant life. She was two-thirds of the way across when the shadow of the drake loomed below. Fear lent her the impetus for speed.

She slipped as she ran, tumbling to the tiles just beyond the opening to the water. She skinned her hands on the stone and tore open her leggings. Ivrian stood above her, spear ready for another thrust.

Behind her, the ledge erupted in a spray of stone and water. The drake had broken the walkway, widening the hole.

Mirian scrambled to her feet. "Go!" She imagined the drake's lightning blasting through the young man.

The floor shook beneath them, and for the first time Mirian wondered about the structural integrity of the lizardfolk tunnels.

She ran, her allies racing with her. The corner they needed was fifty feet on, twenty—

Suddenly there was a roar from behind, then a burst of light and a lance of pain. She dropped to the flagstones beside Ivrian, her body shaking spasmodically.

"Mirian!" Jekka shouted.

The pain tingled through every limb. She forced herself up, knowing the sea drake could spit lightning again soon. Jekka took her arm and helped her forward.

Ivrian lay motionless in the hall, a jagged black mark blasted through his shirt. The smell of burned flesh nearly made her gag. He must have been the target, with the drake's lightning playing off any other living thing in range. That's how their attacks worked; she'd witnessed the creature that had hunted her younger self killing scores of fish while it waited for her and Rendak and her father to emerge from hiding.

Jekka seemed unharmed.

"Help me drag him," she said.

"You can barely move. And he may be dead."

"No one gets left behind," Mirian snapped. She wobbled as she reached for Ivrian. Jekka was faster. He handed his staff to Mirian, grasped Ivrian by the arms, and began to drag, grunting with the effort.

They hurried down the hall and ducked left, halting just past an intersection. Mirian undid the padded flap along her belt and pulled forth the healing potion. She knelt beside the wounded writer and propped up his head, forcing the liquid down his throat.

He blinked and coughed, which meant he must not really have been dead. Expensive as these supplies were, they didn't have *that* kind of muscle.

"Damn," he wheezed. "That really hurt."

"How do you feel?" she asked him.

"Alive," he said.

The floor shook.

"It still wants us," Ivrian said groggily.

The lizard man turned his large eyes to Mirian. "How are you?"

"I've felt better. Did you get hit at all?"

"No."

That was odd. But then, maybe the electrical attacks weren't quite as deadly in the air as they were underwater.

"We have to follow that passage back to the Hall of Records," she said. "Jekka, do you know how far it can reach with that storm breath?"

"At least this far," Jekka told her.

Mirian nodded. "Ivrian, do you think you can run?"

"Um." Ivrian tripped over his own feet as he tried to rise, catching himself on the wall. "Maybe."

"Take a good long breath. Slowly. In and out. There you go."

Again the floor trembled. It was hard to tell exactly what the beast was doing. Did it mean to lure them out of hiding and then pop its head out of the pool to blast them? Or was it trying to nudge them into motion so it could feel where they were, tracking them through the tunnels from below?

"Here's what we do," she said. "We wait until we feel another of those bumps. Then we run like hell for the Hall of Records and hope we can find a way out through one of the towers. We've got to get everybody out before it gets a fix on us." She looked to Ivrian. "Ready?"

The boy nodded.

"Go!"

Jekka was out and running at full speed. Ivrian made a good show of it. Mirian lagged back to run at his side, looking over her shoulder. The entrance to the water certainly seemed a long way back there.

The floor rocked and splintered. A huge crack appeared in the tile.

Ivrian cursed.

As they passed the next intersection, Mirian saw Rendak waiting in the doorway ahead, waving them forward. The floor rocked a second time, and then they were through the red archway and into the brightly lit room beyond.

Gasping, she explained the situation to Rendak and Alderra, who hurried forward to assist her son, immediately proffering her own healing potion. The Karshnaar consulted among themselves.

"How did things go here?" Mirian asked Rendak.

"Quiet, until you showed up. Heltan's found something important, but he's wanting to take about a hundred of these book cones with him. I'm not sure there's even room in Lady Galanor's magical bag."

Apparently satisfied with her son's status, Alderra arched an eyebrow at Mirian. She bent down to undo the ties that bound Ivrian's packs. Her eyes brightened when she gazed upon the sparkling contents, and her smile spread wide. Ivrian seemed to be talking to her about the treasure room, but Mirian couldn't quite hear over the Karshnaar, whose own conversation had grown increasingly voluble.

Kalina and Jekka had taken issue with Heltan and now gestured toward him with some violence. Each of their frills had risen.

"What's that about?" Mirian asked.

Rendak passed her another of the healing potions. "Hell if I know. Drink this."

"I don't need that." The tarnished bronze tube was a great temptation, but she knew they should hold off until they really needed it.

"Yes you do. You look like a devil's dance partner, Mirian."

"We don't have that many left."

"We use them when we need them. And if you got hit by even part of a sea drake blast, I guarantee you need it."

Mirian finally gave into the temptation, pulled the cork free, and quaffed the potion. Mostly bitter with a hint of cinnamon. But she felt almost normal within moments.

One of the walls rumbled. The Karshnaar, seemingly oblivious, continued their argument.

"Hey. Hey!"

All three lizardfolk looked toward her at once, their heads snapping about on their long necks.

"We need to get out of here through one of the towers," she said.

Heltan shook his head. "I think all of them are blocked."

"There's a sea drake down there," Mirian said. "I don't know if you know what those . . ."

Her voice trailed off. The Karshnaar stared at her, expressions unreadable, and she thought of the sea drake sculpture she'd brought with her, as well as of the bones in the cenotes.

Heltan reached up to finger his turquoise necklace.

One of the necklaces all of them wore, their stones the same color as the sea drake's scales.

Mirian's jaw dropped.

"Did you *know* it was down there?" she shouted.

Kalina and Jekka stared at Heltan as if daring him to answer.

"They were city guardians," Heltan said. "I didn't think any could still be alive—"

"But you brought protective necklaces just in case," Mirian finished in disgust. "I asked you what the boggards might be afraid of!"

"We were just discussing that with him," Jekka said, glaring at his brother.

"We didn't know," Kalina explained.

"Of course you knew!" Mirian said.

"Only Heltan knew," Jekka said, hissing. "He did not tell us, either."

"Really, everything is fine," Heltan said. "No one has died. A beast is still down there, but we can get out. Surely you cannot blame me for trying to do a little more to protect my clan when—"

"You could at least have warned us," Alderra told him icily. "You could at least have loaned the necklaces to my son and Mirian when they went diving!"

Heltan bobbed his head. "I was distracted. I—"

"Hey," Rendak whispered from the doorway. "Boggards. Hallway!"

Mirian scowled at Heltan. "Jekka, Kalina, get to the doorway. The rest of you, get your gear." She handed off her spare pack and shouldered into her own. Then she and the lizardfolk pressed themselves to the wall next to the door alongside Rendak.

"Scouting party," Rendak whispered. "Best finish them."

"Yes," Kalina said. One of her disk weapons dangled from her right hand.

They stepped out together.

Down the hall, three hunched green forms with bowed legs and huge, froglike heads looked up. Immediately, the boggards let out an excited burbling, one that rose to a scream as Kalina's disk embedded itself in the head of the one on the far right. Mirian concentrated with her wand and blasted the legs out from under the next. It fell, mouth moving in soundless pain.

The third bounded away. Mirian aimed her wand to fire again even as Kalina dashed to retrieve her weapon.

A wave of boggards poured out of a corridor farther down the hall, feet slapping the floor tiles like drums. Kalina spun, disk in hand, and raced back toward her friends. From below came the thump of the sea drake in response.

"Move!" Mirian roared, flinging herself back through the door as the lizard woman passed her. "Heltan, get us out of here!"

She brought up the rear as the others rushed ahead. The hopping boggards followed. One alone looked ridiculous. A dozen of the things, toothed heads bobbing, weren't remotely funny.

A blast from Mirian's wand felled one with a squeal, but its brethren hopped right over it, advancing with astonishing speed.

She rounded a corner to discover Heltan and the other humans stopped at the pool in the scorched hall. Alderra faced him, hand on her hilt.

"Then give over the necklace, if you think it's so safe!" the noblewoman sneered.

"Belay that!" Mirian snapped. Behind her the boggards' pounding feet sounded like thunder. "They're almost on us!"

Heltan dropped through the hole. Alderra, eyes burning with hatred, shoved her air tube between her teeth and went in after, followed by the others.

They were all swimming within a few moments, following the lizardfolk in the forefront. Mirian half expected the drake to be waiting for them, but the water seemed clear. The only worrisome thing was the rumbling overhead of the boggards nearing their drop point.

On the way in they'd passed a number of exits to the surface; she hoped they were nearby, for boggards were excellent swimmers.

As if on cue, she heard the splashes of boggards dropping in behind her, the sound dulled by the water. She didn't slow down to look over her shoulder.

Heltan suddenly veered left—a left Mirian didn't remember. What was he doing? But the rest of the party had no choice but to follow, and Mirian went after, fully cognizant of the thrashing in the water behind. She passed Ivrian as she turned the corner into the wider corridor.

And there was sunlight, shining from on high into a vast, vaulted space. What this chamber once had been she could not guess, but now it was their salvation. She turned to wave Ivrian on just in time to see the first four boggards swimming furiously after. She blasted one between the eyes. It sank slowly, dropping through a slanting sunbeam.

A wide-eyed Ivrian swam toward her past a row of sculpted lizardfolk standing atop stone columns, his glowing fins briefly tinting them in emerald light. Beyond was the circular light of the pool rim. Heltan had reached it and was already clambering up.

Rendak and Alderra were halfway there, while Kalina held on to the rim, looking back. Jekka hung back, suspended in the water near Rendak, waiting for the oncoming boggards with spear readied.

Then the sea drake appeared, sending a ripple of lightning through the boggards even as it tore through the pack, leaving bloody limbs in its wake. The closest three were caught by the electrical blast.

Along with Ivrian.

Damn it!

As the boy sank, Mirian dove after, knowing it was foolish, that he was probably dead already.

The drake thrashed through the water like a winged eel, set on rending and devouring everything in reach. The remaining boggards scattered, one swimming straight down for Mirian, who paused to blow a smoking hole through its face.

Then she had Ivrian by a shoulder strap and was kicking toward the surface. She saw in surprise that he was kicking feebly himself. The boy was hard to kill.

As she rose, Mirian saw Alderra swimming down, spear in hand, and called for her to get out. But Lady Galanor drove the weapon into a boggard as another gouged her shoulder with a clawed foot. The water was a fury of crazed forms, Kalina and Jekka fighting savagely to keep the path open.

Rendak was suddenly there at her side, grabbing Ivrian's other shoulder strap. With his aid, their speed almost doubled.

The sea drake roared, and the water hummed with another blast of electricity. Mirian silently mouthed a prayer to Desna.

Time crawled. Every heartbeat seemed an hour, the water filled with bubbling and screams. She tasted blood as she breathed in.

At last she broke into the air. She and Rendak grasped the stone rim and pulled Ivrian up.

A reptilian hand thrust out toward her from the blinding surface world. Heltan. She grasped it, and between his clasp and her knee upon the stone, she leveraged Ivrian out.

A dripping Rendak scrambled up beside her, tube hanging beside his mouth as he gasped in air. The three of them dragged the weak, coughing Ivrian farther back from the edge.

Kalina and Jekka were out in the next moment, and Mirian whirled, coughing fluid. She hadn't been able to fully empty her lungs.

Alderra swam furiously just a few feet below the surface. The drake was only a body length behind, and rising fast. Below, scattered boggard body parts drifted in billowing crimson clouds.

Mirian aimed the wand at the drake's bloody maw, commanded it to fire.

Nothing.

The creature's mouth closed around the noblewoman's lower body, engulfing her to the navel. Mirian saw the astonishment in the woman's gaze as she was dragged off, disappearing in a welter of blood.

"No!" Mirian screamed, and fired again, then once more. Each blast of acid burned into the drake as it lashed away and out of sight. Too late.

Too late.

21
Missing Friends
Mirian

Rendak grabbed her shoulder and pulled her away. "Mirian, get back! That thing can crawl right out of there!"

He was right. Sea drakes were amphibious. If it wished, it could follow them into the sunlight. She allowed herself to be led away, stumbling. Alderra. What if she'd made Heltan turn over the necklaces to the humans? Alderra might be standing beside her now.

She pulled herself together and spun to take in their surroundings. Her eyes had finally adjusted to the brilliant noonday sun. Kalina and Jekka were on guard, him standing post to the north, her to the south. The ruins stretched away in every direction.

Mirian put her anger at Heltan aside for a moment. "Heltan, how close are we to the tower? We need to tend Ivrian."

The boy was huddled to one side, coughing water out of his lungs. "My mother," he said weakly, "has a potion on her belt." He could barely hold up his head.

Rendak and Mirian exchanged a quick glance.

"She didn't make it, lad," Rendak said.

"What?" Ivrian fell into another coughing fit.

"Heltan?" Mirian prompted.

The Karshnaar leader was turning this way and that. Finally, he pointed south.

With Kalina and Heltan leading, Mirian and Rendak carried the wounded young man through the empty, weed-choked courtyard and around the dilapidated towers. Ivrian tried to ask about his mother, but Rendak shushed him gently. Jekka brought up their rear.

The sun was hot on Mirian's shoulders; she could practically feel the water steaming up from her exposed skin. It wasn't especially pleasant making their way barefoot across the rough ground, but they had no other recourse.

They found the first of the boggards about ten feet out from the tower, transfixed by a spear. There were four others about its base.

She knew then the creatures must have been watching from the jungle since this morning, or maybe even the evening before. She grimly climbed the tower with Rendak and Jekka to seek the bodies of her friends.

But the only bodies were two more boggards, lying amid a great deal of blood that may or may not have been human. Human belongings were scattered haphazardly about the room. Anything fragile was broken, and much of their clothing was in tatters, but mercifully their footgear was still intact, and while some boggards seemed to have taken delight in smashing each of Tokello's glass bottles, a single healing potion in its brass tube had survived. Mirian clambered down to pass it off to Kalina, who'd taken it upon herself to guard Ivrian.

He was weak enough that even downing the potion was a challenge. While Kalina assisted him, Mirian consulted Jekka. "Can you find their tracks?"

"Tracks?" Heltan asked. He had donned his robe, marred now by a run of boggard footprints near the waist. He stretched his neck forward, eyes wide. "There is nothing you can do for the others."

"That's where you're wrong. I mean to find them. Jekka?"

"It should be easy," Jekka announced, and crept away, head low.

"I am sorry about these others," Heltan said, "but you know as well as I that they are probably already food—"

"You know as well as I they'll probably be dragged back to the village for torture!" Mirian snapped. "You think I don't know how boggards act? We can save them if we reach them in time."

"How are you going to do that?" Heltan's voice grew challenging. "Three humans against an entire tribe of boggards?"

It hadn't occurred to her that the Karshnaar wouldn't help. She stared at him, torn between a desire to punch him in the snout and the urgent need for his aid.

Kalina stepped between them. "First, I wager fully half the warriors of the tribe are food for the drake." She paused and eyed her mate. "Second, the humans will *not* go alone."

Heltan responded in the lizardfolk language.

"This is a council of peers." Kalina sounded angry. "You will speak so we all understand."

Heltan hissed. "That is a very noble thing to consider, Kalina, but we cannot risk this venture. Not now. We have come through, alive, and done what we were asked. I don't want those humans ended, but we did not agree to help them."

"So your precious library is more vital than your allies?" Kalina countered. "Maybe *that* is why our people are dying out. Because our leaders don't know what's important."

"But if we die now, all of this will have been for nothing!"

Jekka loped up to them and interjected without preamble. "Their tracks are simple to follow. Very fresh."

"Numbers?" Mirian asked.

"Probably two tens."

"Right." Mirian faced the dwindling members of her expedition. "Who's coming?"

"You know I am," Rendak said. He clapped a hand to his sword hilt. Ivrian, revived but haggard, stepped up behind him.

Jekka and Kalina both nodded their assent and fingered their weapons.

Heltan hissed, showing his teeth. "Brother, beloved—"

"Say nothing more, beloved, lest it be agreement."

The lizard man all but gnashed his teeth. He stared hard at the other members of his tribe, then faced Mirian. "Very well. Do you have a plan?"

"My plan is to sneak in close and then arrange a distraction."

"What sort of distraction?" Heltan asked.

Mirian smiled thinly. "I think you'll like it."

22

Reunion
Ivrian

Of that time, I shall not speak.
—From *The Collected Writings of Lord Ivrian Galanor*

One foot before the other. Later, Ivrian would try to remember how he pressed on so easily after the death of his mother, and recall that it was by moving forward. There might have been more to worry about, but he didn't. Mirian was calling the shots and the lizardfolk were guiding, so he just held his weapons and looked forward to killing something.

He'd never really imagined his mother's death, except as an abstract possibility. He'd never thought about how it would affect him.

Alderra Galanor always had a plan, but it hadn't saved her this time. Somewhat dully, Ivrian realized *he* was the head of the family now. Someday, perhaps soon, he *would* have to find some woman with whom to produce an heir. Gods. He couldn't even adopt, for fear the inheritance might be contested and the property handed on to some remote cousin.

He realized, too, that he was now effectively an agent of the Sargavan government, and that all of the others were his employees. Probably, then, the best action would have been to back Heltan. The success of the mission was his responsibility. They had what they needed, and to venture deeper into the jungle toward an enemy stronghold was probably a little mad.

Yet he didn't want Gombe's smiling face planted forever on the end of a boggard stake, and he didn't want grumpy Tokello tortured and eaten.

And so he followed along in a fog, wiping both sweat and tears from his face.

A half hour into the jungle, Kalina found the first of the boggard snares, a tripwire that would have swung a limb stuck with spines into their chests. She guided them past that and two others before motioning them quiet. She and Jekka then split up to survey the terrain. Mirian had the rest of them ready their weapons, urging them to remain silent.

Jekka was the first back, returning to crouch beside the spade-leafed olanga bush that shielded them.

He pitched his voice so low Ivrian had to strain to hear him. "The village is close. Your healer and Salvager Gombe are being tied to stakes, and the boggard chieftain is walking back and forth before them. We haven't much time."

"He'll boast a little before he gets to the torture," Mirian said.

A moment later Kalina materialized out of the brush. She whispered her report. "There are many more scouts posted than I'd usually see." She showed her teeth in pride. "I think they fear us. They are on high alert."

"Are any of the scouts close?" Mirian asked.

"One is very near.

"I want him alive," Mirian said.

"Alive?" Jekka hissed. He seemed to find the idea abhorrent.

"I want to know numbers. And I want them fast. Unless you don't think you can capture him."

"There is no need for insult." Jekka drifted soundlessly away. Kalina let out a gentle coughing laugh and followed.

Ivrian listened intently, but apart from the swish of something moving through a nearby bush, nothing disturbed the omnipresent trilling of jungle creatures. It seemed only moments later that Jekka and Kalina returned dragging one of the hideous frog-people. They tossed the boggard roughly to the ground, and Jekka leveled the spear end of his staff at its throat.

"Shelyn guard me," Ivrian said, surprised at how strained his voice sounded. "It reeks."

The boggard goggled at them with huge eyes. Its mottled gray flesh was slick, completely naked save for a filthy loincloth.

"Rendak," Mirian said, "stand watch. Kalina, scout the perimeter."

Both stepped away, and Mirian turned to the boggard. "What are your numbers?"

Jekka translated for her.

The boggard's pointed teeth gleamed as it jabbered, then Jekka spoke calmly. "Hundreds are hunting you. Soon they will creep up from behind and we will feast."

"Your people are food for vermin," Mirian replied. "We killed them. How many are left?"

The boggard's eyes shifted up to Jekka while he relayed her words. Then he looked at Mirian and gabbled some more. Ivrian thought his voice had taken on a wheedling quality, and Jekka's response bore that out.

"I did not realize you were so powerful. Do you seek to conquer our lands? Surely such mighty warriors need guides. Servants."

"Maybe."

"Then you will not kill me?"

"Not if you give us truth."

"Oh, you can trust Uthla." It showed its teeth in what might have been an attempt at a reassuring smile. "I will give you truths! What would you know? How may I serve?" Jekka paused in his translation. "He is lying."

"I'm sure," Mirian said. "Ask him what is being done with my people."

Jekka asked, listened, then answered: "The chief is asking them of their numbers and their plans before they're cooked. He says they wouldn't do that since you our friends now."

"Since we're allies now, ask him how many of our new friends await in the village?"

"Two dozen. He isn't sure," Jekka said. "And I think he may be telling the truth this time."

Mirian looked to Jekka. "Very well. Knock him out."

Jekka promptly dove his spear through the boggard's throat. The boggard thrashed like a fish on a line as it bled out.

Ivrian gasped in surprise.

"I said to knock him out!" Mirian snapped.

Jekka's head turned, though the rest of his posture remained rigid. "I did."

"I meant to render him unconscious!"

"Oh." Jekka withdrew his spear and stared at the still twitching body. Its absurdly long tongue lolled out of its hideous mouth. "Why?"

"I gave my word not to kill him if he spoke the truth!"

"You said you would not kill him," Jekka said. "I made no such promise."

Mirian scowled. "You might have a future as a lawyer."

The lizard man looked confused by Mirian's anger. Ivrian sought quickly for a means of explanation. "If she speaks for the group, her word binds us all."

Jekka considered this, then bobbed his head toward Mirian. "I have dishonored you. I apologize."

Mirian nodded slowly as Kalina returned. She took in the dead boggard, then cleared away brush and insects on the jungle floor and quickly sketched out a map of the village with one long finger. She pointed to where the primary huts lay, where most of the boggards were clustered, and where Gombe and Tokello were staked—near the village center, naturally.

Ivrian was all for getting the people out, but he didn't have an inkling of how they could pull it off until Mirian removed, with infinite care, the ruby lizardfolk heads she'd taken from the hall of treasure.

"You activate these by pressing their frills. Or by roughly jostling them. Kalina, take Ivrian to a tree overlooking the village to the south. Jekka, take your brother to a tree overlooking a village to the north. Kill any scouts you spot along the way."

"Yes," Kalina said. Jekka nodded.

"Give Jekka a slow fifty count because his position's further out, then throw these heads to the jungle floor."

Jekka hissed. "I begin to like this plan. The boggards will run to investigate, but their numbers will be split."

"That's my hope."

"And we will slice them down as they come."

"Right. Rendak and I will reach the center and cut our friends free. If we don't survive this, it's been an honor. If it goes wrong, no more rescue attempts. Get back to the shore with your lives and the treasure, which must be returned to the baron himself. Is that clear?"

"Too damned clear," Rendak agreed.

The lizardfolk bobbed their heads, birdlike.

"All right." Mirian handed over a cloth-wrapped packet to Ivrian, who accepted the carvings gingerly, then passed on another to Heltan. "Let's do this."

23

The River Run
Mirian

As plans went, it wasn't one of her best. Apart from having smaller numbers, they were on enemy ground that might be littered with traps her scouts hadn't detected.

In their favor was surprise, the natural cowardice of the boggards, and the sheer audacity of the attack. At least Mirian hoped it was audacity. She supposed that's what Ivrian would call it if she succeeded.

Rendak waited with her, sword ready, still as death no matter the sweat trickling down his face. Both stared past the single bush that separated them from the west end of the village and a half-dozen mud-daub huts. Leaning to the left, Mirian could just see the backs of a crowd of boggards listening to their chieftain harangue Tokello and Gombe. She would have liked to have known what they were saying, although she couldn't imagine any circumstance when she would have occasion to learn their language. She wondered if some Pathfinder, somewhere, had done so.

Mirian's fingers tightened on the wand in her right hand. It wasn't the fighting she hated so much, but the waiting beforehand.

All at once the sound of lizardfolk laughter rolled out from the south side of the camp. Mirian saw the boggards rise up and search the brush, and then an even larger burst of lizardfolk laughter erupted into laughter from the north.

The chieftain roared. Boggards grabbed spears and charged away.

"Now," she said, and she and Rendak were running as one down the lane of huts.

In no time at all they'd arrived at the central clearing. Tokello and Gombe were knotted by neck and wrists to blackened poles. Gombe, facing her, lit up with more amazement than delight.

Five boggards remained, including the chieftain. Two were poking fingers at Tokello's robed stomach, almost like butchers evaluating a steer to find the best cut of meat.

Mirian's luck held with the wand this time. Acid streamed forth and blew one boggard's eye into glowing emerald ruin. The creature fell, gobbling even as Mirian pivoted and aimed at the chieftain.

He stood a head taller than the others, and was nearly twice as wide. She caught him as one of his bodyguards frantically grabbed his shoulder.

He howled and clutched the bubbling mark in his chest, then howled all the more as the fingers touching the injury began to burn.

Mirian tried to fire a third time, but it didn't work, so she thrust the wand into its holster and charged the chieftain's guards.

Boggards were inveterate cowards, and these two had seen her work magics that burned their leader. They turned and bounded toward the greenery. Their chieftain screeched plaintively after them.

Mirian slashed through his head.

He dropped, spewing blackish-red blood. Mirian scanned their surroundings, found no boggards watching. She whirled to see how Rendak fared.

She needn't have worried: her first mate was more than a match for two boggards. Both of the amphibians were down and twitching, and Tokello was already free, somewhat dazedly rubbing her wrists.

"Glad you showed up," Gombe said. "This ceremonial necklace was a little tight." He made a good show at sounding casual, but his voice shook a little.

Rendak cut his friend's rope free as Mirian heard the boggards calling to one another. Their heavy bodies crashed through the brush.

"Are you good to run?" Mirian asked.

"I think so." Tokello shook her head in wonder, deep voice thick with gratitude. "May Gozreh bless you, Mirian. I should have known you'd come back for me."

"Well, unless we get moving, we may still be on the menu," Rendak said. "Come on!"

They ran, Rendak leading. Mirian drifted a little to the rear, wand at the ready.

Within half a league they were joined by Heltan and Jekka, who reported that the boggards were still scattered. There was no sign of Ivrian or Kalina until they reached the tower, where they found the two already waiting.

Mirian, Gombe, Rendak, and Tokello slipped on the haversacks while the others grabbed what little remained intact among their survival gear. Seeing Heltan struggle with the bag that held his books, Ivrian shouldered it.

And then they were off, for Mirian assured them the boggards wouldn't remain disorganized forever.

She was right.

They had their first sign of them as Rendak and the lizardfolk wrestled their raft out of the weed bank. A spear arched out of the woods and stood quivering along the rail. The tip glistened—no doubt dipped in some form of poison.

Mirian whipped around and leveled the wand. Hoping to cow their pursuers, she blasted an innocent bush into melting ruin.

It bought them enough time to slip the raft into the river and board it, but it didn't deter the boggards from their next rush. The expedition had poled almost to the middle when boggards erupted from the forest. Some hurled spears. Others leapt into the water.

Most of the weapons fell short. One struck the raft near Ivrian's foot.

Gombe turned to call back at them. "Nothing but your own meat for your pots tonight!"

But his gloating proved premature. The boggards proved faster in the water than they were on land, closing until they were only a few body lengths from the raft.

More spears rained down, one taking Tokello in the side and sending her stumbling into the rail.

Mirian grabbed for the healer. Her fingers brushed Tokello's robe but failed to grasp it as the older woman plunged over the side into the murky water. Even as Mirian cried out Tokello's name and stretched down for her, pain exploded through her shoulder. She gasped, back arching, and twisted her neck to find a boggard spear lodged beside her shoulder blade. Blood welled as she pulled it out.

Tokello shouted. The healer had managed to grab hold of the raft to keep from being swept away.

Around her, the water began to churn.

Poor Tokello didn't even have time to scream as the piranha closed in.

Behind the raft, boggards broke off their pursuit, swimming frantically for shore lest they fall prey to the ravenous school. Of Tokello, there was no sign, other than the furiously boiling water.

Sobbing in pain and remorse, Mirian rolled from the edge. "Tokello," she mouthed, though she couldn't hear. The world was growing shaky.

Ivrian snatched up her wand and shouted the activation word again and again. As Rendak dragged her from the raft's edge. She saw Ivrian loosing deadly acid blasts at the boggards lining the receding shore.

She had the sense that they grounded on the far side, heard Rendak reassuring her that she'd be all right. And then everything whirled away into velvety blackness, free of stars, pain, and fallen friends.

24
Blood Ties
Mirian

Mostly she slept deeply, without dreams. Sometimes she woke to find scaled faces leering over her, jabbering and flashing teeth. Other times she found herself floating past dancing trees. Once her mother walked at her side and sang a mournful Bas'o lullaby.

She was too tired to care that her name was called until it grew more and more insistent. Mirian opened her eyes to discover Kellic leaning toward her. That couldn't be. Kellic hadn't gone into the jungle.

Yet as her consciousness shambled in the direction of lucidity, she understood that he, at least, was real. She lay on a ship's bed built near a bulkhead, the air laced with salt and a faint reek from a distant bilge.

She tried sitting up. Immediately stars bloomed in her field of vision.

A green hand settled on her arm, steadying her. She followed it up the scaled arm flecked with orange to a bare shoulder, then shifted to take in a reptilian snout and two unwinking amber eyes. "Jekka. Where's Kellic?"

Her voice was the faintest whisper. Why was she so weak?

"I'm right here." Kellic shifted back into view. He sounded petulant. "You need medicine and Jekka won't let you take any."

"I don't trust him or his mate," Jekka said.

Kellic's mate? Mirian maneuvered the fluffy scarlet pillows piled on the narrow mattress and managed to prop herself upright against them. Kellic rattled on about his frustrations: how he didn't want to hurt Jekka, but that he'd have to order sailors to march him out if the lizard man wouldn't let Mirian be treated. None of it quite made sense, and didn't seem particularly important.

"Where am I?" she asked hoarsely. "Where's the rest of my team?"

"This is the *Wayfarer*, Sylena's father's ship." The deck planks creaked as Kellic knelt beside her. "She came looking for us, praise be to Desna, and anchored off the coast until your men stumbled out of the jungle with you."

It took Mirian a moment to understand he meant Sylena had come looking, not the ship. Her comprehension was slowed, but she didn't like the sound of Sylena's involvement. And Kellic still hadn't answered the most important question. "What about my team?"

"The humans are in quarantine, under the orlop deck," Kellic said, then hurried on: "Sylena says they've been exposed to sensun fever and are still suffering the effects. You're lucky you don't have it, too. You're very weak from some injuries." He pointed at the lizard man. "And Jekka here won't let you drink any of Sylena's broth."

It took a great deal of concentration to draw conclusions from that information, and she saw Kellic fidgeting under her stare. "What about the rest of the lizardfolk?"

"We do not have this fever," Jekka said. "I do not think the humans have this fever, either. And we are only hours out from Crown's End. We will have a proper healer look over you there."

Sensible, she thought, and while Kellic protested she forced her tired brain to sift through the information she'd heard. She ached abominably, especially her shoulder, and her face felt flushed.

"Kellic." He didn't stop talking, so she was forced to raise her voice. "Kellic!"

Finally he closed his mouth and looked at her.

"Don't you think it's odd that Sylena happened to turn up looking for you? How did she know where you were?"

"She felt like taking the ship out," Kellic said. "It was pure chance—lucky chance."

"Or she's a Chelish spy," Mirian said.

Kellic scoffed.

"Where's the treasure, then?"

"In the chests in her cabin," Kellic said. "For safekeeping."

Mirian stared at him.

"She's not a spy!"

Mirian massaged her temples. "Ancestors, grant him sight."

"Ancestors." He snorted derisively.

"Kellic, Sylena could scarcely be in a better position. She's locked up my team and taken the treasure."

"They're not locked up!"

"They are," Jekka said.

"If she's a spy, why hasn't she simply killed us all?" Kellic asked.

"She might yet," Mirian said.

"She's left the lizardfolk free."

"They're confined to the forward deck," Jekka said. "Mirian, is he always this blind?"

"He didn't used to be."

Her brother scowled.

"Kellic, listen to me. Lady Galanor suspected Sylena was a spy. That's why I kept our destination secret from you."

"That's why? You thought I was a *spy*?"

"No, but I thought you'd tell her where we were going. She found out anyway. Doesn't that seem suspicious? Don't you see that we're—" she was starting to finish the sentence with the word "prisoners" when her eyes lit on the ring that still glinted on Kellic's hand. The one Sylena had given him.

Finally her thoughts seemed to tumble into place at something like normal speed. She knew powerful wizards and witches could spy upon people at a distance—she and her venture-captain, Finze Bellaugh, had once hired a wizard to do exactly that to help track a thief into the wilds. The job of scrying, the tanned old man had explained, was far simpler if the spell's subject carried something belonging to the spellcaster.

Mirian wasn't versed enough in magic to know exactly what was possible. Could the ring act as a magical beacon? Was it letting Sylena eavesdrop on them even now? She decided explaining further wasn't worth the risk. Their lives might depend upon Sylena wishing to remain in Kellic's good graces, though she wasn't sure why the woman thought Kellic worth the trouble. If Mirian convinced him Sylena was a spy, she might well end up getting all of them killed.

"That we're what?" Kellic demanded. "How could you say anything against Sylena? You've never even met her!"

"Maybe you're right," she said.

Kellic's eyebrows drew together peevishly but he held off speaking. Mirian glanced at Jekka, found his expression unreadable.

"Lady Galanor would have said anything to get the expedition moving," Mirian said, which was almost true. Mirian improvised as she went. "She wanted me in charge, not you, because you weren't giving her what she wanted."

Kellic nodded slowly.

So she was convincing him at least; but if Sylena were listening, would she be fooled? Mirian forced a smile, hoped it was reassuring. "It's hard to think clearly. I'm sorry if I insulted you."

"You need to take the medicine, Mirian." He reached over and patted her shoulder gruffly, but there was honest concern in his eyes.

If nothing else, Kellic's worry was sincere. He might be a coward and a dupe, but he wasn't a traitor. She took small comfort in that. "How far out from Crown's End did you say we were?"

"Only a few hours."

"You should wait," Jekka said.

"I'm going to pray," Mirian said, "before I do anything else."

"Pray?" Kellic repeated in astonishment. "Since when did you get so religious?"

"I lost two women under my command. I haven't prayed for them yet, or asked the ancestors for guidance."

He didn't sniff his disapproval, but it was writ large on his face.

"You have as much Bas'o blood as I do," she said. "You should honor both traditions."

He frowned.

"But you're in charge, Kellic. You need to make sure the lizard-folk are well cared for. Check in on them and see that they have water. They may be too polite to ask for it."

Kellic's frown deepened.

"And you have to look in on Gombe and Rendak and Lord Galanor." Strange to refer to Ivrian like that.

"I don't want to get sick," Kellic protested.

"Then check on them through the door. And take Sylena with you so that if they have any needs she can help them right away."

"Are you really sure that's necessary?" Kellic sounded as though she'd just asked him to cross through the deepest jungle in monsoon weather.

"You've got to take care of your people," Mirian said. It was something they'd heard their father repeat countless times, and he nodded glumly.

"Very well. So long as you get some medicine into you when I get back."

"I'll consider it."

He sighed and climbed to his feet. He seemed to find a little more of his spine as he stepped to the door of the narrow cabin. "Are you going to keep loitering there?" he asked Jekka.

"I remain until Mirian dismisses me," Jekka replied tonelessly.

Kellic glared, then opened the door and departed. It clicked shut behind him.

She spoke quietly to Jekka. "Thank you."

"I have done right?"

"Oh yes. I'm just not sure how to get us out of here. Are we truly on course for Crown's End?"

"I cannot say. I do not know the ways of ships."

"Is the coast on our port side? I mean, the left side of the ship?"

"Yes."

Mirian pushed covers aside and discovered herself in her sleeping gown, white and rather conservatively high-necked. She had left it with her dunnage, expecting it to be carried back to Sargava with her brother along with the rest of her clothing. "Is my chest in this cabin?"

"Your chest?" Jekka sounded confused.

"A wooden container. With clothes."

"Oh. I am sitting on it."

Mirian climbed uneasily to her knees so she could look out the narrow porthole. Evening. They were making east, with a good wind. A long coastline loomed to the north, only two or three miles out. A hard swim, but with their gear, not an impossible one.

If she were in her normal shape.

She almost asked Jekka to turn around while she dressed, then realized the absurdity of the request. What would a lizard man care about a naked human? His people barely even wore clothes. Her arms felt leaden and her vision occasionally swam as she moved, but she forced speed.

Her gear belt had been returned to the chest, though not her sword, or her wand. Or, she realized, her rings. How stupid was her brother? Hadn't he been suspicious that all her tools were kept from her? Or had he kept those things for himself?

"What do we do, Mirian?" Jekka asked.

"First, you're going to go to the weather deck and create a distraction. Not a violent or dangerous one. Just something that will attract a lot of attention."

He didn't ask why, which she appreciated. She didn't have a lot of spare energy to explain. "What should I do?"

"I bet if you and your brother and cousin sang it would draw all kinds of attention."

"Shall we sing our death songs?"

"Your death songs? No. We're not dying today. Any of us," she added with a conviction she hoped would make her declaration true. "I just need all attention pulled from me. I'm going into Sylena's cabin to get our gear."

"And then?"

"Then we go over the side."

"What about the others?"

"No one gets left behind. I just don't know how to free them yet."

"You will make another distraction."

"Probably."

"If someone can do this, it is you," Jekka told her, which brought a brief smile to her lips.

"Here's hoping. I'm going to try and get my brother out of here as well. It's not his fault he's stupid."

"My brother disappointed me, too, Mirian."

"You and me both."

Jekka hissed and tilted his head to one side. "When Kalina said that Ivrian claimed her friendship, I told her he lied. But I do not think so now. Do you think humans and lizardfolk can be friends?"

"I know it," she said. "Now let's get moving and save our team."

25

Complications
Sylena

It doesn't sound as if you had much success." Sylena leaned against the back of her cabin chair and carefully watched Kellic's face.

The Sargavan waved the criticism away. "She's agreed to think matters over. And she apologized."

"Apologized?' Sylena pretended ignorance. She'd naturally been listening via the ring.

Kellic cleared his throat, glanced at Atok standing silently beside Sylena. "She's a little suspicious of you because of your Chelish heritage, but she's starting to rethink her opinion." He laughed, a little strained. "I guess she saw the hypocrisy."

"Indeed." Sylena settled back in her chair.

"I'm sure it's all because of her illness. She said she needed to pray, but I fully expect her to take your ministrations soon."

"We can hope." Sylena doubted Mirian's change of heart. She studied Kellic, who stood uncomfortably in front of her.

"She reminded me of my duty as head of the family business. She suggested I check in with the lizardfolk and the salvagers."

"They're being taken care of. You can't visit the salvaging team without exposing yourself to fever. Not only is the disease contagious, they're likely to be raving."

He nodded. "All the same, it's my duty."

Sylena tapped fingers on the surface of her desk. This was an irritating time for Kellic to insist upon anything.

Until now, almost everything had proceeded according to plan. Once she arrived she sent the rest of the sailors away via the Ijo boats with assurances she'd pick up the salvage party, and Kellic had reassured their leader there was no need to send Lady Galanor's letter along. She'd easily tricked Kellic into thinking the salvagers were sick by casting a minor spell shortly after they boarded, then locked them away.

She'd thought of several contingencies for the lizardfolk, but two proved so interested in the black cones they'd brought back that Sylena left them on deck without restraint. Once night fell she'd render them harmless with a sleep enchantment. They'd fetch a good price at the Crown's End arena.

The one wrinkle had been the lizard man who refused to leave Mirian's side or permit her consumption of any food or liquid until she was seen by a mainland healer. That made poisoning her problematic unless she killed the lizard man, which might rouse Kellic's suspicions. As would refusing his current request.

"I understand, of course," she said finally. "I'll have Atok escort you below. You can talk with your salvagers through the door, if they're even awake. Atok will check on them first. Gillmen are immune to sensun fever."

Kellic looked the gillman up and down, as if searching for signs of his immunity. He had never liked Atok, and she knew the feeling was mutual.

She gave Kellic her best smile. "We'll arrive at Crown's End in only a few hours, and then they'll receive the finest care. For now, please, you must only check on them through the door. We can't risk you becoming infected as well. And when you're done, you can meet me on deck to talk to the lizardfolk."

Kellic nodded.

"You also might want to stop by your quarters and grab some-thing to use as a face mask. A scented kerchief, perhaps, that you can press over your nose and mouth when you get close, just to be safe."

"Oh. Of course."

He bent and raised her hand to his lips, then departed, closing the door behind him.

Atok listened to his footsteps retreat, then bowed to her. He couldn't quite mask his surprise. "You really want me to take him to the men you've imprisoned, mistress?"

"I want you to go in first and stress to them their lives depend upon their answers."

"Very well, mistress. I don't think I'm actually immune to sensun fever."

He could be so literal. "Good thing they don't have it, then."

"I suppose so."

"Is there something else?"

"No, mistress."

"Perhaps you think I go to too much trouble for him?"

"If you still believe you might be better placed as a landholder in the new Sargava with Kellic Raas twined about your finger, then it's probably worth some trouble."

"But?"

"But perhaps not too much more."

He was probably right. She had to be honest with herself: marriage to Kellic was no guarantee his property would remain hers after Sargava's reconquest, though she was certain it would help legitimize her claim.

The uncomfortable truth was she had grown fond of Kellic. He was simple and pleasant and thoroughly devoted. He was no Chelish title-seeker who'd start sparring over money and land the moment they signed betrothal papers. He simply enjoyed her company.

Why couldn't she hold on to him? Didn't she deserve a little something extra after all of her hard work? She frowned at Atok.

"You may go. Don't give him much time before you lead him back to the lizardfolk."

"I'll do my best, mistress."

26

Chains and Challenges
Ivrian

To have come so far and suffered so much, only to end up chained in a smelly ship's hold . . . When I saw Kellic and the shore party, I'd assumed we were safe at last, but the Chelish sorceress worked her magics upon us while our backs were turned. The next thing I knew, I was waking to the shake of Gombe's hand, chained and manacled to metal plates bolted to the deck!

—From *The Daughter of the Mist*

It was very dim in the cramped space beneath the orlop deck. Intensely focused shafts of bright sunlight streamed in through gaps between two planks overhead. All else in Ivrian's world was dark, and everything stank of sweat and urine and sea brine.

"What do you think's happening to everyone else?" Ivrian shifted, and the chains rattled as he tested the manacles around each wrist. Neither was remotely loose, and the right one bit into his skin.

Rendak's voice was grim. "I think that pretty little captain threw a spell on us. Leovan's boy sold us out. The gods alone know what they've got planned for Mirian."

"And the lizardfolk?" He wanted to ask if they were still alive, but he couldn't bear to do it.

"No idea."

Ivrian reflected on that glumly for a moment, then pushed the thought from his mind. Right now there was only mental space to worry about their own situation. "So what do we do?"

Rendak rattled his chains.

"Are you saying we're trapped?" Ivrian asked.

"I'm not saying that at all," Rendak said. "This ain't my first dance."

There was enough slack in the chains that they could raise and lower their arms, and Rendak fiddled with his belt buckle.

"What are you doing?" Ivrian asked.

"Well," Rendak answered, huffing a little with effort, "one of the things a salvager has to be an expert with is locks. Think on it, lad. A lot of chests and doors and such bar our way when we're in the middle of a drop."

"It's not just about glamour and grateful, gorgeous women," Gombe added.

Ivrian felt hope dawning.

"So." Rendak paused to grunt. "A simple wrist lock like this"—he waved a hand in the air, now bereft of chain—"ain't no problem at all."

"Isn't any," Gombe corrected.

"Isn't any what?" Rendak asked.

Ivrian breathed out in relief. "Sweet, sweet Shelyn. How did you do that?"

"Years of practice."

"Plus a lock pick hidden in his belt buckle," Gombe added.

"You're going to give the boy all our secrets." Rendak was already hard at work on his second manacle.

"So what's the plan?" Ivrian couldn't keep the excitement from his voice.

"Well, first . . ." Rendak paused, concentrating. Ivrian heard a faint click as the second manacle opened. "We get ourselves free, although if any sailors come with slop for us we'll have to pretend we're still chained. We'll stay in this fine hotel until things get dark. Come the dog watch, that's when we make our move."

"What's our move?" Ivrian asked.

"He has no idea," Gombe explained.

"There you go, giving away our secrets again."

"Seriously," Ivrian insisted, "what's the plan?"

"Lad, we've got to free Mirian. We've got to free the lizardfolk, and we've got to get our gear." He leaned over Gombe, who offered a chained wrist.

"Don't forget the treasure," Gombe said.

"Aye, and we've got to get the treasure. Somehow we've got to sneak out in the darkness and get all of that done without getting caught."

"Or killed," Gombe added.

Rendak grunted, bore down on the lock. "That goes without saying."

"I think it needed saying." Gombe lifted one hand free of a manacle, flexing his fingers as Rendak moved to the next.

"I think not being killed should always be first on the list," Ivrian said.

"You're wrong there." Rendak was suddenly serious. "The way I see it, we owe Mirian for pulling our fat from the fryer."

"She ran into a boggard village to get me," Gombe said.

"That she did. And poor Tokello too. And then she took a spear for us on the way out. And I've lost count of how many times she saved your ass, Lord. No disrespect intended."

It still felt odd being referred to as "lord," though Rendak, Gombe, and even the lizardfolk had called him that over the last days. "No offense taken," Ivrian said, although not getting killed still seemed important.

Rendak finished with Gombe's second wrist manacle. He set it gently on the floor. "My point is that goal one is getting Mirian out alive. We owe her that. Second is getting the treasure out of here and away from Sylena and Kellic. 'Cause if they get the money, Sargava's got nothing to pay off the pirates with."

"You don't know that," Gombe objected.

Rendak had moved over to Ivrian, who held his wrist upright on his knee. The salvager clasped the metal in one hand and dug with his pick.

"Then you tell me why Lady Galanor headed into the Kaava Lands. The boy here will tell you the truth of it."

Ivrian felt Gombe's eyes on him. "There might be other ventures in the works," he said. His mother's absence was like a great pressure upon his heart. "But no. You're probably right. I think Mother was one of the few people of sense the baron had, and I think things must be really desperate or she wouldn't have gone out to manage things." He fell silent, lest his voice crack.

For the entirety of their journey, he'd been so caught up in the tale, and the wording of it, and how the whole thing affected him, that he'd given almost no thought to the larger picture. "I've been so selfish," he muttered.

The manacle popped free and he methodically removed his hand, placing the other on his knee.

"She was proud of you," Gombe said.

"I don't think I was proud enough of her."

"That's the way of things, though, lad." Rendak paused to shake one hand out. "My fingers aren't as nimble as they used to be," he said, then went on. "You can't see who your parents really are until you get to that point yourself, or they're not there anymore."

Ivrian felt his eyes well with tears. "She wanted to make a man of me. I heard her saying it to Mirian."

"Then she couldn't see you," Gombe said. "Because you were a brave rake from the first. You never hesitate. You just throw yourself into the middle of it."

"That's not what she meant. Anyone can be reckless. She wanted me to think beyond myself."

This time Rendak answered him. "Seems to me you've been doing that all along. You could have stood back when those harpies attacked, but you leapt right in."

"That's not what I mean."

"And you could've stayed on the shore like a coward," Rendak continued

"Not to mention any names, like Kellic's," Gombe added.

"But you came in with us."

Ivrian was still shaking his head.

"And when Gombe and Tokello were captured, you risked your life to save them. So." Rendak popped the other manacle free. "You're a better man than you think you are." Rendak clapped him on the shoulder. "One I'm proud to have fighting at my side."

"Aye," Gombe agreed.

Ivrian wiped the moisture from his eyes. A week before he would never have guessed that the praise of these two rough-hewn men would affect him so deeply.

"The escape," Gombe said in the sudden silence, "is going to be the hard part. But if we've got a calm ocean and our gear, we can get where we need to go."

"All we need is one air bottle," Rendak continued. "We can share it."

Ivrian looked down at the blank spot on his finger where the Raas family ring used to rest. The gods alone knew where that or his writing desk or his rare Ailson Kindler volume had gone. The last he'd seen, the desk and book had been stuffed into the bag Heltan was carrying.

None of the material objects seemed especially important now except for the ring. And the treasure—the freedom of his people, as defined in sparkling gems.

"What about the lizardfolk?" he asked.

"We'll get them free too," Rendak promised.

"No, I mean, how will they breathe underwater if we only have one bottle?"

"I think they've got it easier in the water than we do," Rendak answered.

"You saw how well they swim," Gombe added.

"So really it's just a matter of getting out of here."

"Right." Gombe nodded. "And maybe dying in a heroic final stand."

"No," Ivrian insisted.

Gombe's teeth glittered in a grim smile. "I thought my time was out when the boggards got me. If you survive to write about this, you'll give me a few good lines in your play, won't you, Ivrian?"

It was the first time the salvager had addressed him by his first name, and it brought a smile to his lips.

"I will."

From the decks above came a peculiar trilling noise, something like the call of birds, but lower-pitched, mixed with occasional guttural noises. They heard sailors calling out questions, and then a second strange voice joined in.

"The lizardfolk," Gombe said.

"What are they doing?" Ivrian asked.

"I can't be sure," Rendak said, "but it's a fine distraction. Maybe it's time we try this lock on the door."

As Rendak slid forward, there was a sudden flurry of steps, and all three scrambled to shove their hands behind their backs, near the manacles. With a little luck, no one would notice they gaped open. The sound of their movements was concealed by the rattle of a key chain and the rusty turn of the lock.

Light spilled in on them. There in the doorway was a burly Chelish sailor and, holding a small ship's lantern behind him, the archly handsome bald man that seemed to be first mate. Another figure lurked in the darkness beyond. Kellic.

"Wait here for a moment," the bald man said. "I'll go in first and—"

Rendak threw himself at the speaker. There was a heavy thunk and a low-voiced oath. Gombe came immediately on his heels and soon had a knee in the other sailor's gut.

The sailor gagged and struck out at Gombe, then Ivrian woke from his paralysis and drove his hand into the fellow's face. He hadn't meant to drive the chain as well, but there was a loud crack and the sailor groaned.

"Nice!" Gombe said.

Judging by the commotion outside, Rendak had his hands full, so Ivrian clambered out the door.

The bald first mate was partly turned away, a wicked knife in one hand. Rendak was hunched in the hallway. A length of freed chain lay next to the lamp, which had somehow landed on its side without breaking open.

Kellic watched, frozen in astonishment.

Thinking Ivrian meant to charge him, the mate turned with a flourish of his knife, which was enough of an opening for Rendak. As the mate spun to stab, Ivrian grabbed his knife hand and Rendak drove a calloused fist into the curious fleshy flaps along the fellow's neck.

That apparently hurt, judging from the way the gillman curled up, but Rendak hammered him in the same place again. The bald man went limp, moaning, and Rendak wound up for a third strike.

"He looks finished," Ivrian said quickly.

"Right enough."

While Rendak and Gombe dragged the sailors into the hold, Ivrian turned to Kellic, who had backed furtively into a dark corner, pressing a cloth to his face.

"Stay back!" Kellic cried. "You'll infect the whole ship!"

"We're not sick," Ivrian snapped. "We were being held prisoner. Isn't it obvious?"

Kellic didn't answer immediately, but his eyes widened.

Ivrian picked up the lamp. "Are you working with them, or us?"

"You're really not sick?"

"No. Where's Mirian, and what's going on with the lizardfolk?"

"Mirian's in a cabin near Sylena. I have no idea what the lizard-folk are doing. Is that them making the noise?"

"I'm pretty sure," Ivrian said. What other explanation could Kellic suggest?

Ivrian heard Rendak and Gombe talking behind him. "You know," Rendak was saying, "I bet you could fit into that gillman's shirt."

"No one's going to mistake me for him," Gombe objected. "Perhaps you've noticed that he's devilishly handsome and whitish. I'm devilishly handsome and *brown*."

"Don't bother," Ivrian said. "We need to move fast. Kellic's going to take us to his sister, and we'll see about getting off this ship." He shone the lantern at Mirian's brother. "Where's our gear?"

"In the captain's cabin. By the gods—Sylena really is some kind of spy?"

Ivrian couldn't decide if Mirian's brother were stupid or naive or a healthy mix of both, but he feigned good fellowship with a broad smile and a pat on the man's shoulder. "Love makes fools of us all. I'd muster more sympathy, but right now we're trapped on a ship surrounded by enemies. You've got to get us safely back to Mirian and the lizardfolk."

"Um. " Kellic hesitated, then, shaking his head in disbelief, started down a dark passage. "This way."

27

Expiration
Mirian

Sylena's quarters took up the entire aft deck save for the narrow spaces that served as officer cabins, in one of which Mirian herself had been recuperating.

Though her legs still trembled with the lingering effects of the boggards' poison, Mirian's hands were steady as she worked the lock. In moments she was inside and closing the door behind her. Light streamed in through leaded glass windows in a thick lattice screen. A lovely, nearly full-length mirror in a gilt frame hung on one bulkhead, and there were other fine appointments, including carved devils holding sconces.

Mirian noted the chests stowed under the galley window bench. Looking through the aft windows, she saw the ship's wake, a brighter ribbon across waters stained by the golden light of the sinking sun. She could just make out the dim outline of the north shore. She had downplayed the difficulty in her earlier estimation. It would be a challenging swim even if she were in top condition and regained her rings. And nearly impossible if they had no gear at all.

Her brother had said the treasure was in the chests. Hopefully the gear was as well.

The locks were intricate, but Mirian was hardly a novice, and they soon yielded to her ministrations. Only clothing lay in the first chest. The second, though, held two of the haversacks, including one with an air bottle, as well as Mirian's sword and belt, which she buckled into place. The third chest contained the final pack.

From the sound of things above, Jekka had taken her suggestion to heart and been joined by at least one of the other lizardfolk in an impromptu concert.

Mirian hoped she hadn't sent him off to his doom. Those three at least could drop overside and swim for a good long while before needing to surface. No gear was required. She had little idea how she was going to get the rest of her team to safety, but luck was working in her favor so far. Now she needed to find the rings, and as she struggled into her haversack she cast about the room, her gaze settling on a desk built into the bulkhead beside the door.

It was carved from dark wood and boasted a number of locked drawers. It might be that Sylena had secret cubbyholes, but Mirian saw no point in searching for them when the rings could lie just beyond another lock.

And so she set to work on the desk and found its protections the most complex yet. That gave her hope she was on to something good, although she cursed under her breath in frustration. There was a babble of concerned human voices on the weather deck. How much longer would she have alone?

The third tumbler yielded to her at last. Mirian wiped sweat from her face and gently pulled the drawer free.

It was deep and heavy, with room for a sturdy black book with gold foil, a sheaf of papers, and various writing instruments. But her eyes slid immediately past those to the wands lying beside them.

One was hers, handed to her by her father on her sixteenth birthday. She could still remember his solemn expression as he declared it her birthright.

The other wand, nearly identical, was her father's.

Mirian felt her heart race. There was only one explanation for her father's wand lying there, and for the collection of four Raas family rings that rested in a line beside them.

Both the wand and the second ring had been thought lost with Leovan's death. His mutilated body, recovered by Rendak and Gombe, had been missing most of its right arm. Someone, or some*thing*, dispatched by Sylena, had killed her father and taken his belongings.

Mirian felt her lips peel back in a snarl.

Without thinking, she put the rings on her fingers, and had just reached for the wand when she heard the creak of footsteps in the corridor. She tensed at her brother's voice, then heard Rendak telling him to quiet.

She stepped to the door and opened it a little unsteadily, found herself staring at a disheveled parade of figures turning upon her with menace.

"Mirian!" Rendak said. "What are you doing here?"

She smiled in relief and waved them in. "Get in here! I've found our gear."

It was only as she stepped back that she realized she no longer heard the lizardfolk.

28

The Drop
Ivrian

When I was young, I used to constantly disappoint myself. I'd end up scolding my reflection and telling him how he should have handled himself better. And then, one day, I did the right thing without thinking. But not because of my self-loathing. I'd simply learned loyalty.
    —From *The Collected Writings of Lord Ivrian Galanor*

Ivrian and his companions joined Mirian in the cabin, which, large as it was, began to feel a little cramped.

Kellic turned to his sister. "I'm such a fool." His voice shook. "I just didn't want to believe it."

"I'm glad you understand," Mirian said briskly. To Ivrian she still looked peaked. "We're out of time. We've got to get over the side and hope Jekka and the others can follow."

"Over the side?" Kellic repeated. "Do you realize how far we are from shore?"

"We can hardly wait for Sylena to take us to Crown's End, and I'm willing to bet her sailors are trained warriors. Gombe, Rendak—gear up. Two of the satchels still have air bottles."

She stepped to the galley window as the others pulled on the satchels. "Ivrian, I've got another set of rings. We'll have to—"

Whatever she said next was lost in the sudden crash of the door behind them.

Ivrian whirled to find it smoking as it slammed into the bulkhead.

The captain's face was ugly with anger. Ivrian glimpsed a host of sailors behind her. She shrieked a curse at Mirian, then shouted: "You've ruined everything!" She plucked something from her necklace and hurled it at Mirian—a brilliant scarlet bead.

Kellic threw himself in front of his sister.

The bead struck his nose and widened into flame, like a flower bud partly open. Ivrian stared in slack-jawed horror as Kellic was engulfed in a wave of fire that traveled forward, catching Mirian even as she turned away.

She and Gombe burst through the gallery window and plummeted, followed by broken shards of glass and wood.

Without really thinking about what he did, Ivrian took two steps and dived to aid his friends. As he cleared the window he saw Gombe flailing weakly as he hit the water, his clothes smoldering. Mirian was limp.

The water was a lot farther down than he'd imagined.

He hit the waves with a painful belly flop and scrabbled to get his head above water, to suck in a deep breath for air.

Then he dove. As his vision cleared, he hunted frantically for Gombe and Raas, only to find the salvagers dropping lifelessly into the depths.

He gritted his teeth. No way was he going to let them die.

"Definitely," he swore to himself.

29

Atok's Dive
Sylena

Everything was spoiled, and now Kellic was dead.

First she'd had to resort to spells to silence the lizardfolk. Then, hoping to head Kellic off before he saw what she'd done, she raced to the orlop deck and discovered Atok dazed and chained.

Sylena knew then things were bad, but she'd harbored hope her sister might know some spell to erase or alter Kellic's memory, or that she herself could still explain everything.

And then he'd flung himself into the fireball.

"Put him out! Put him out!" Kellic was clearly beyond help, but there was a fair chance the burning corpse might set fire to the deck. The sailors hurried to smother him with her expensive pillows.

Atok and another sailor piled into the remaining salvager and took him down. Rendak struggled, cursing, and Atok lifted a knife to his throat.

"No," Sylena snapped. She might yet profit from him. "The treasure was blasted over the side with Mirian and the others! Atok, retrieve it!"

"Yes, mistress."

Atok sheathed his knife and rose, a little unsteady. He stepped past the smoking cushions and the burnt lump they hid. He dove through the broken window.

In addition to his own considerable prowess as a warrior, Atok wore an enchanted anklet that granted him the power to summon and command sharks. Even wounded, he'd make short work of Ivrian Galanor. And Mirian Raas and the native salvager were probably already dead. The trick would be getting their treasure-filled satchels before they sank too deep.

Sylena pointed at Rendak. "Pull the pack off that one and chain him back up. Don't leave any slack this time! And use more chains!"

Rendak glared as three sailors dragged him off. "Your gillman's not coming back!" he shouted from the corridor.

The lowly salvager's opinion was beneath notice. She paced over to the sailors ruining her pillows, and they looked up from their work. The fire was out, and she became closely acquainted with a nearly unbearable reek of charred flesh. Her sister was a powerful wizard, but even she couldn't bring back the dead. Even if they could find a cleric powerful enough for that feat, her superiors would never approve the expense.

If only the idiot hadn't jumped in front! "Take that away and throw it over the side."

The eldest sailor knuckled his brow with a calloused hand. "Yes, mistress."

"And throw out the pillows as well. There'll be no getting rid of that stink."

"Yes, mistress."

The four burly men hastened to obey, but even after they'd transported the body the smell still lingered.

Scowling, Sylena stepped to the galley window. A last amber beam of sunlight lit the surface of the ocean where she hoped to see Atok surface. He did not—but then, he hadn't been gone long, and it might take some time to recover the treasures.

She turned on her heel, bent to open the pack the sailors had pulled off Rendak. The first thing she touched felt like one of the sculptures.

Surely not.

She pulled her hand out and stared at the ruby lizard head, which coughed. The thing's teeth were bared, and for a moment she imagined it was laughing at her. It was all she could do to keep from smashing it into the blackened deck planks in frustration.

This was the worst of the bags, by far. The jewels that filled the others would be more valuable in any city. Only a collector would pay full value for sculptures, and the mocking lizard head seemed to know that.

"Atok will come back," she told it, and pushed the thing into the haversack before setting it firmly on the planks. Atok would surface with the lost bags. And then all the jewels would still be in her possession, and her sister would be pleased, and so would their masters back in Cheliax.

Kellic was dead, but she might still claim some kind of property reward once Sargava was retaken. After all, she knew the city. It was a shame about him, but there would be other pretty men.

Deciding the smell was too overpowering, she left the cabin and moved up top, remembering only then to instruct the helmsman to drop anchor, and to tell the ship's captain to lower the rope ladders, one to starboard and one to port.

She went to stand by the taffrail, peering into the dark water.

Sylena watched for long moments, but it was one of the hands who saw the shark fins a quarter league east and pointed them out to her.

She grinned to herself. That meant Atok had finished off Lady Galanor's boy and was probably watching his minions feast.

"Go tell the crew to keep watch for Atok," she instructed. "He may need help climbing the ladders." Atok would have to manage two satchels, after all.

"Yes, mistress." The sailor saluted and hurried off.

But Atok didn't rise.

Night fell in earnest, and she stared out at the waters in disbelief.

How dare he fail her!

For a long time she gripped the rail, seething, but as the moon rose her anger was mixed with a sense of loss. What would she do without Atok? He hadn't been a friend, exactly, but he'd been the only person she trusted. He had always apologized when he irritated, and his advice had never failed to be sound.

And now he was gone, with the treasure. She felt a tightening in her chest. What would she tell her sister?

She'd allowed a fortune to slip through her fingers. Sylena could make a little selling the lizardfolk to the arena in Crown's End, and maybe Rendak, too, if she claimed he were a murderer. Given his disheveled state and lack of identification, no one would be likely to believe any protests he offered.

Those four could scarcely make up for the money lost, but it would be something.

The important thing, she reminded herself, was that she'd kept the treasure from the Sargavans. The salvagers were surely dead on the ocean floor or currently being digested by sharks, and so long as the jewels were with them, they wouldn't be paid to any pirates to hold off the Chelish fleet. She hoped her sister would like that. She wished now that she'd never contacted Rajana to brag about her success over the mirror. Atok himself had suggested she surprise her.

She would be surprised now, Sylena though bitterly.

30

Deep and Dark
Ivrian

*I could not let them die. Not when we had come so far
together. Not when the very future of Sargava lay at stake!
I summoned reserves I'd never known and dove deep, my
lungs straining.*

—From *The Daughter of the Mist*

Ivrian glimpsed the emerald glow of Mirian's gills and fins and
knew she could breath if she weren't already dead. It was Gombe
who needed help first. The salvager was struggling feebly with his
haversack. Ivrian kicked through the waters for him and got the
stiff black air bottle hose free from its housing pocket. He mouthed
its end to suck in a deep breath of pure, clean air, then put it to
Gombe's lips. He went swimming after the figure sinking farther
and farther. The magical glow about Mirian's neck, arms, and feet
gleamed in the darkness.

Mirian had said she bore the other two rings. Reasoning that
because she was right handed she'd probably place them in her
right pocket, he explored there first.

Nothing, apart from the feel of a muscular thigh. Her left
pocket was likewise empty.

Then he remembered the equipment belt she wore about her
waist. It had many containers. He didn't think he could hold his
breath long enough to check every one of them, but he set to work.

It wasn't in the first, the second, or the third. The fourth contained a vial that felt the same size as the healing potions, which he planned to use on her as soon as he got her to the surface, providing he didn't drown.

I'm definitely not drowning, he vowed to himself.

His lungs strained with effort. He couldn't hold his breath much longer. It would have been wiser, he now knew, to drag her to the surface. If he surfaced, would he be able to get back down and find her again?

An object above blocked the limited light and he made out a man-shaped figure coming toward him. Gombe?

Distracted by the shape, he wasn't watching when his fingers closed on Mirian's drifting hand—and felt not one ring, but two.

Of course! Why would she put the rings in a pouch? He attempted to slide the ring off her finger, only to slip and send it spinning off into the darkness.

Damn! What if that was the one he needed? He quickly found Mirian's other hand. This time he took extra care, touching his fingertip to Mirian's as he slid the ring off of her and onto him.

Emerald fins flared into existence along his arms and over his feet. He risked a breath, and the magic gills about his neck pulled air from the water.

Gombe reached him. Ivrian pointed to the surface and dragged Mirian by one strap. Gombe grabbed the other, and they kicked hard for the surface. As they rose into brighter waters, Ivrian saw the black scorch marks burned through Mirian's blouse and into her flesh

Ivrian surfaced first, remembering to blow the water from his mouth. He removed the healing flask from Mirian's pouch, dug the cork out with his teeth, and poured the liquid into her throat.

Mirian blinked slowly, gagging a little. Ivrian pushed her back under, then looked to Gombe. The right side of the man's shirt had been burned, and the skin there was blistered, but he'd live.

Ivrian surveyed the ship, more than a hundred yards distant. At that very moment, a familiar figure hurtled through the broken window in an expert dive.

Ivrian cursed. Atok was a gillman, born to the water. Ivrian ducked below, trying to pantomime a warning to Gombe and Mirian. Neither of them seemed especially alert.

His eyes fastened upon the wand holster on Mirian's belt.

He'd used it before, back in the jungle. All he had to do was grip it the way Mirian did and whisper the word she used.

She seemed surprised by his sudden proximity, and pushed weakly at him as he took the wand.

"What was the word?" he asked. "Sterak?"

A lance of green acid shot straight out of the end of the instrument and missed his booted foot by a toe length. The energy drifted down and away, a deadly stain in the waters.

Apparently the wand was easier to use than he'd known.

Atok came surging in. Flanking him, one to a side, were the tigers of the sea; finned monstrosities with dagger-sharp teeth and beady eyes.

Ivrian could see the victory in Atok's eyes as the gillman pointed the sharks toward the salvagers.

Ivrian raised the wand. For a brief moment Atok's face registered concern. Then the bolt tore through his face. Even beneath the waves, Ivrian heard the scream of agony. Ivrian blasted him the second time.

The gillman stopped making noise.

Scenting blood, the sharks stopped their charge, circled back, and nudged their master's body.

Gombe touched Ivrian's arm and motioned him away. They grabbed Mirian's arms and swam off many yards, and then Gombe shouted at him underwater. Ivrian had to draw close to understand him.

"Thank you!"

Ivrian nodded. He figured he'd be forever haunted by the sight of that ring drifting slowly into the depths, and his own incompetence in dropping it. A real hero would have managed both the rescue and the retainment of a priceless treasure.

Gombe swam close, so that they could hear each other, though they had to speak slowly and clearly. "What do we do?" he asked. "Where are the others?"

"Back on the ship." Ivrian shook his head. Something must have gone wrong, or they'd have followed instead of Atok. "We need to get to shore. Hire Ijo to take us to Crown's End."

Ivrian looked down at Mirian, who regarded them through hooded eyes that seemed to have trouble focusing. She'd been injured before she'd been blasted out the window, and even a healing potion only did so much.

They'd have to transport her themselves. It would be hard enough going on one's own for three or four miles. And then there was the problem of getting to Crown's End to free their friends, on the off chance Rendak and the lizardfolk were still alive. Both Kellic and Mirian had mentioned Sylena planned to sail there, apparently to visit her sister. Hopefully the woman would stick with her plan.

He'd worry about the rest once they got there.

31

Relative Safety
Ivrian

*I thought that I'd known fatigue and hardship. I was wrong.
Nothing I'd ever done prepared me for that night. The
aching muscles. The constant worry for my friends. The fear
that some terrible predator from the deeps would hunt us.
Between the mental trauma and physical exhaustion, I was
sorely pressed, and to this day I'd be lying if I told you I knew
what it was that drove me on. Was it loyalty? Friendship?
Fear of death? It might even be that I was simply too stubborn and stupid to give up.*

—From *The Collected Writings of Lord Ivrian Galanor*

Either because Gombe lacked a ring or because the salvager
was still injured, Ivrian tired far less swiftly. Yet Gombe never
complained. He insisted they push on, kicking and kicking mile
after mile, surfacing from time to time to keep the shoreline in
focus. There was a frightening moment when Mirian stopped
moving altogether, and they had to surface so Gombe could press
his ear to her chest. Her heart still beat. She was simply spent, too
tired to carry on after multiple injuries, none of them fully healed.

After the first few hours of the swim Ivrian was numb, any
thoughts of sea predators far from his mind. They saw few large
fish, close as they were to the surface. Once a pod of squids the

size of his torso streamed below him in a line, but the odd-looking creatures seemed eager to avoid them.

On and on they swam, until both men were gasping. Their legs and arms were heavy as anchors. They had to stop and drift to clear cramps. With the help of the magical rings and Gombe's air bottle, they couldn't drown, but Ivrian was beginning to think they might well pass out from exhaustion. To make matters worse, he hadn't eaten well for days, and hunger gnawed insistently.

Yet neither man complained. There was too much at stake: Their leader and friend, carried between them. The treasure on their backs that could save a kingdom. Their friends, trapped still in the hands of their enemies.

And so in the late hours of the night they staggered out of the sea and onto a rocky beach, dripping wet and cold. The moon was high, or Ivrian would have stepped right onto a spiky sea urchin. He croaked a warning to Gombe, and then the two swayed like drunkards as they carried Mirian past a little tidal pool and up a rocky beach. They lay her down as gently as they could, then sank together near a palm tree and looked up at the stars.

"By the gods, I'm hungry." Ivrian's voice was hoarse.

"I . . ." Gombe breathed in and out slowly, "used to think . . . a moonlight swim was romantic."

Ivrian considered their surroundings. They'd come ashore a quarter mile from a cluster of huts.

"I never realized how comfortable lying on rocks could be," Gombe said. "If only I weren't so thirsty."

"Come on." Ivrian forced himself to his knees. His legs ached in protest. "We've got to find a healer for Mirian. Find transport. Although perhaps we should stow this treasure."

"Lad," Gombe said without moving in the slightest, "we can't risk this. Let me go in, alone. I've got some Ijo blood. And the Ijo know about the Raas family. Leovan dealt with a lot of villages over the years."

"Then you'd best get moving. It's getting cold, and Mirian needs help."

"Just enjoying the stars a bit."

"Come on!"

"All right, all right." Groaning, Gombe climbed to his feet and staggered toward the huts. Ivrian supposed Mirian knew how to start a fire in the wilderness, but he didn't want to wake her, and was uncertain she'd be capable of instruction even if he did.

His mother could have managed a fire, he was certain. Thinking about her again was like opening a fresh wound, and he forced her from his mind.

Fortunately, Gombe returned with some brawny, broad-backed Ijo before too long. The villagers proved friendly and gregarious—not unlike Gombe himself—and were more than willing to lend aid. Soon they had everyone seated around a fire pit.

The real trick was getting them motivated to lift anchor at night and set out for Crown's End. They thought the idea rash and dangerous, especially given Mirian's condition, and urged delaying until morning, when a healer could be summoned from a nearby village.

But Ivrian insisted, and offered a sapphire in payment. They looked insulted, but went back to fetch a boat anyway.

"What did I say?" Ivrian asked when they were gone.

Gombe shook his head. "Ijo don't need bribes to care for their guests, lad."

"Oh." Ivrian felt a pang of regret about bullying them onto the ocean at night. If he survived all this, he promised himself, he'd see this village further rewarded. Somehow.

The winds were with them. Ivrian was hard put to stay awake for the two-hour trip, but he'd resolved to monitor Mirian the whole way, ensuring she stayed wrapped in blankets. Her terrible shoulder and arm wounds had been sealed by the healing potion, but he was certain the raw, burned skin would have stung terribly if she fully regained consciousness. Once she woke and asked about Kellic, Rendak, Jekka, Kalina—even Heltan. He assured her that they were all alive, and she rose up to look for them before her eyes rolled and she fell back asleep.

Gombe dozed off once or twice, then kept himself awake talking quietly with Ivrian in the bow of the little boat. The four Ijo sailors were busy manipulating the sail and rudder and had little to say in any case, resenting their guests for asking a favor so far beyond what should reasonably have been expected.

"When we arrive," Gombe said, "we'll head to the temple of Iomedae."

The idea surprised Ivrian. "Shouldn't we go straight to the governor?"

"In the middle of the night? And have you seen yourself? I mean, *look* at us. You think any guard is going to let us near the manor house?"

Ivrian looked down at his dripping sleeves, his torn and stained leggings. He'd left his boots drifting in the ocean. He touched his face and felt days of beard growth. And he smelled rather strongly of the ocean. "I suppose you're right." He hadn't thought of any of these particular difficulties. He'd been so fixated on getting to the shore, turning the money over to the governor, and freeing his friends that he had somehow overlooked further challenges.

"My uncle's a priest here," Gombe said. "Of Iomedae. The head priest."

"You're kidding!" The news was like a welcome thunderbolt. Weary as he was, Ivrian felt a surge of energy.

"Oh, yes, a fine joke."

"We'll go to him, get Mirian healed, get cleaned up, then see the governor!"

"Exactly what I was thinking," Gombe said.

"Will the temple even be open?"

"No, but my uncle lives beside it." Gombe looked down at Mirian, stirring fitfully. "It's going to be a long walk up the bluff."

"We can hire a cart."

"At this time of night? This is Crown's End, not Eleder."

They arrived a little before two bells, putting in at the end of one of dozens of long quays where ships were moored. Ivrian supposed that somewhere nearby he'd find Sylena's ship, if he cared to look.

They thanked the Ijo, who gruffly replied that it had been their duty, though they looked none too happy about it. And then Gombe and Ivrian stumbled out onto the dock, supporting Mirian between them.

Despite Gombe's pessimism, they did find a cart for hire, though the halfling who drove it looked dubious until they tendered him a small jewel. Ivrian had nothing else to pay him with. After that, the driver was the soul of courtesy, and conveyed them promptly beyond the port and up the cobblestone road to the little walled town on the cliff.

Iron gates and a stone watchtower guarded the settlement. The soldier on duty waved them past. Just beyond, to the right, was a narrow building of stone, complete with steeple and columns. It was clearly a temple, though the shadows were too deep for Ivrian to discern any further details. The halfling let them off, though he reminded them the temple was closed and suggested a variety of hostelries.

Ivrian thanked him, and then he and Gombe hoisted Mirian between them and trudged past the wide front entrance, diverted to the side and through a sagging metal gate. It creaked as it swung open, and then Ivrian shut it behind them, wincing a little both from the noise and the agony of moving his aching legs.

Gombe was already knocking on the door of the small stone home beside the temple. There was a brief exchange with grumpy servants before the door opened and a bevy of assistance whirled them forward. Mirian was whisked one way, Gombe and Ivrian another. Before long, an old, dignified Mulaa man with rich black skin and short white hair was in earnest discussion with Gombe, promising that Mirian would make a full recovery.

Ivrian rather wished to hear the assurances in more detail, but he was led to where water had been pumped into an austere but immense bathing tub, which he soaked in gratefully before climbing into a set of clean clothes. Afterward, he was taken to a narrow, high-ceilinged dining hall with a long cedar table to behold a wondrous sight: half a cormorant breast on a bed of rice beside a bowl of coconut soup.

Ivrian gratefully dug in. He'd finished off the bird and nearly half the soup, seasoned with lime and filled with chunks of tender crab, before the white-haired fellow entered the room. Ivrian wrestled himself to his feet.

"There's no need for that," the man told him, voice heavy with dignity and age.

Ivrian bowed. "You are a priest of Iomedae."

"And also uncle to Gombe." The older man stepped closer, and Ivrian noticed for the first time that he walked with a limp. He was clothed like a colonial, in tailored pants and a shirt, but wore a colorful red-and-yellow vest, and aged slippers. "From everything I hear, you are a very brave young man." The priest gripped Ivrian's shoulders with two powerful hands and pulled him in close. Startled, Ivrian belatedly grabbed the priest's shoulders.

"My nephew is so tired from what you have endured that he fell asleep sitting upright, but I believe I understand the gist of the matter. My given name is Onwu, and that is what I wish you to call me. I will join you. Please. Eat."

So saying, Onwu pulled out one of the high-backed chairs and lowered himself to the cushion—with some pain, Ivrian thought. After a moment, Ivrian took his seat, his own aches rendering his motion a mirror to the priest's.

"I can't thank you enough for your hospitality, Fath— Onwu. And Mirian is going to be all right?"

"I have personally tended her injuries. She will be fine, so long as she can have rest. Which you need sorely as well. I need be no healer to see that."

A woman he hadn't noticed behind him passed a goblet Ivrian's way, then stepped to hand one to Onwu.

Ivrian drank gratefully. Fermented coconut milk mixed with brandy. Sweet, with a burn at the end. It felt good in his throat.

"You have a warrior's soul," Onwu told him. "To fight sharks. To risk all for your friends."

Ivrian shook his head. "There are people, friends, who still need our help. I've got to speak with the governor and get them off the Chelish ship."

Onwu set the goblet aside. "It is not so simple. You cannot take these treasures you brought to the Icehand."

"Icehand?" Ivrian repeated.

The woman answered, her voice low. "My grandfather means the governor. Ilina Ysande. They call her the Icehand."

Ivrian glanced over at her, but in the poor light he saw only a slim figure in one of the long yellow skirts of the Mulaa, a dark-red blouse hanging over a bare and muscular midriff.

"This is Jeneta, my granddaughter. And she speaks true. The Icehand will take your money. You will have to get it to the baron without her."

"And what about our friends?"

"I've looked into it," Jeneta said. "Three lizardfolk and a single man were sold to the arena by the ship Wayfarer."

"How did you find out so fast?"

"My granddaughter is resourceful," Onwu said. "But this information was not gained as swiftly as you might think. You were long in the bath."

Ivrian put his hand to his head. Fatigue beat at him like a hammer. "Do you know if the man was named Rendak?"

Jeneta turned her head slowly from side to side. "No one remarked upon him, only that he was a murderer. They recalled the lizardfolk."

"Those four are the ones we must ask the governor to free. We don't have to mention the money."

"The governor will not care," Jeneta said. "It's unlikely you'll get them back, particularly if they've been judged."

"Judged?"

"Those presented as criminals to the arena are given a chance to explain their case to a 'judge,'" Onwu explained. "A man who takes a cut from all those brought in for combat. You can guess why he very rarely rules in a victim's favor."

"Then we'll just pay off this man."

"It doesn't work that way. Once past the judge, any prisoners are auctioned to agents who represent the arena stakeholders. You'd have to track down the agent, or the actual owner, and bribe *them*."

Ivrian was too tired for all this complexity. "Surely there's some other way."

Onwu leaned forward, his dark face grimly serious. "As a priest, I could gain entrance to offer final prayers. But getting anyone out is problematic. No guards would accept bribes to release prisoners, not when the wrath of the arena's owners would fall on them."

"Gombe says you have magics that allow you to breathe underwater," Jeneta interrupted.

"Yes," Ivrian said, a little annoyed by the change in topic.

Jeneta continued. "A sewer exit drains from the arena and out into the bay. It's tied to an underground stream. A lot of blood has to be washed out of the arena every week. People have tried to escape that way, but they always drown. With your magic, though, they could live."

Ivrian felt the first flash of hope. "That may be our answer. We have two rings that allow the breathing of water. And an air bottle." He frowned in thought. "Do you know how long the tunnel is?"

"A quarter mile, perhaps? Maybe longer."

"That might be a bit long for the lizardfolk," Ivrian said. "They can hold their breath for a good long while, but they can't breathe underwater." He remembered those eerie green-lit tunnels beneath the ancient city and tried to estimate how long the Karshnaar had gone without surfacing. How far could they swim if pressed to their limit? He couldn't really guess. "It may be our best chance. Onwu, can you get me in to see them?"

"I will take you," the woman declared firmly. She stepped forward, and Ivrian had his first clear sight of her. She was tall and strapping, long-chinned. A bronze headband held back a mass of tightly curled hair from her face.

There was no missing her determination, just as there was no missing her age. He had been deceived by both her height and her low, sonorous voice. She couldn't be much older than sixteen.

Tired as he was, Ivrian's patience was razor thin. Still, he managed politeness. "Lives are at stake," he reminded them. "I mean no offense, Father Onwu, but as head priest you'll have far more authority than your granddaughter. Won't you have better luck getting me in?"

"I will be using my 'authority,' such as it is in this snake pit, to find a legal way to free them. If not, I'll find you a way out of the town. If you must visit them, Jeneta is up to the task. She is a cleric of Iomedae herself."

The girl stepped closer and bowed her head with dignity. "You may have faith in me, young lord."

Ivrian started to object further, but Jeneta cut him off. "Grandfather, the lord looks as though he needs rest."

"I've never been more tired in my life," Ivrian admitted, and it was true—he hadn't been so weary since he'd stayed up for almost forty-eight hours straight writing sonnets to that damned Varisian actor. What a crashing waste of time.

"To bed, then," Onwu said. "May your dreams be blessed. Sore trials lie before you and your friends tomorrow."

32

Death Songs
Sylena

The arms of the vendors hawking meat on a stick and candied nuts were so streaked with filth Sylena couldn't imagine why anyone would purchase anything from the trays they carried. Yet the merchants did a brisk business among the folk in the viewing stands. At least with those who couldn't afford seats beneath the awnings.

She'd been in an arena before, but never one quite like this. It was a huge rectangular structure of old stone. Chipped rock benches swept up in stair-steps on its two longest sides, and one of its smaller. The north side was a raised platform that trailed the Sargavan banner down to the tallest of the barred arena gates. Smaller grilled doors were set into the walls beneath the stands at semi-regular intervals. In the early morning light there was little to be seen through them, but Sylena caught an occasional glimpse of some monstrous eye peering out.

Rajana carried a parasol despite the protection of the sagging crimson awning over their expensive front-row seat. She didn't want to risk any stray rays reaching her arms or neck. Sylena had sneered inwardly the moment her elder sister opened the pretty little thing, but she'd refrained from comment.

Her sister and her smug Garundi bodyguard had been unaccountably quiet all morning.

She addressed Rajana with forced cheer. "How many people are there in Crown's End? I can't possibly imagine how much money it must have taken to build such an arena. It must usually be empty."

Rajana's left eyebrow arched, and she answered coolly. "Perhaps you failed to notice the age of the stone."

Sylena masked her embarrassment with a smile. "This was here before the settlement?"

"Yes. A temple compound, long abandoned. Some accommodation was made in converting it to an arena." An idle hand swept toward the barred openings built into the wall across from them. "I understand that some of the pens were added, and the images of savage gods removed."

Sylena strove for pleasant blandness, her eyes roving over the stadium. "It's hard to believe the crowd could be gathered so early."

"It's hard to believe *any* of us are here so early, isn't it? I'd not expected to have to be here at all, sweating under this ridiculous awning."

Sylena bit back a rejoinder. Rajana didn't have to be here. Her sister worried that Rendak or the lizardfolk might somehow jeopardize their cover in Sargava, despite Sylena's assurances to the contrary.

The more she'd thought about it, the more she realized her only real mistake had been Kellic. Seeing as how she hadn't told Rajana about her plans for him, Rajana could hardly count that as an error. "That's not fair, Sister. We earned plenty of gold for the lizardfolk and the human—"

"A few purses is not 'plenty,'" Rajana corrected. "And selling any of them to the arena, especially a human, was simply stupid. I can't believe it didn't occur to you to search their belongings! Anything carried by Galanor's son or the salvager could have been used to scry the location of their bodies."

"Under fathoms of water," Sylena corrected. "And we don't have any salvagers."

Her sister spoke through gritted teeth. "A king's ransom—no, a *kingdom's* ransom—is lying on the ocean floor! I could have found a way if you hadn't thrown their luggage into the water! You're an idiot."

"I don't think you realize the challenges I've been under."

Rajana's eyes narrowed. "Praise Asmodeus that my superiors know the challenges I'm under, working with you. The little you've brought back will *probably* be enough to pay our extra expenditures, providing I make the right connections back in Cheliax."

"Two bags full of treasure," Sylena countered.

"One of which holds mostly strange carvings, and the other unreadable writing of a useless race. To get any worth from them I'll need to find a collector."

"I think you miss the point, Sister, and are unduly harsh. I thoroughly wrecked the salvager mission, and Lady Galanor and her son are dead. And that money they found will *not* go to the Free Captains. That was the most important goal. Our superiors should be pleased."

"They may be content," Rajana said. "Perhaps enough to let us leave this place for good. I, for one, will be pleased when that day comes."

A trumpet blast sounded.

Sylena, Rajana, and the rest of the crowd turned to face the musician standing on the platform atop the fourth wall. He lowered the trumpet with a flourish and made way for a corpulent colonial in a shiny blue shirt.

The newcomer grinned and spread his arms. "People of Crown's End and visitors, I bid you good morning!" His voice boomed through the arena. "We've quite a spectacle planned today, starting with a very special treat! Your friends will wish they'd gotten out of bed early like you when they see the savage frillbacks who'll be facing one another any moment!"

The crowd stirred, clearly unused to drama in the early slots, which were usually given over to executions. Sylena's heart raced as Rajana turned with burning eyes.

"You said," Rajana said with slow deliberation, "that this Rendak was scheduled for execution first thing."

"That's what I was promised. Believe me, I'm very upset about this. Do you want me to get up and complain?"

"To whom?" Rajana asked icily.

The crowd muttered excitedly as the announcer elaborated on the ferocity and cunning of the frillback warriors they were about to witness in a bitter battle to the death.

The trumpeter stepped forward to blow another fanfare, and then two lizardfolk were forced into the enclosure by the lash of whips. The spokesman continued to stress the untamed savagery of the imminent conflict.

Sylena was too disciplined to sputter, though she very much felt like doing so. Why weren't the human prisoners being introduced first?

Fortunately, the announcer's next words put her at greater ease. "These two will battle to the death, and then the winner will be set loose against the prisoners!"

"Ah." Sylena smiled. "You see, it'll all work out."

"Let's hope so."

Weapons were thrown out from behind the grills, the clack of axes upon swords just audible over the rising bloodlust of the hundred or so spectators scattered through the stands. This early in the morning there were many empty seats yet.

It was the two smaller frillbacks they'd released first. Kellic had told her the one with the smaller snout was a female, although there were no obvious gender differences. Neither wore anything but a long loincloth that hung almost to their knees. Their frills were fully extended, and they stood near one another. The male raised his arms and called out to the people in the stands, saying something about injustice.

"Excellent," Rajana said. "He's bound to mention you soon."

But the first was silenced as the second threw back her head and began a strange chirping, warbling song. The other's head sank, along with his frill, and he plodded toward the weapons.

"Let's get this going!" a man shouted from higher in the stands.

Now the frillback handed a sword off to the singer and began a melody of his own. Their songs sometimes clashed, sometimes met in weird harmony.

It was certainly peculiar, and diverting enough that the catcalls briefly died down.

An old woman in the awning beside theirs put hands to her mouth and shouted: "We didn't come for frillback opera!"

Roars of laughter swept through the viewers, and the announcer cried out to the frillbacks that neither would live unless they got to the fight.

"It's always disappointing when someone underperforms, don't you think?" Rajana asked.

33

Song and Sword
Mirian

She was tired, so very tired, but when Ivrian shook her awake, Mirian's eyes slid open, and she wondered briefly whether she were alive or dead.

Concisely, sharply, the writer conveyed all that had transpired, leaving her little time to marvel over her miraculous survival, and less time to formulate a proper thanks.

Ivrian shook his head at her mumbled gratitude. "I only did what you would have done for any of us, and done better. I'm sorry I lost your ring."

"A ring I thought already lost." Mirian sat up. "Do we still have both wands?"

"We do. And the haversacks with most of the gemstones."

She took stock of her surroundings for the first time. She'd woken in a narrow room with a high window. Wooden carvings hung on all the walls, though the gloom beyond the lantern light rendered all but the nearest indistinct.

"I'm sorry about your brother," Ivrian said. "He tried to save you. Honestly, you'd probably be dead if not for him."

She nodded glumly. In the end, Kellic had proved less than she had hoped and more than she had feared. How was she going to tell their mother?

"I've got to be honest, Mirian. Father Onwu tells me you're fully healed, but you look like you've been dragged through hell. I'm not sure this rescue mission is good for you."

"You don't look that great yourself."

He chuckled with an ease of manner she hadn't seen in him a few weeks ago. "I've been chewing chalva root. I couldn't sleep now if I wanted, though I'm going to be down for a while when the effect wears off."

"Maybe I'll do the same." Mirian threw off the covers and set her feet to the cold, red-tiled floor. She discovered herself in an unfamiliar ankle-length nightgown. "This is the second time I've woken to find someone else has dressed me."

"This time it was definitely women," Ivrian said.

"All the same, I'd rather avoid it in the future. Has any of my clothing survived?"

"Your blouse was ruined. Our hosts have donated another. And some footgear that will probably fit. Oh, and some for Rendak."

It was hard to believe this confident person was the same one she'd left the harbor with. "It seems you planned ahead."

"I knew better than to think you'd stay behind when your people were in danger. Rather," he said after a brief pause, "your team."

"No one gets left behind." The memory of Tokello dropping into that churning water was overlain by Lady Galanor chewed in half by the drake. Swept by anguish, she closed her eyes and prayed to her ancestors for calm. At least the gods had seen fit that she not witness Kellic's death.

When she opened her eyes, she found Ivrian rubbing a hand back through his hair. It was an unguarded moment, and there was no missing the fatigue and grief etched there. She wasn't the only one who'd suffered loss. She reached out and squeezed his hand. "Your mother would be proud of you."

He flashed a smile that showed even teeth. He'd grown gaunt in the last weeks.

"Come." Mirian pushed to her feet.

Garbed in the white-and-gold robes of Iomedae, driven in a coach emblazoned with the sigil of the warrior goddess's sword, Mirian, Ivrian, and tall, spare Jeneta left for the arena. The golden tropic sun swept up over the ocean and threw long shadows before them.

Mirian had never been to the arena in Crown's End. It was apparently part of a wider circuit, the dubious crown jewel of which was a pit fight held somewhere in the Shackles. There, monsters and oddities were thrown against each other before cheering crowds. At many outlying arenas, like the one in Crown's End, creatures were pitted against criminals intended as practice targets, though there were a few warriors who earned glory weeding out lesser monsters.

The arena itself was an ancient stone structure resembling Kalabuto's temples, though there were certain architectural oddities Mirian would have gladly examined some other time. The town's folk of Crown's End were already filing in for the dawn showing, where prisoners were usually put to death prior to a day of bloodshed punctuated by musical interludes.

Mirian knew Rendak was probably slated for execution in this opening event, and it was all she could do to remain silent, hood shadowing her face, while Jeneta spoke with the pair of surly guards at the side gate.

They proved less than receptive. "Sister, these murderers don't want any word from Iomedae." The broken-nosed guard picked at a tooth with a dirty fingernail.

Jeneta's response was solemn. "Iomedae's call is insistent."

"She can insist all she wants," the other guard said, laughing. He was a light-skinned Ijo man, probably of mixed blood, his dyed hair a bright yellow.

"Perhaps this insistence is more to your liking." Jeneta extended her hand and turned up her palm to reveal a small coin purse. "A donation to your fraternal organization."

The blond laughed while his companion took it and peered inside. "Well, well. Looks like maybe you can save some souls, if you hurry. Normally I don't like to rush in the mornings, but I'm feeling pretty thankful for your fraternal generosity and all."

"Especially thankful," said the blond to his comrade, "so long as you remember me."

Broken-nose grunted, then unlocked the gate behind him and motioned the trio to follow. They were led into the corridors below the arena, where they were greeted by an astonishing mixture of aromas, none of them pleasant. Strange beasts growled and hooted in the distance.

"You're in luck," their escort said over his shoulder. He carried a battered lantern in one hand, and it shined on the pitted stonework floor as they walked. "Usually the humans are the first ones out and there'd be no one to pray for. But we got in a troupe of bloodthirsty frillbacks last night, and we're letting them entertain the crowd. Shake things up a little, you know?"

Mirian felt her nostrils flare and her voice rose. "You mean the lizardfolk are already on the arena floor?"

"Out or on the way." The guard stopped before a long span of rusty metal bars, and the scent of unwashed humanity increased. He lifted the lantern and shined it into a mass of men blinking in the sudden onslaught of light. A dozen of them huddled against the walls.

"On your feet, boys! I've been paid good coin to get your souls saved by Iomedae!"

Mirian spotted Rendak immediately. He sat rubbing his eyes with a grubby hand. Shirtless, dirty, disheveled, he looked little different from his companions.

"We want a word alone," Mirian said.

"I can't do that, I'm afraid."

Up top, Mirian heard the roar of the crowd and a flare of trumpets. At any moment her friends were going to be released into the arena, against what the gods only knew what monstrosity.

It was time to improvise.

She drew the wand without really thinking. The guard stared at it, then reached for his hilt. Ivrian grabbed his arm.

The guard was far stockier than Ivrian and easily fought him off, but in the intervening moment Jeneta stepped forward and thumped him on the side of the head. He staggered, and in an instant the priestess had him pressed to the bars, left arm raised between his shoulder blades.

The guard gasped in pain. "You're no priestess!"

Jeneta gave Mirian a dark look. She had specifically asked that no violence be done to the guards.

"No one has to die." Mirian took the guard's sword. "So long as you have sense."

In moments the prisoners were milling in the corridor and Ivrian told them to make their way out through any exit they could. Likely there were real convicts among them, but Mirian had no time for niceties, and she hoped their escape would add to the confusion. She ordered the guard to pull off his shirt and armor before she locked him up, then ordered Rendak into the garb.

The salvager stared wide-eyed at them as he dressed. "I can't believe you're alive! Did Gombe make it?"

"He did." Mirian started to say more, but she heard a plaintive, soaring melody from the arena above. By now she recognized the birdlike sound of a lizardfolk song, and guessed its meaning.

"What's that?" Ivrian asked.

"A lizardfolk death song." Mirian cursed and searched the surrounding halls, which stretched darkly in every direction beyond the pale pool of lantern light. The rest of the prisoners had already run on. "Damn it! Which way to the arena?" She spotted a faint light to what she assumed was the north, nodded to herself even as Rendak was spoke.

"Mirian," Rendak said soberly, "it's too late for them. What can you do?"

"Oh, I'm good at distractions. Ivrian, give me your ring."

He pulled it off. "You'll need help—"

"Get out. Get Gombe and get the jewels to Eleder. We'll follow if we can. Meet us where the tunnels empty. Just like we planned.

Mirian left them with the lantern and hurried toward the distant light, and the death song of a people.

34

Blood in the Sands
Sylena

The crowd pitched meat and fruit at the frillbacks, booing and hissing, and guards deployed along the wall leveled crossbows and shouted threats at the creatures, who continued their song.

"At least they haven't said anything," Rajana said.

The frillbacks brandished their swords at the crowd.

One of the guards along the bank shouted a command, and a crossbow bolt thudded into the thigh of the male frillback. He shouted and threw his sword almost to the top of the fourteen-foot wall.

There was a trumpet blast and the disgruntled crowd shifted its attention to the harried-looking announcer. "You wanted killer lizards? Well, I'll give you one! A thunder lizard from the savage, beating heart of the Mwangi Expanse!"

The large gate directly beneath the speaker's stand ground open and a yellow-and-green-striped lizard twice the height of a man stalked out, upright on huge clawed feet. Its great head swiveled to examine the arena and the crowd. Its maw opened to reveal sword-length teeth.

And then it caught scent of the frillbacks, roaring a low, deafening challenge, and trotted forward, its clawed front arms twitching.

"This will be the end of them," Sylena said. Below, the male frillback limped for the wall where his sword lay. The thunder lizard hooted and dashed at him.

The female dove, waving her own sword, but the beast paid no heed. Just as the male frillback turned, sword raised, the monster's great maw swept down over his head and chest. The frillback's rib cage disintegrated in a single pulverizing blow. The beast lifted him into the air and blood sprayed into the stands. Women screamed.

The female frillback roared defiance. She ran forward and slashed the front of the monster's leg.

It let out a choking roar, dropping the half of the frillback body it hadn't swallowed, and swept its tail at the female, who threw herself aside.

"Yes, yes," the spokesman cried from his platform. "We try to find you only the bravest here at the Crown's End Arena. It seems the first frillback was a lover, not a fighter. Too bad for him, eh? But we have more surprises in store for you today. Much better surprises. Feast your eyes on this!"

The female dived to the left before one huge foot could stomp her to paste. The great head snapped at her, missed.

"Don't think we just mean to have you watch the creature eat! No! For you see, we have *another* frillback. A killer among killers! A man-eater! Think what he'll do when confronted by the beast who slew his nestmate!"

And the third lizard man stumbled into the arena—the problematic one they'd called Jekka. They'd given him the strange axe the female had carried. He held it in his left hand. In his right he bore the frillback staff, a scythe-like blade attached.

Jekka's tongue snaked out and his mouth widened to reveal sharp teeth. His skin color darkened and spots of red appeared among dark green scales as his frill rose. He let out a low growl.

The thunder lizard snorted at the sound and turned. Its tale whipped into Kalina and sent her flying into a wall. She struggled to rise.

Jekka trotted forward as if he meant to meet the monster head-on.

"Look at his daring!" the speaker cried. "This one's no coward!"

The thunder lizard's attention was distracted by the crowd's cheers, and it raised its head to snuffle along the arena rim. By straining, its small eyes could just see over the top, presumably finding the noisemakers of great interest. Sylena knew a tingle of fear as it stepped within ten feet.

Jekka ran on, lifting one of the weapons. Sylena was a little startled to see it had changed from a scythe to a spear. How had that happened?

The frillback was looking at her.

No. Surely it studied the thunder lizard, which had finally turned to face him with a roar that shook the stands. The crowd shouted approval.

Jekka released the spear, but the cast flew wide of the monster's head. It was a terrible throw, arcing up over the stands, up—

"Atok!" she screamed. It was pure reflex, because she *knew* Atok was dead. It was just that he had been there for so many years to shield her.

Rajana's black-clad bodyguard put his hand to her shoulder and leapt onto the railing, knocking the spear aside with a sheathed sword. The spear clattered harmlessly along the stony bench.

Sylena gasped in horror and shoved her sister's bodyguard aside, peering over the rim. Unfortunately, the monster completely blocked her line of sight.

"Sister," Rajana hissed. "Get down! Get back! You'll call attention to yourself!"

"I want to see him die!" Sylena leaned out and to the left, far enough that she could just see the frillback sprinting. The thunder lizard pursued, its footfalls shaking the walls, head thrust forward to snap Jekka in half.

Suddenly a huge, white-furred ape thing with four arms climbed out of an open cage door. It reared back and beat its great chest with two of its fists.

The thunder lizard growled and halted to consider the new development. Jekka bolted clear.

The crowd murmured in puzzlement, and Sylena glanced at the speaker, who was in frantic consultation with a red-robed official. Clearly the events weren't going according to plan for anyone.

Two rhinos charged onto the field, the sun gleaming from scythe blades fitted over their horns, and the crowd shouted in joy. It looked like things were shaping up for a bloodbath.

Sylena leaned down and picked up the lizard man's spear, ignoring her sister's demands that she stop making a spectacle. Jekka was in plain view. If he got close enough, she wouldn't even have to wait for something else to kill him.

And then she heard her name, shouted from below. She looked down.

Impossibly, Mirian Raas stood directly beneath, alive and well and pointing a wand. As the glowing emerald bolt streamed for Sylena, she almost managed a scream.

But then the bolt struck her face. Wailing through her ruined mouth, she lost her balance and plummeted to the arena floor.

35
The Thing at the Shoreline
Mirian

She blasted the nearest guard in the face. As he dropped to the hallway floor, Mirian brandished her sword at the other. She'd hoped he'd back away, but these men were professionals, armed and armored, and he apparently thought he stood a good chance against a woman in a robe.

She parried high in his swing, shouted the wand's activation word, and sent him clawing at his bubbling neck.

She'd never get used to what the weapon did to people. She stepped past the dying man and depressed the lever in the pillar beside him before finishing him off with a merciful thrust. The cage opened into the arena, and the two large rhinos tramped out into the rectangle of sunlight, pawing and snorting, swinging their metal-tipped horns left and right. The moment they were gone, Mirian used the jailer's keys to open the pen and enter the stinking enclosure.

She'd already opened one cage to set loose a huge, four-armed white gorilla. Between the monsters she released outside and the prisoners she'd freed within, chaos reigned. She hadn't even been challenged until she arrived at the rhino pen.

She worried about setting such dangerous monsters loose in the arena with her friends. But without a distraction, they had no hope at all.

Now, as she peered out the open doorway, she saw the gorilla turning to roar at one rhino even as the thunder lizard chased another. She looked up along the rim, and that was when Desna truly smiled, for who should she see but her brother's murderer.

"Sylena!" she cried.

The moment that pale face looked down at her, she blasted. The wretched woman fell screaming, landing with a crunch six feet to Mirian's left. Even over the rest of the arena noise, Mirian could hear the sizzle of the acid as it ate away at Sylena's face.

For once she felt no pity for a victim of the weapon's work.

"Jekka!" she shouted. "Jekka, over here! Kalina!" She'd spotted the lizard woman limping along the side of the enclosure, hand pressed to one arm.

But Jekka still hadn't seen, or heard. He was running from the thunder lizard, which seemed to have caught the attention of the four-armed gorilla. Closer at hand, one of the rhinos saw something it didn't like and swept its head low to gore Sylena's body. It flipped her into the air, and Mirian realized in horror that the woman was still alive in the brief moment before she hit the arena floor and was thoroughly trampled by the rhinoceros. The crowd seemed uncertain what to make of that particular spectacle, for there were both enthusiastic shouts and screams of terror.

Kalina reached the doorway, and Mirian saw blood trickling from both her arm and her thigh. "Go on," Mirian urged, "get out! Where's Heltan?"

"Dead! Mirian, what are you doing?"

Mirian pushed Kalina toward the open gate. Jekka still hadn't seen her. She lowered her wand and fired again. The acid spray hit the sand just past Jekka's shoulder, right at the foot of the four-armed gorilla.

She had Jekka's attention finally, but had to fire once more to distract the thunder lizard as it lunged for a bite. Mirian tagged it in the snout and it lifted its head to growl in pain.

"Jekka!" Mirian waved from the open gateway, and the lizard man turned on his heel, sprinting at full speed. He fell as the gorilla slapped him with one of its hands, but tumbled to his feet and kept running. Thankfully, the monster seemed more interested in challenging the thunder lizard and pushed into it with a demented scream of fury.

Jekka was almost there when Mirian smelled brimstone.

She whirled, sidestepped to avoid the bite from the massive, flaming hound with burning eyes that had appeared beside her.

Mirian had neither the time nor energy to care who had summoned the thing. It caught her sword slice with its burning maw and tore the weapon from her grasp.

Jekka charged in with Kalina's laumahk. His was a mighty blow, backed up by the momentum of his long sprint, and sheared through the creature's side. The flaming hound opened its mouth to howl as Kalina turned back and ran it through one burning flank.

Mirian rushed past, the wounded lizardfolk following. She heard the devil hound shamble after, moaning in something between pain and ecstasy.

With Kalina and Jekka beside her, she slammed home the bar on the pen. "Come on!"

She scanned her friends in the light trickling through the bars. Jekka looked to be in better shape, though a crossbow quarrel stuck out of one shoulder and a shallow claw mark stretched across his chest.

Kalina bled from half a dozen wounds, and there was a chunk carved out of her shoulder. Mirian fumbled with her hand and slipped the extra water-breathing ring onto the lizard woman. "You may need this. To breathe underwater."

"Mirian." Kalina breathed heavily, as though she were working up energy to say something.

"No time." Mirian led them around a corner toward the largest floor grate only to find a squad of spear- and torch-bearing guards running their way. They ducked back as a spear clattered past.

"You came back for us," Jekka said. He laid a clawed hand, softly, upon her shoulder. "But I think we will die together."

"Not yet, damn it." They raced past where the devil hound pushed against the door to the rhino pen, howling at sight of them. She was sure she'd seen a smaller grating.

There.

Just beyond the guards she'd slain lay a rusted metal grill through which dark water gleamed. She bent to it. Jekka dropped with her and the two gripped it by the bars and hauled.

The grating was exceptionally heavy. She heard something pop. It wasn't her back, though, but rather one of the bars bending in the hound's pen.

Mirian lowered the wand and fired, three times in succession. The first shot didn't work, but the other two opened a steaming gap in the grill.

The guards rounded the corner.

Jekka planted his feet wide, swept a spear from the air with the laumahk.

The hound roared, and the door to its pen slammed open.

"Go!" Mirian shouted at Kalina. The lizard woman dropped through, narrowly missing the steaming acid.

"You go!" Jekka sent another spear clattering. "I'll be right behind!"

The guards at the end of the hallway screamed at the appearance of the flaming, howling hound as Mirian dropped through the sizzling grate. Too late she remembered the air bottle she'd tucked into a pocket of the robe. She'd meant to hand it to Jekka, but under the constant assault there'd been no time.

She hoped he'd be able to hold his breath.

The old stone tunnel was even worse than she'd imagined. It sloped down and away, completely unlit and filled with not just water but offal. She didn't want to breathe the stuff, so she held her breath as long as she could and let the current carry her.

It wasn't very wide, either. She kept brushing her hand against the wall. Fearful that she'd damage or lose the wand, she thrust it inside its housing on her belt. The movement sent her off course, and she bashed her head against an old stone. At the same moment she heard a shattering noise and knew the air bottle had broken.

If she hadn't been wearing the rings of her ancestors then, she would have drowned, for she was stunned and dizzy. The water didn't taste quite as foul as it smelled, but she found herself coughing anyway. She could hear nothing now but the rush of water on stone, and she wondered if the young priestess had really known where this spillway led. Suppose she were merely descending deeper and deeper into the bowels of the world?

And had Jekka come with her? Did he trail yet, or had he sacrificed himself so they could escape?

There was a burst of light, and suddenly she was sliding into open water. Salt water. She swam up toward the light, then saw movement below her. She turned to find Kalina struggling away from a clawed, slime-coated creature like a man-sized crab.

Mirian kicked toward her friend and struggled to free her wand. The monster released Kalina to float in a cloud of blood and pushed up—not toward Mirian, but toward Jekka, out now and straining for the surface. The beast stretched with its two great claws and the writhing mass of tentacles that extended from its mandibles. She heard it chittering in excitement as it closed.

Mirian finally put hand to wand as the creature grabbed Jekka's left leg in a huge pincer. Jekka swung desperately with the laumahk.

He missed, and the scavenger's tentacles brushed his tail.

The lizard man went limp, drifting helplessly as the creature pulled him toward its maw.

Mirian shouted the activation word, but the damnable wand didn't fire. Just when she thought she was getting better with the thing. Was it out of charges?

Kalina swam in and stabbed the thing's eyes with her fingers. The scavenger dropped Jekka and lashed out at the lizard woman with both tentacles and claws. Blood gushed from the lizard woman's side.

Mirian caught the sinking Jekka and wrestled the laumahk from his stiff fingers.

The monster had three or four hundred pounds on her, and was born to move in the water. But because of her second ring, she could move just as naturally.

At last, a fair fight.

The monster abandoned the motionless lizardfolk and churned after her. She swung Kalina's weapon two-handed and slashed into the hideous tentacles. The monster pulled up short.

But even though the dreadful wound released ichor, the beast was undeterred. It stretched toward her with snapping claws. Mirian kicked away, risking a glance back at Jekka and Kalina, who still floated motionless. Ancestors, she thought, give me strength to save my friends. If she didn't move fast, Jekka would drown, and Kalina might be dead already.

She bit deep with her second swipe of the laumahk, but then the beast wrenched the weapon from her hands. She backpedaled, lifted the wand, and commanded it to fire.

And again she failed.

With a powerful surge of its back legs, the scavenger swept in. She pulled away, but the tip of the claw snipped her shoulder. Blood billowed, and she knew pain as well as raw panic as the tentacles stretched for her face.

She had overestimated her own competence, and now she and Jekka and Kalina were all finished.

No. She raised the wand until the tip of it actually touched one of the tentacles. The creature grasped the weapon's end even as it received the blast of green acid.

The creature let out a high-pitched wail and swam backward. Mirian fired again, and again and again as it attempted retreat, until at last the weapon stopped responding.

The monster moved only spasmodically. Mirian shook herself to life, kicked up to Jekka. She tried not to think about the thing below, and how it might recover and rush up to slice her feet off at the ankles.

She reached her friend, grabbed him by the hands, swam to the surface. She pushed his head into the air.

The steep, rocky shoreline lay only ten feet off. With her hand beneath Jekka's chin to keep his face above the water, she kicked to it, then dragged him out across the rough stones, past a cluster of mangroves.

There she rolled him onto his stomach, wrapped hands about him, gripped fingers in a double-fist just above the muscular solar plexus, and pushed. Her shoulder throbbed in agony, but she pushed again.

He coughed up water once, twice, then groaned. He struggled to his knees, hands flat on the sandy soil, and vomited more water as Mirian beat his back with the flat of her hand.

He waved her off and continued to cough water. She turned, steeled herself, and dove after Kalina.

The monster was as motionless as the paralyzed lizard woman. Mirian tried not to focus on the deep gouge through Kalina's chest. She grasped her under the chin, near the point where magical gills glowed, and swam for the shore.

Somehow, she reached it. Gasping from pain and exertion, she dragged Kalina by the arms over to her cousin, then stood panting, hands on knees. She considered the enormity of the lizard woman's wounds. The pale green of her scales.

Kalina wasn't moving. Wasn't blinking.

"She's dead," Jekka said weakly. He had climbed to one knee.

Mirian shook her head. "Paralyzed. Like you."

"No, Mirian," he told her, gently.

Was he right? No. Kalina had simply taken a larger hit from the creature's paralyzing tentacles.

Mirian was no healer, but she knew how to take a pulse. She threw herself down beside the lizard woman, sucking in a painful breath as a clam shell dug into her thigh. She pressed her ear to Kalina's chest.

Nothing. But maybe lizardfolk hearts were located in a different place.

She put her hand to Kalina's neck. Did they have the same big vein as humans? They were built on similar lines. "Where do you take pulses? Jekka?"

Jekka joined her and spoke quietly. "If her heart worked, her open wounds would still spout blood."

Gods. He was right. Mirian stared down at the graying lizard woman, sank back on her haunches.

She was too stunned even to cry. "I don't understand. The ring should have allowed her to breathe."

"She was too badly hurt."

Mirian was cool, dripping with water, and she stank all over. But these were minor irritants, like the bites of insects. She rose, scanning the ocean beyond the spindly legs of the mangroves. She spotted her wand among the rocks by the shore and numbly stepped out to grab it before a low wave swelled in.

When she returned, she found Jekka sitting beside his cousin.

"Mirian," he said softly, "what happened to Salvager Rendak?"

"He got out. And Ivrian and Gombe live. My brother is dead."

"Your brother. He worked with our betrayers."

"He was weak, and foolish. But he died trying to protect me."

Jekka nodded. "My brother, too, was less than I wished."

"Yours watched out for his own clan, at least."

"Writer Ivrian's mother might be alive if my brother had warned her. It wasn't just."

"Like I said. Heltan was just looking out for his family."

Jekka hissed. "You defend him? You, who looked out for all of us. Past race. Past clan."

"I was your leader."

"You came to save us, when our bargain was finished. Why did you come, Mirian?"

"Because it was my brother's fault."

"So it was your duty."

She tried not to think of the still form beside them that had been so full of vivacity and charm. "My clan failed you. Now let me see that arm. We should get the crossbow quarrel out. And keep our eyes sharp for Ivrian. He'll be coming after us."

Mirian took the knife from its sheath and reached for his arm.

Jekka, though, seemed uninterested in letting her examine the limb. He kept it stiff beside him, and she frowned at the bruised ring where the bolt stood out from his fine scales.

"What will I do now?" His eyes were wide and bright as they met her own. "Where will I go?"

The quarrel, she saw, was lightly embedded, and judging by the feel of the scaled skin, she didn't think it was barbed. "You're lucky. This could have torn straight through your arm."

It occurred to her that if she were to cut out the bolt, they'd need bandages. The only cloth anywhere nearby was on her and the lizardfolk, none of which was clean.

"There's no point, Mirian." Jekka reached up and put a hand on her arm. "You work too hard to save me. There's nothing left."

"What do you mean?"

"I have no clan. I have no brother or sister or cousin. What am I to do?"

She stared into those inhuman eyes and saw their pain, their loss. She felt tears form in her own, and put her hand to her wounded arm. When it was wet with blood, she pressed her fingers to the crimson gash across Jekka's chest. He gasped in pain, his tongue sliding out in astonishment.

"Put your blood to mine," she said.

Hesitant, Jekka dragged his fingers through that same wound, showing his teeth in a grimace, then touched scarlet-stained fingers to Mirian's shoulder injury.

"Our blood is mingled," Mirian said. "Now *I* will be your sister."

Jekka stared. Slowly, his head bobbed up and down. "You *are* my sister. And I am your brother."

Mirian's wiped tears away with a bloody hand. "And right now your sister's got to get our wounds bandaged. And then we've got to rendezvous with the rest of our friends."

"And then?"

"Then we get the treasure back to Sargava."

"Will your people want me in Sargava?"

"I don't even think my people want *me* in Sargava, Jekka. But I'm a Raas, and the land is mine. And you're my brother. So to hell with them."

36

Wheels and Vigils
Ivrian

*Against all odds, we had dragged Mirian Raas from the surf
alive, so you can imagine my reluctance to let her dash off to
almost certain doom. But what was I to do? At that point,
the jewels were my responsibility, as was Rendak's survival. I
had little choice but to obey her orders and lead the others to
the exit, hoping our luck would hold.*
—From The Collected Writings of Lord Ivrian Galanor

Four men in guard armor hurried down the steps into the arena's
lower level just as Ivrian arrived with Jeneta and Rendak.

"The prisoners have escaped," Rendak said. "I'm escorting the
priests to safety."

The scarred fellow in the lead nodded as they hurried past.
From somewhere nearby came an ear-rattling roar.

Ivrian and the others were up the stairs and almost to the open
doorway, a rectangle of light more welcome than a lover's touch,
when he heard the shout behind him.

"That's not a guard!"

Ivrian turned to find all four guards halted at the foot of
the stairs. The imitation blond from the side gate was pointing
to Rendak while the other three turned. "He's not wearing any
shoes!"

Rendak lifted a dirty bare foot and laughed. "Come on, Sister!"
He charged with Jeneta up through the doorway. Ivrian bolted

after, whirled to see the onrush of the guards, and slammed the door as the pursuit was still halfway up the stairs. He looked in vain for the board that should have been nearby to bar it closed. Jeneta and Rendak ran on.

Ivrian spied a heavy table strewn with cards, leapt it. He shoved the table at the door, gaining momentum with every step. Three feet out, the door started to swing open, a hand gripping its edge.

The heavy table struck the door, slamming it shut with a heavy thud. There was a long wailing scream from its other side. Ivrian winced in sympathy. He really hadn't meant to hurt anyone.

He turned and raced after his friends. Once in the sun, he joined a stream of frightened Sargavans fleeing the arena. Jeneta and Rendak dashed for the small carriage emblazoned with the golden-haloed sword of Iomedae.

Jeneta threw the door open for the limping salvager, who clambered inside, then hopped after and turned to reach down for Ivrian. As soon as his feet were inside, she knocked on the carriage wall, shouting for the driver to go.

They heard the crack of the carriage whip and the vehicle lurched forward.

"How far is it?" Ivrian asked, panting.

"Down past the harbor." Jeneta eyed Ivrian keenly.

"I'm sorry about how that went," he said. "If there'd been some other way—"

"I'll have to leave Crown's End." She sounded matter-of-fact. "You didn't tell me your friend was a madwoman."

"Mirian's not mad," Ivrian objected.

"She has little chance, but I salute her bravery. We should all hope to have friends as loyal, some day."

"Amen, sister." Rendak pushed his lank dark hair back from his forehead, struggling to render himself more presentable. "I'm Rendak, by the way. Thank you for your help."

The young woman nodded, her long face the picture of dignity. "I am Jeneta."

"No offense, Jeneta," Rendak said, "but Mirian's going to make it. You don't know her."

Another nod. "I hope you're right."

The cart jounced and bounced down the steep road, and Ivrian peered fitfully through the curtains as they drew near the harbor. The driver advanced at a more leisurely pace through the port. They passed mule teams pulling cargo wagons, and strolling sailors, their occupation obvious from their rolling gaits.

"Is it just me," Ivrian asked, "or does everyone here look like a pirate?"

"If you're looking to find something, no questions asked," Rendak said, "Crown's End's your best bet."

"It's a snake pit," Jeneta said. "It will be a pleasure to leave this place. Though I will miss Grandfather."

"You can come with us, if you like," Ivrian volunteered.

"Where will you go? To Eleder?" Jeneta shook her head. "I would have no place there."

"You can have any room in my mansion."

The woman considered him for a moment, as if wondering whether he were serious. "You're a generous man, Lord Galanor."

Him, a lord! He laughed a little, but said nothing. All he could think about were his friends. Could Mirian really pull the lizardfolk out of the arena and escape with them alive? It would have seemed impossible. And yet they'd done a dozen impossible things in the last weeks.

Down one quay he spotted what he thought were the masts of Sylena's ship. He couldn't help wondering if their other treasures remained aboard, and if there were some way to get them back, but he supposed he was already asking for too many miracles just to get Mirian and the lizardfolk out alive. He closed his eyes and offered a prayer to Shelyn. When he opened his eyes he discovered Jeneta staring at him.

"You were praying."

"Yes."

"A wise idea," she said. "Your friends need all the luck the gods can give."

"Aye," Rendak said glumly.

Jeneta bent her head and began speaking in her native tongue.

The cobblestones ended abruptly, and the carriage thumped onto a road now consisting solely of packed dirt.

On the carriage rolled, jolting and thrashing them thoroughly before it finally stopped. The driver called to them: "Sister, the road pretty much ends here. The bay's about a quarter mile through those mangroves."

Ivrian and Rendak hopped out. The younger man reached into his robes to free the wand Mirian had given him.

A forest of tropical foliage stood in the sun, leafy upper limbs waving in a breeze. The water was gray and choppy.

The driver, a curly-haired Mulaa man, tipped his dented brown hat and pointed. "If your friends made it, they're somewhere in there."

"Ivrian," Rendak said, "you stay here and watch for pursuers. I'll go in and see what I can find."

"I'm coming with you."

"If they did make it out, and anyone saw how they exited, they'll send riders to follow. We need someone to stand guard. And you've got that wand."

Ivrian looked back along the dirt track. The view of the harbor and the city was blocked by a mass of palm trees and an intervening hill. "All right. Good luck, Rendak."

"It's our friends who need the luck, lad. My part's easy."

Ivrian watched the sturdy older man stride into the mangroves, still limping slightly, and briefly wondered how he could ever have thought to judge in one glance what a hero looked like.

He turned to the driver and the priestess, to whom he gave a polite nod. "I'm going to go watch from that hill." He indicated it with a vague wave and started to climb.

37

Meeting of Minds
Rajana

Guards had surrounded her as she left the arena carrying the lizardfolk staff. The first two Rajana restrained with a tentacle spell, but she recognized the blue livery of the governor on the next three, and saw others rushing to back them up. It would still be easy enough to escape—she never left her quarters without a scroll of teleportation for just this sort of event—but she decided there might be some profit in allowing them to escort her.

She was glad now that she had, for after listening to them talk, she understood exactly how to get what she needed.

She stood with her bodyguard, Narsial, in a cluttered arena office. Seated at the table across from her, flanked by two brawny guards, was the Icehand herself, a pockmarked woman with brilliant blue eyes. Her clothes were finely tailored but mannish, half hidden by well-tended ring mail. She must be suffocating in this heat, Rajana thought.

A pale, balding colonial with yellow eyes stood at the governor's side. Rajana had waited patiently while the Icehand listened to the reports of the arena officials. They had laid the expensive destruction at the feet of the man who'd purchased the lizardfolk, and, through him, her foolish sister. And thence to her. Along with several of the governor's guards, two stout arena men, middle-aged merchants encumbered by an excess of rings and necklaces, waited nervously to one side as the Icehand mulled over her response.

"How interesting," she said when she was through with her questions at last. She gestured toward one of the arena men. "While Gordof here is a sniveling coward who'd sell out his own mother to suck up to me, Nalden assures me he's telling the truth."

The advisor's unsettling yellow eyes focused squarely upon Rajana. This must be Nalden, then. A priest of some kind, Rajana surmised, for he'd apparently thrown a lie-detection spell. That might make matters more challenging.

"This all means," the Icehand continued, "that the fee for this incident falls squarely upon your shoulders."

Rajana shook her head. "I can hardly be blamed if your people didn't take better charge of the prisoners they purchased. And lest we forget, I was not involved in the arrangements. Those were made by my poor sister, who perished in the events herself."

"I can tell you're pretty broken up about it."

"I find profound displays of emotion vulgar."

Icehand grunted and crossed her arms. "I think you'll find what I'm about to say very vulgar, then. Rajana, is it?"

"Correct."

"Well then, Rajana, perhaps you can explain how someone dressed as a priestess of Iomedae came in to free these prisoners of yours?"

"I don't know anything about that."

The yellow-eyed man leaned close to the Icehand and spoke, low-voiced. "Her confusion is genuine."

"They had outside help," the Icehand went on. "Someone got them free, and you can bet someone was waiting to pick them up when they got out of the tunnels. They'll be long gone by the time the lazy-ass arena guards finally remember where the drain empties." She waggled her finger at Rajana. "I'm guessing this means you know who that somebody is, and that you know a lot more about what's going on than you've told me."

"I do."

The Icehand leaned forward and steepled her hands on the desk. "Why don't we dispense with the bilge water and cut right to the good stuff. Who were these prisoners, really?"

"They were doing some work with my sister," Rajana answered calmly. "Some salvage work, and they had a falling-out. Sylena was less accustomed to holding her temper than I, and when things went badly, she sold them into slavery. I would have had them killed."

Icehand glanced to Nalden.

"She's speaking truth," he relayed.

More or less, Rajana thought. She knew how lie-detection spells worked. So long as she kept certain answers broad, she could maneuver the conversation as she wished.

"Let's get to specifics. What kind of work were they doing for your sister?"

"They were salvagers." Rajana thought quickly. "And there was a great deal of money involved."

"How much?"

Rajana smiled. "How much do you trust your guards?"

"Any of these here would die for me. They know what I'd do to them if I didn't like it. Answer my question."

"I will. I just think it would behoove you to consider the rest of the people listening and realize what I'm about to tell you really shouldn't be shared with anyone who isn't a close confidant."

The Icehand glared at her, but Rajana refused to look away. Finally, the governor muttered a foul curse. "Gordof, Mirok, piss off." She pointed to the guards. "You two, outside as well. But Rajana's guard has to go, too."

The arena stakeholders departed, though they looked reluctantly over their shoulders. Rajana's bodyguard eyed her questioningly. She gave him a nod.

He was the last one out, closing the door after the Icehand's guards had left.

"I already know you can cast spells, Rajana," Icehand went on. "So here's a heads-up: I have any number of protections on me. You try anything fancy, and you'll find it real hard explaining it away with your throat slit."

Rajana made a sour face.

"Told you I was vulgar. Which is why I'll come right out and ask you a question. Are you a Chelish agent?"

Rajana froze.

The governor waved a hand. "Don't bother trying to find some half-truth. There are a dozen ways to get around a lie-detection spell, and I know them all. So now that we've cleared *that* up, why not tell me why Cheliax is interested in salvaging from our waters? There must be a lot of gold involved."

Rajana made herself smile. "Very astute, Governor. But it's not gold—rather, a hoard of gems. Enough to buy a small city. Or ransom a kingdom."

Icehand's eyes widened at that.

"Three allies of the prisoners went overboard during the dispute with my sister. They were far from shore, and she assured me they drowned, because two were badly wounded."

"You think your sister was wrong," the Icehand guessed.

"Yes. Two had equipment that allowed them to breathe underwater. I believe at least one of them made it back. Which means some of the treasure made it back with her."

"Underwater breathing, huh?" The Icehand checked with her advisor, who nodded at her. "All right. Go on."

"Who else would have known what my sister had done with the salvaging team? Or cared enough to intervene? It had to be one of them disguised as a priestess."

The Icehand tapped her fingers on her tabletop. "It's really not hard to guess things from here on out. You're going to offer me a cut if I help you track them down. But why should I cut you in for anything? You think the frillbacks are still alive or you wouldn't have been trying to leave the arena with the spear the one threw at you. Or at your dear sister, I guess. Whose body I understand you weren't going to retrieve."

Rajana couldn't care less about Sylena's body. Her sister had been an incompetent. "You may think you don't need me, but you do."

"How's that? I have a wizard on staff who can use that spear to scry for the frillback."

"I'm sure someone could. But what if word should get out that you intercepted money intended to pay off the Free Captains of the Shackles? Whereas if I recovered the money—supported by, say, a small band of mercenaries who happen not to be wearing your colors—it's all on me."

The Icehand stared at her, then her mouth turned up into something that was almost a smile. "I want eighty percent."

"Governor, that's hardly reasonable. You wouldn't even have the treasure on your lands—"

"—if you hadn't destroyed Crown's End's amphitheater."

"It's hardly destroyed. I say we split it."

The Icehand snorted. "I can send my own mercenaries."

"But you won't be able to blame it on a Chelish agent if things go wrong. Fifty-fifty."

"No. You can keep a fifth of it."

"Sixty-forty."

The Icehand muttered another vulgarity. "Seventy-thirty is as low as I'm going to go. Any more bargaining, and I might just decide to curry favor with the baron by turning over a Chelish agent for interrogation." She gave a malicious smile.

"Very well. Thirty percent. So long as none of your seventy percent gets anywhere close to the Free Captains."

"Oh, Crown's End will pay its yearly tithe when it comes due. But no more and no less than usual. If the baron needs more money he can squeeze his damned nobles. I have plans for this treasure. So you'd best get with your casting. And you can leave your man behind. I'm sending my best officer with you. You'll like Karvak. He'll keep you safe."

There were always challenges, but Rajana was certain she could best any presented by a soldier. "I'm sure. Now if you will be so kind as to return the lizardfolk spear?"

38

The Fortress of Fangs
Mirian

Mirian's distraction had saved Jekka, but it had brought the city guard out in full force, and they were far more organized than Mirian would ever have guessed. They'd already completely shut down the harbor. If Gombe and his grandfather hadn't arranged a backup plan, all of them might already be in custody. Instead, they'd managed to slip out of Crown's End on horseback and now rode into the wilds under cover of a morning rainstorm.

There'd been a little trouble getting the horse used to the scent of both Jekka and Kalina's corpse. They'd overcome that by rubbing the lizard man down with horse blankets and wrapping Kalina's body in them. That problem solved, they still had to address the challenge of Jekka's distinct lack of riding skill, so one of the others always rode close beside him.

Mirian elected to keep them a mile in from the coastal road, knowing it was a haven for bandits and would leave them in easy sight of any ships. Fortunately, the coastal plain was fairly dry along the hundred-mile stretch between Crown's End and Eleder, so going off-road in the daylight wasn't particularly troublesome. There was no jungle terrain to contend with.

The skies grumbled threat but never delivered more than a wet blanket of mist. All the better, as far as Mirian was concerned. Limited visibility worked in their favor.

By evening the rain leveled off, though the sky was still overcast. Mirian could just make out the long spur of the Bandu Hills arcing eastward from the sea. The distant, higher peaks were shadowy outlines in the fog.

She motioned to Jeneta, and the young priestess guided her dun mare to Mirian's side. "Jeneta, is the Fortress of Fangs still abandoned?"

The woman's slim eyebrows shot up her high forehead. "That ground is dangerous, Mirian. Great lizards still stalk the hills, along with the Bandu themselves."

"All the more reason to take shelter in the old fortress."

"They say it's haunted."

In fact, Mirian had visited the ruins before as part of a Pathfinder expedition to investigate precisely those claims. But all she said was, "All the better, then. Ghosts worry me less than bandits."

Jeneta nodded and said no more. The girl might be young, but there was an economy and dignity in her carriage and words that Mirian was coming to respect.

Mirian turned her horse's head to face more westerly, and the rest of the troop followed.

Most wild animals seemed to have taken shelter from the approaching storm, but as they rode they saw hares and lizards and other smaller game. It wasn't until nearly twilight that they came upon anything larger, and when they did they all started in amazement.

Mirian had seen herds of the great lizards before, but only in the deep jungles had she encountered any quite this large. There were dozens of the big horned brutes, each with armored, upswept crests and long trailing tails. Any was easily two or three times the size of a full-grown rhino.

The riders were downwind of the creatures, but as their mounts snorted in concern, the creatures looked up from where they rooted among the scrubby grasses. One of them roared a warning, and then all of the lizards raised their heads as one.

"Let's give those a wide berth," Gombe said softly.

"You're a man of good sense," Rendak said in a mock aristocratic accent, "and I concur without acrimony."

"Acrimony?" Gombe said. "Can you even spell that?"

It was good to hear the two bantering again, but Mirian silenced them with a motion and led them east.

"How close are we to the ruins?" Ivrian asked. He rode like a champion, and Mirian expected he'd received riding lessons along with the sword instruction his mother had mentioned.

"Not as close as I'd like." The bluffs were a darker shadow against the night and the clouds, and she guessed a least a half hour farther out.

She was wrong. It wasn't until another hour had fled that Jeneta spotted the old stone road leading up the hillside.

They guided their animals along the weed-coated flagstones, and Mirian couldn't help imagining again what the path might have looked like when the city was at its height. She'd drawn it once, and she supposed the picture existed still, in one of her old sketchbooks stored at the manor.

That put her in mind of her mother, who might even now be sitting at the courtyard fire. What would she say when Mirian came trotting back into the city with news that home and ship were safe, but Kellic was dead?

She shook herself out of her reverie and focused on the here and now. Just because the fortress was familiar didn't make it safe.

The Fortress of Fangs stood at the head of the trail, in the mouth of a natural break in the hills that opened onto a low plateau. Long, slim horns and fangs projected from the crenelated height of its walls. The wooden gate had long since rotted away, but the stones remained, twice the height of a man. She and Finze Bellaugh, Pathfinder venture-captain for Eleder, had supposed the fortress must once have protected an important trade route. There were remnants of other buildings in the grasses beyond, including an ancient temple that remained partly intact. There had probably once been an entire town on the plateau, one of many time-lost settlements dotting the region.

Mirian dropped from her weary animal and stretched sore legs. "Jekka, let's take a look around. The rest of you stay by the shadow of the wall. Rendak, post sentries."

"Right."

A half hour's search showed the place empty of anything particularly dangerous, though Jekka found a snake nest in the southern tower.

The most defensible spot was the tower beside the front gate. The second floor was dry and sheltered and empty, apart from a few spider webs. Next to it was a squared, shoulder-high rectangle outlining what she and Finze had determined were once stables. Gombe blocked off the single entrance by stringing a rope across it so they could corral the horses for the night.

Jekka and Ivrian volunteered for first watch, on the tower height. Everyone else bedded down in the room below. They had precious little baggage—just a few days' worth of food and Kalina's blanket-wrapped body, preserved from rot by one of Jeneta's spells.

Jekka hadn't understood the necessity of bringing the body along, for lizardfolk looked on the dead as meat, even if they had no plans to eat it. But Mirian told him burial was the way her people honored those they valued, and he'd accepted the explanation.

Mirian knew she should lie down for a few hours with the rest of her expedition, but she was seized with nervous energy, and returned to the tower height.

Jekka and Ivrian sat back to back, the lizard man looking over the empty city, the young lord staring out through a broken gap in the tusk-encrusted merlons. The storm had blown out, and the stars were bright, obscured only now and then by tattered streams of cloud, as though shredded by a great clawed hand.

Jekka was whittling at a piece of ivory. Mirian wondered if it came from the tower's adornments. "What are you making?"

"A calling horn," the lizard man said.

Mirian squatted down to look closer. "I'm not familiar that concept."

Jekka raised it, letting Mirian see. It was the size of a drinking horn, and hollow. "When you blow, it makes the sound of a thunder walker. Good for scaring off intruders. But only if you make it properly."

"Really?" Ivrian turned around.

"You should be watching the trees, Writer Ivrian."

Ivrian looked chagrined and turned back around.

Mirian grinned. "Jekka, that's amazing. I had no idea you were a craftsman."

Jekka's tongue flicked out. "It is a thing a warrior should know."

"That could come in handy. If you want to focus on it, I can take your watch."

Jekka hesitated, then nodded. "I will go below. Others may have better tools."

When he was gone, Mirian sat down on the cool stone and stared out through a gap in the tower at the city. The ruined temple sat nearby. As before, she didn't have the time to make a proper study of it. She wondered if Finze had ever sent someone back to sketch the friezes they'd glimpsed upon its walls.

Ivrian addressed her quietly. "Mirian, what are you planning to do when we get back?"

If we get back, she thought, but she didn't want to put doubts in his mind or dwell upon those in her own. "I haven't had time to give it much thought." Make sure that her mother still had a house, and that the ship was paid for. But who would be running the business?

Ivrian guessed her thoughts. "My mother said you were going to turn the business back over to your brother." His voice faltered. "I'm sorry."

"For what?"

"I guess I didn't think the question through. I didn't mean to bring him up."

"He's been on my mind. And so has your mother." She spoke slowly. "And Tokello. And Kalina. And Heltan. And the living. I don't know what I'm going to do about the *Daughter*, Ivrian. Maybe I'll sell it to Rendak." Yet even as she said it, she had a hard time believing herself. Rendak was capable and dependable, and practically family, but it still didn't sit right. "What are you going to do when we get out of this? Work with the government, like your mother?"

"I don't think so." There was no missing the vulnerability in his voice. "I was wondering if you needed another salvager."

Mirian was too startled to respond.

He continued, cautiously: "I think I've proven myself pretty dependable."

Ivrian thought she still doubted him! "I'd be honored to have you," she said solemnly. "I'm just not sure that I'm going to be salvaging."

"You were born to this, Mirian."

"I'm a Pathfinder. Before I came back I was in the middle of a cave dig."

"Is your team there as good as this one?"

"Yes and no," Mirian said, then decided to be honest with herself. "No."

"Can't you be a salvager *and* a Pathfinder? They both search for lost things, don't they?"

"They do." And then it was as though a damn had broken, for she found the words pouring forth. "I've missed the smell of the salt air, and the roll of the waves, and the sights of the deep. My father swore it was in my blood, and I swore I was never coming back."

"But you did." Ivrian lowered his voice. "These people need you, Mirian. Rendak is a fine captain, but you're a better leader, and you know it."

She was flattered, but she shook her head. "I just want to get us home. We can talk about the rest when we get there." She fell silent and leaned forward to peer out at the grasses. Then she swore.

"There's someone moving out there."

39

Surprise Attack
Rajana

She should never have trusted anything important to her sister. Sylena always had extra motives apart from serving her country and adding money to the family coffers. Thanks to her sister's foolishness, Rajana now wasn't entirely sure she could do either herself.

Certainly it would be a trick getting her hands on the treasure she was owed by her agreement with the Icehand, for she no more trusted the woman than the Icehand trusted her. Of course, the most important thing was keeping the money from Sargava's government.

She had two things in her favor. First was the cool weather, so different from the blasting heat typical of Sargava. The conditions almost rendered the journey pleasant. The other was careful preparation. That morning she'd wisely readied two scrying spells, and had used them to great effect over the course of their trip. With her last she determined that the lizard man rested in a stone tower. With that information, she and the Icehand's captain, Karvak, had narrowed the possibilities down to one of the structures in a ruined native fortress.

Thinking the main approach to the ruins would undoubtedly be watched, Karvak led them to a back trail too steep for the horses.

Karvak seemed a good man to have on her side, at least for now. All the same, she still had her teleportation scroll tucked up one sleeve, and expected to use it soon.

Four soldiers were left below with the animals. Rajana hated to leave her mount, for hidden in her saddle gear was the extradimensional bag with all of those lizardfolk book cones and the pack of gems and statuary her sister hadn't managed to lose.

One way or another, she planned to put her hands to all of the treasure at the same time, then use the scroll to vanish away to Cheliax. Leaving any of the treasure aboard her ship would have just about guaranteed its loss, for the Icehand moved quickly. Possibly the ship was already being searched.

Once they reached the narrow plateau, Karvak halted and stared at the outline of the fortress looming against the sky a half mile north. He split his forces into two groups and then led them forward. She asked him about the wisdom of attacking in full darkness, but he only tapped an amulet engraved with an owl. "I can see in the darkness pretty damned clear."

Karvak and his guards moved carefully through the mix of low foliage. There were occasional clusters of palm trees and, more rarely, lines of stone from some edifice older even than the ruined fortress. Rajana scanned the distance, and the moon hanging a lance-length higher than the ruin's longest tusk. She saw no one, but that meant nothing.

Rajana didn't hope for complete surprise, or even desire it. It would be far simpler to escape with the treasures if Mirian Raas and her expedition thinned out the soldiers. Unfortunately, Karvak's people seemed as skilled as he, and they made only an occasional sound as they threaded their way through the terrain. Could a good sentry see their movement, or the occasional shift of plant life as they pushed it aside?

Maybe not.

She told Karvak she must stop to ready a spell, and the captain warned her not to delay long. Rajana waited only until the men had their backs turned, then pushed against a young palm tree so that its trunk swayed. She pushed it twice more before moving forward. Two of the guards looked back at her as she stumbled deliberately against a jeerenberry bush. This produced only a little noise, but more movement.

Sylena picked herself and muttered embarrassed thanks as one of the men helped her to her feet. Her faint smile was genuine. If there were sentries looking this direction, they couldn't possibly have missed what she'd done.

Bit by bit, they closed upon the partly collapsed wall of the fortress. Rajana peered at its four towers and wondered which housed the sleeping lizard man.

As they drew closer, one shape proved not to be a hill or cluster of trees, but a ruined building, still partly roofed. Karvak sent half his force to look it over and advanced with Rajana and the rest toward the silent towers.

A thunder lizard trumpeted a challenge from their left.

Rajana had heard the beast call in the arena, and this one sounded nearly as close. She jumped in surprise as the guards pulled at their weapons.

Rajana cast her invisibility spell and vanished.

The beast roared again. The three men in the vanguard broke and ran, even as Karvak shouted to hold position. She could see the moonlight silver their fear-stricken faces as they raced back the way they'd come.

A scream rose from the east. She whirled to see a man whose chest armor bubbled in a sizzling green circle. "Help me!"

A green bolt raced out of the darkness and took another soldier in the helmet. She dropped, crying out in terrible pain.

Mirian Raas must lie nearby with her acid wand.

"It's some kind of trick," Karvak shouted, then looked in vain for Rajana. "Cursed witch! Where did you go?"

Smiling to herself, Rajana stepped away even as a lizard man erupted from the foliage and brought a blade crashing down on another of Karvak's guards.

Beautiful, she thought. She left the two groups to whittle each other down and went to find her treasure.

40
Duel with a Monster
Mirian

Mirian lay hidden in the palms where Jeneta had just used the lizardfolk horn, so she was more than a little surprised when another call trumpeted somewhere to the east. She glanced to make sure Jeneta remained beside her. The young woman sat motionless, hand to her long sword.

Once more the other horn call blasted.

"Is that a real one?" Mirian whispered.

Jeneta nodded.

"Sound our horn."

"And call it here?"

"And even the odds."

Three soldiers had raced into the darkness after Jekka, leading them straight into an ambush from Rendak and Gombe. That left ten more. One of those dropped as a well-placed acid bolt from Ivrian tore through him.

Their leader pointed his sword and sent two men scurrying toward the cluster of bushes that hid the lord.

Jeneta raised the instrument to her lips and sounded it once more. In comparison to the real thing, this call seemed ghostly, hollow.

"They're over there," the leader cried, pointing in their general direction.

But one of his warriors cried out because the ground rumbled. A heavy creature was closing, and let out a sustained roar to announce its arrival.

Mirian looked out to see the leader marshaling his people into a line and presenting bladed weapons even as another distant scream sounded. Jekka and his team had worked their ambush.

From out of the darkness loomed a great reptile tall enough to peer into a second-story window. While the invaders nervously stood their ground and shouted, Mirian leveled her wand and took one of the men in the side. He dropped, his scream sounding more like fright than pain. He struggled to tear off his armor. The remaining soldiers flinched, and the monster roared at them.

Suddenly a flaming hound popped into existence a few feet to Mirian's right, identical to the one that had appeared near her in the arena. It let out a fiendish howl and pushed into the brush.

So the Icehand had sent a spellcaster.

The monster was almost as tall as Mirian's shoulder, the shadow of a hound wreathed in red and yellow flames. Its pointed teeth bared in a sadistic grin.

Naturally, Mirian's second wand blast didn't work.

Jeneta rose and spoke in a sonorous, commanding voice. The creature briefly halted its approach. The black leaves through which it had thrust its body began to smoke.

Mirian backed away as she fired a second time. This time the emerald blast caught the creature in the side of its skull and the air was immediately filled with the scent of smoking flesh. Jeneta slashed the beast with her blade even as it leapt to claw her leg. The priestess dropped to one knee, and the monster bore in.

Mirian stepped to the side, brought her sword down across the back of its neck. The hound threw back its head to howl in terrible disappointment, then dissolved in black smoke.

Mirian bent to Jeneta, but the warrior priestess was fighting to her feet already. "Find its summoner! I can heal myself."

Mirian scanned their surroundings and spotted the caster almost immediately. She was ten feet back of the line of men still brandishing weapons at the thunder lizard, launching a red bead of flame that grew into a ball of fire as it soared toward the giant lizard's head.

The light of the flame permitted a brief glimpse of the woman's face, one so like Sylena that Mirian doubted her eyes. How could the woman possibly have survived her arena injuries?

If it was her, she wouldn't be standing for much longer. Mirian whispered the activation word, and the acid blast streamed forward from her wand, exploding against the wizard's blue dress.

Except instead of burning through, the acid just stuck there, sizzling. The caster pivoted sharply, her sinister smile lit by the shimmering green energy. "Did you really think you could use the same trick twice?" She raised a hand in a cryptic gesture.

Mirian mouthed the words to activate her wand. It failed again, but the woman's arm was painted by another harmless acid blast from her right. Ivrian, may Desna bless him. He'd escaped from the soldiers sent to kill him.

But Ivrian's blast neither eliminated the woman's magical protection nor disrupted her concentration. Mirian dashed and dove behind a boulder just as a powerful fireball exploded over its front.

She pulled herself up, thrusting the wand back into its holster, and peered around the boulder.

The great lizard had stamped backward, whipping its tail in agitation. Sylena's lookalike advanced through the rubble toward Mirian's position, clutching a wand.

Fabulous. Mirian very much doubted the spellcaster would miss as frequently as she herself had, if at all. Mirian crept backward and almost fell sideways over a broken stone that ringed a yawning hole. She clutched at a palm tree, brought herself upright behind it, and considered the black circle into which she'd almost plummeted. From below wafted the musty scent of wet stone. A well?

Mirian heard the distinct sound of Ivrian's magical wand, then the crashing blast of some other sorcerous energy. From out of the darkness, a shape emerged, moving swift and low: Jeneta. The priestess arrived to crouch at a palm tree beside her.

"Sound the horn," Mirian said.

Jeneta raised the horn to her lips, and once more the call rang out on the night air, to be answered by the deeper, full-throated blast from the monster.

Mirian peered out in time to see the thunder lizard advance against the soldiers, who scattered in all directions. It reached down to snatch one of the fleeing figures and leaned its massive head to snap at another.

The spellcaster set it reeling with a powerful blast of blue-white energies, directed from a wand. The monster lizard reared back, pulping the man it carried as it clenched its clawed hand in pain. It moved off to chase the running prey, the ground thundering beneath it.

Mirian blasted again at the spellcaster. She'd seen enough wizardry to know protective spells could be worn down, but there was no knowing how strong this woman's was. Mirian threw herself flat as the woman leveled her own wand. A cone of ice swept up against boulder and palm tree and blasted Mirian's side with cold so intense it stung like a sunburn. She staggered to her feet even as the woman charged toward them, wand leveled.

Jeneta stepped forward, blade high, and took the full brunt of the next ice blast. She collapsed, covered in deadly, shimmering frost. Mirian stepped to the back edge of the well even as the spellcaster advanced.

Mirian lowered her sword. "Spare my people," she called, "and I'll tell you where the treasure's hidden."

The woman came closer, closer, and the moonlight showed Mirian a face that was only similar to Sylena's, not identical. A sister?

The caster's wand pointed steadily at Mirian's chest. "Do you think I somehow failed to notice the hole in front of you?"

"I'd hoped," Mirian admitted. "But I'd counted on you missing the lizard man to your left."

The woman spun as Jekka reared up, his cousin's laumahk in both hands. His blade lashed out, catching the wizard in the side.

The woman screamed in pain, but before she could complete an incantation Mirian lunged and struck. The sweep of the blade sent the woman's wand and three of her fingers flying into darkness. The woman shrieked and tottered forward into the well.

Her fall was silent. Mirian had hoped for a satisfying splash— or better, a crunch. But then the thunder lizard came up from behind, its stride shaking the ground. She threw herself to the right even as her friends went left. She rolled through a screen of rough bushes and emerged upright, scratched and torn.

Behind came the clomp of great feet. She diverted right again and found herself near the shell of the temple.

The monster ripped the sky apart with its call of rage, all but deafening her. She expected those teeth to close over her head any moment.

She felt rather than heard the falter of its step, and risked a backward glance.

The monster had turned, and the slapping tail missed Mirian's head by inches. Jekka faced it, laumahk raised and glinting in the moonlight.

He'd distracted it from her, and it was time for a return favor. She slipped past the beast's tail and drove her cutlass deep into an immense ankle.

Once more the animal roared and pivoted, moving so fast she didn't have a chance to pull her sword out. Heart pounding, she sprinted for a gap she'd seen in the temple's wall.

The ground rattled and the tread drew closer.

She reached the temple, reached the gap formed by the fall of a pillar through a decorative temple frieze. She caught a quick glimpse of graceful, slender folk bowing to a god descending on moonbeams.

She flung herself into darkness. There was a brief instant that felt suspended in time. Before she hit, a dozen horrible possibilities flitted through her imagination. What lay beyond? A fall of thirty feet? A nest of venomous lizards? A giant spider web? A pile of rusted weapons?

Her hands touched ground first, for she was a practiced tumbler. She landed on a salting of rubble and somersaulted over smashed tiles, popping to her feet beside a broken pillar.

The wall collapsed in a rumble of stone as the beast pushed its head in to reach her. She dashed on through the darkness, stubbing her foot on a fallen stone. Overhead, the roof swayed and a vast section fell inward, raining tile. She backed farther into the black recesses. Her ringing ears faintly detected the sound of a distant roar she knew for Jeneta's horn. Through the gap in the ceiling, she saw the great silhouette of the thunder lizard's head turn as the creature sought the noise.

Jeneta's call rang out once more, and Mirian's attacker opened its massive maw to roar a curious response, then stomped away to investigate.

She knew she should go out there and help, but she remained in the shadows for a moment longer, straining to catch her breath. As her pulse slowed, she noticed just how much her right foot actually hurt. She wondered if she'd broken a toe or three.

The remnant of the roof creaked ominously. More shingles crashed down to shatter into fragments, and there was moonlight enough to show her an upright column tilting.

She just couldn't seem to catch a break.

The only safe course was toward the already ruined wall. Gritting her teeth against the pain, she ran ahead of the rolling thunder of collapsing masonry and threw herself clear. The building disintegrated behind her.

She landed on her hands and tumbled awkwardly down a short flight of stairs. She lay gasping, looking back to see the last temple wall collapse in a calamitous crash that hurled an immense cloud of debris into the starry sky.

So much for drawing those particular friezes.

She forced herself to her feet, pulled out her wand, and limped out to check her team. In the distance, the dark shape of the great lizard trod after a phantom caller, occasionally stopping to roar in answer. She might have been imagining it, but the beast sounded confused.

Who, she wondered, was doing that?

Not Jeneta. She found Rendak cradling her head in his lap as he raised a small gray vial to her lips.

Gombe knelt beside his cousin, rubbing her hand. For once he couldn't joke. "Mirian." He gave her a troubled smile. "I wasn't sure you'd made it."

"I'm all here," she breathed. "I'm just not sure all of it's working." She pointed at the vial. "What's that?"

"The officer was trying to down this after Jekka wounded him," Rendak answered. "I figure it's a healing potion."

"What if it's not?"

Rendak grimaced. "Looking at her, I don't figure she has much to lose. Helluva thing, to freeze to death in Sargava."

She nodded her blessing, and Rendak tilted the vial to the young woman's lips. Mirian bent her head in prayer. "May Iomedae give you strength, girl. You surely showed her your bravery this night."

Jeneta gasped once, then sucked in a huge breath. The next one sounded far better, almost normal.

"Praise Iomedae," Jeneta said, softly.

"Praise Rendak," Mirian said, then addressed her first mate. "Where are Ivrian and Jekka?"

"Jekka took the horn back and ran off with it."

Mirian blinked in surprise. "How's he going to outrun that thing?"

"He's pretty fast," Rendak offered, although he sounded doubtful. Swift Jekka might be, but how could he outpace a monster that could beat a running man in a couple of strides?

"Where's their spellcaster?" Rendak asked.

"At the bottom of a well," Mirian said. "Dead or dying. Have you seen the rest of the Icehand's troops?"

"They bolted. Those that we didn't kill, I mean. Or that the monster didn't stomp."

Mirian eyed Jeneta. "She still looks woozy. Why don't you see if the Icehand's officer had any more healing potions on him."

"Will do." Rendak rose slowly so that Gombe could shift to cradle his cousin's head.

Mirian bent down to retrieve the priestess's sword. "You don't mind if I borrow this, do you?"

Jeneta's answer was weak, distracted. "Not at all."

A few minutes later, Ivrian joined them, moving a little stiffly. He'd taken a sword cut in one arm, and Mirian helped bandage him. She and Gombe and Rendak then helped the other two back to the tower, before she and Gombe returned to scout the area.

There was no sign of living soldiers, and no Jekka until nearly dawn, when he trouped back carrying not just the laumahk, but a familiar shoulder pack, a larger bag, and his gray staff.

Mirian was so pleased to see him alive she hugged him. She felt the lizard man's body go rigid in her embrace.

He cocked his head at her and slung down the gear. "This is a human greeting?"

"Between those who are fond of one another."

"Ah." Stiffly he imitated the gesture, then stepped away. "It's good to see you." He bobbed his head at Rendak. "And you as well, Salvager Rendak."

"Just Rendak," the man said, amiably. "Or Filian, if you want. Though even my friends call me by my last name."

"Rendak," Jekka repeated.

The first mate pointed to the pile of belongings. "Where did you find all that?"

"I thought this would please you. I led the al'k'ring down a steep hill, and it chased horses the soldiers left. I found this on one of the ones it stepped on."

Mirian laughed in disbelief. "That's the third bag, isn't it? And your book cones?"

"It is."

She could scarce believe it, and couldn't quite imagine why the treasures had been brought on the journey. While she was puzzling over an explanation, Jekka questioned her further.

"Everyone else is well?"

"Everyone else is alive," Mirian said. "And healing."

Jekka tapped the ground with his staff. "Then we did very well."

"Thanks for your help with the thunder lizard." She smiled. "Jekka, have you ever thought about being a salvager?"

He cocked his head to one side, as though he hadn't understood the question. "I am a warrior."

"Salvagers have to be warriors as well," Mirian pointed out.

"Does this mean you're staying?" Rendak asked, his voice tinged with a certain shy tenderness.

"Ivrian says it's the thing I do best. And it seems to me our little team does a pretty good job of keeping each other alive. Besides, how can I captain the *Daughter* if I'm wandering the Mwangi Expanse?"

Rendak grinned crookedly.

"So how about it, Jekka?" Mirian asked. "You want to join the family business?"

"I will go where my sister goes," he said simply. "And with my friends."

41

The Sweetest Wine
Ivrian

*Riches and fame were ours at last, but triumph was a
bitter salve. All of us had lost much and suffered greatly.
Yet the story was not yet finished, and a final surprise still
awaited us . . .*

—From The Daughter of the Mist

Ivrian wasn't sure he'd ever get over the luxury of clean sheets
and a soft mattress. But as wonderful as it was to be safe at home,
he was surrounded by reminders of his mother. Grief he'd thought
expended rose afresh with him each morning.

Playing host to solemn Jeneta and seeing to the writing of
what proved a very difficult letter kept him fairly busy for the first
two days. He finished it in time to have it delivered to the Ministry
of Defense the afternoon after their return. By that evening, he'd
received a formal summons to the court the following morning. The
letter bore the baron's own signature, and requested his presence
alongside that of Mirian and Jekka—and naturally, the treasure.

Ivrian was tempted to take Rendak and Gombe and Jeneta as
well, but all three demurred. The priestess had necessary duties
at the local temple to Iomedae, and neither Rendak nor Gombe
felt comfortable mixing with "blue bloods." Ivrian couldn't help
smiling a little when Rendak said that, for it took the salvager a
moment or two to remember Ivrian himself was a lord.

It pleased him very much that these two men viewed him as one of their own.

When they disembarked from the carriage in front of the capitol building, Ivrian thought he and Mirian and Jekka made a rather fine spectacle. Ivrian wore the most conservative of his dark suits, with only two spots of color, a scarlet kerchief and a matching belt sash he thought gave him a rakish air.

Mirian looked lovely and refined in her red dress, cut in colonial style. Eyebrows rose at sight of her, then lifted even higher as Jekka stepped out.

The lizard man wore a light brown robe, one Ivrian had overpaid a nervous tailor to alter the previous afternoon. It was belted at the waist with the striking turquoise stones that usually supported Jekka's loincloth.

Jekka's matching necklace adorned his long throat, and in one hand he carried the carved staff, which lent him the air of a visiting sage or scholar.

Each of them carried one of the expedition haversacks.

White-garbed guards advanced to meet them, nervously fingering the hafts of their halberds.

"We're expected," Ivrian said. "I'm Lord Galanor."

"Of course, Lord," said the eldest of the three, a scarred man in his mid-thirties. "The undersecretary said to expect you at nine bells."

"And here we are," Ivrian said, even as the nearby temple of Desna tolled the hour. They started up the steps. The guards trailed behind.

Beyond the dark teak doors lay a grand hallway hung with frowning portraits of pale men and women in black. Dark doors stood closed in long lines to right and left, and harried-looking men and women bustled in and out of them and down side corridors, carrying sheaves of paper.

One of them, a handsome matron of middle years garbed in a brown dress and lacy white blouse, drew to a stop and gave Ivrian a crisp nod. "Lord Galanor, I presume?"

"Yes. You must be Lady Felham?"

"Indeed." The Undersecretary of Defense took in Ivrian and his companions with a practiced gaze, then cleared her throat. "Please come with me."

She turned on a heel and started for the grand staircase leading to a row of windows looking east, almost blinding in the sunlight.

The undersecretary stopped a few paces short, glanced back at them. "Perhaps we should speak privately downstairs." She stepped to one of the dark teak doors, rapped it peremptorily, and poked her head inside. "This will do." She thrust it open and gestured for them to enter.

Ivrian did so, a wan smile on his face. He pretended not to notice that the three guards still trailed their little group.

They'd been led to a dark-paneled conference room with high, north-facing windows. Two elaborate chandeliers hung over an oaken table polished so thoroughly it gleamed.

"My apologies," the undersecretary said, not sounding the least bit apologetic, "but I wish to examine the contents of your satchels before I conduct you forward. I hope you understand."

Ivrian frowned. "Their contents are solely for the view of the baron."

Lady Felham's expression was stony. "I'm afraid the baron's safety is my concern, and that I'll be viewing their contents first."

This wasn't at all the sort of treatment they had earned, nor deserved. Ivrian was opening his mouth to object when Mirian touched his sleeve.

"It's all right, Ivrian. Let's show her what we have." Mirian undid the straps of her pack and removed the sculpture of the sea drake. She set it carefully on one end of the table, and even Ivrian had to admit to himself it was a thing of beauty.

One by one, Mirian removed the three ruby lizardfolk heads that had survived their encounter with the boggards, then deposited jewel after jewel in ordered rows as the little idols began their choking laughter.

Ivrian smirked at the undersecretary's growing interest. He'd described the treasures only in the most general of terms.

Two of the guards lingered in the room behind the undersecretary, and they looked even more impressed than she did.

"Jekka," Ivrian suggested, "let's turn out the rest, don't you think?" And he unceremoniously shook out his pack so gems clattered onto the table in a waterfall of riches: rubies, emeralds, and diamonds of all shapes and sizes. Felham and the guards let out a collective gasp of amazement. The younger of them even swore, and the undersecretary and officer were so stunned they didn't seem to notice.

Jekka let out a coughing laugh and dumped out the contents of his own haversack.

As the wealth streamed down, Ivrian grinned. "This is next year's payment to the Free Captains, and probably the year after. Do you think your superior will be interested in speaking with me now?"

It took the woman a good five-count to close her mouth. "Corporal," she said without turning, "if you will relay my compliments to the baron, suggest that he attend me at once. As a matter of fact, feel free to describe the specifics of this particular incident."

"Right away, m'lady." The younger soldier executed a smart salute, pushed past the gawping soldier leaning in the doorway, and could be heard running down the hall.

"Do you mind if we sit?" Mirian asked.

"No, of course not," the undersecretary said.

Ivrian realized he was taking perhaps a little too much delight in rendering the woman speechless.

Lady Felham cleared her throat. "Your pardon, Lord Galanor, but is that all real?"

"It's all real," Ivrian answered confidently. "Every last bit of it."

"Well. I must say, this is rather impressive."

"Quite," Ivrian said, mimicking her tone.

The corporal returned and stepped to one side, coming crisply to parade rest. The commanding officer, looking out the doorway, stiffened and brought his hand up in salute.

Ivrian had seen Baron Utilinus, Grand Custodian of Sargava, at a distance, but he'd never actually observed him up close. The man was tall, his dark hair flecked with gray, a blocky, clean-shaven man in his early middle years, garbed in a blue short-waisted coat and breeches of the finest cloth.

Mirian and Ivrian stood quickly, followed almost immediately by Jekka. The lizard man might not understand every human social cue, Ivrian thought, but he was smart enough to copy those he didn't know.

The baron advanced, his blue eyes twinkling, uncertain whether to look at the table or his guests.

"This is Lord Galanor," the undersecretary said hastily. "And guests."

Ivrian bowed formally. Mirian curtsied. Jekka, unfortunately, copied the latter rather than former action, but no one commented upon it.

The baron met Ivrian's eyes. "So you're Alderra's boy." His voice was husky but pleasant.

"I am, Baron. It's an honor to meet you."

The baron advanced to clasp his arm, expression somber. "I was sorry to learn of your mother's death, Ivrian. She was a dear friend."

"Thank you, Baron." He was surprised the words affected him so deeply.

The baron nodded once, then extended his hand toward the lizard man, an action that elicited a gasp from the soldiers.

Jekka gripped the baron's arm in return.

"I have never met one of the lizardfolk in person," the baron told Jekka. "But Lord Galanor reported that you served with great distinction. I thank you."

Jekka seemed at a loss. "My friends required help."

"And I am sorry, too, for your own losses," the baron went on.

"I thank you," Jekka said, then bowed his head, slowly. He was learning.

The baron turned to Mirian.

"And you're the daughter of Leovan Raas. I understand that without you, no one would have returned at all."

"That might be a bit of an exaggeration, Baron."

"No," Jekka said, at the same time that Ivrian said, "It's not."

The baron laughed. "I think your friends say differently. I wish I didn't have to offer my condolences to you as well. You three risked much, and lost much." He looked over to the table. "But you have done the state a great service. Lady Felham and her staff will conduct a thorough accounting of the moneys and award you the agreed-upon percentage, minus that amount you asked for the church of Iomedae. I wonder, though, if you three might do me the honor of joining me for a late breakfast? I'd like to hear the details from your own lips."

Ivrian searched the faces of his friends, saw Jekka bob his head and Mirian nod.

"We would be honored."

"Excellent."

The baron left word that the room was to remain under thorough guard, and that the undersecretary would drop all matters and see to the cataloging and tabulation of the treasure immediately, assisted by only her most trustworthy aids.

And then the four of them headed up the stairs to a very fine suite overlooking a private garden, where they were treated to such an elaborate breakfast that Ivrian rather wished he'd eaten nothing beforehand.

They were catered to by servants garbed more finely than Ivrian, men and women so practiced in dignity that he couldn't detect even a trace of consternation when they asked Jekka what wine or food he might desire, and the lizard man asked if they might bring one of each. They obliged him.

While they ate, the baron asked about their journey. Ivrian tried not to dominate the conversation, but his friends frequently relied upon his narration. Occasionally, the baron interjected a question or remarked upon their skill or luck, but mostly he listened, nodding and sipping his wine, or nibbling at the steady stream of delicacies.

"And that's nearly it, Baron," Ivrian finished.

"And the rest of your team? Are they recovering?"

"They're well," Mirian answered. "Happy to be home with their families."

"And the young priestess? She's fully healed? We owe her and her entire family our thanks."

"She's fully mended," Ivrian answered. He cleared his throat delicately. "Will you be saying anything to the Icehand?"

The baron smiled in distaste. "She'll disavow any involvement, I'm sure, but I imagine I can smooth things out for your priestess friend if she does wish to return to her home."

"I'm not sure she does, Baron," Mirian said.

"If she does," he said, "you have but to contact me, and I'll arrange things. Now, as for you three . . ." He set hands to the table. The servants cleared away the plates and departed, leaving them alone in the well-appointed dining room. Ivrian grew conscious of the sound of a ticking clock, and spied it upon a desk to the table's right.

"I can't tell you what a tremendous pleasure it is to have had you work for the state. There are a number of sites that could stand investigation, and I would reward you for looking into them."

Ivrian looked eagerly to Mirian.

She cleared her throat. "With all due respect, Baron, while we'll be happy to work with you again, Jekka still has some unfinished business."

"Oh?" The baron looked to Jekka, then back to Mirian.

"We recovered the book cones of his people, but we've had little time to review them."

"I see."

"If he learns any information about where other members of his clan live, I think we owe it to him to make getting there our first priority."

"Of course. I would expect nothing less. Most of the sites I'm aware of would be more speculative ventures anyway, and perhaps not as remunerative. If you learn of one yourselves, I hope you'll keep the needs of Sargava in mind."

"Naturally, Baron."

The baron brought his hands together in a soft clap and met Mirian's dark eyes. "While your share of what you've brought back is no doubt enough on its own to take care of the matter, I want you to know that, regardless of the total, your family's debts are no longer a concern. I've written your mother, to offer both my condolences and my thanks."

Mirian bowed her head. "She will be honored, I'm sure."

The baron smiled a little sadly. "Jekka, in honor of your assistance, I am awarding you Sargavan citizenship. If Mirian Raas has taken you into her family, then allow me to invite you into the larger family of our nation."

From his pocket he produced a bronzed medallion on a chain and passed it across the table. "This symbolizes your status as an official diplomatic ambassador to Sargava. No citizen or officer of the state can ever question your right to enter any Sargavan settlement, so long as you keep that upon you and show it when questioned."

The lizard man took the object and lifted it in clawed fingers. Ivrian leaned close, but couldn't catch all the words engraved upon the circle—something about the bearer, and rights and full honors.

"And as for you, Ivrian, I've lost one of my best agents. Do you have any interest in following in her footsteps?"

"I know it was her fondest wish that I take up government work," Ivrian said. "But I'll echo what Mirian's said: I'd like to assist Jekka before I make any decisions."

"Then I'll repeat that I hope you'll keep us in mind, Lord Galanor, when you finish helping your friend."

"You are very kind, Baron."

Sargava's ruler rose, straightening his jacket, and then escorted them down the hall and stair and chatted with them in the entryway while a coach was brought around.

The carriage arrived. Ivrian watched Jekka, who hadn't seemed to find any special significance in the sigil of Iomedae emblazoned upon the door. Ivrian noticed Mirian and the baron studying him surreptitiously as well.

The door swung open, and Jeneta stepped out, offering a low bow to the baron and his guards. Then she held the door open as another robed figure dropped down

Jekka hissed and stepped back. "You were dead!"

"I was," Kalina agreed.

Any number of things could have gone wrong, Ivrian knew. There'd been a fair chance that even with the finest priests of Iomedae working the resurrection magic, it might not be enough. No one had wanted to give Jekka false hope, so no one had mentioned what they'd hoped to accomplish by bringing the body back with them.

Jekka turned to Mirian. "What magic is this?"

Mirian put a hand on his shoulder. "The good kind, Jekka. The good kind."

Jekka stepped forward and bobbed his head formally. "Kalina. My heart speeds at the sight of you."

Kalina bobbed her own head, first to Jekka, then to Mirian and Ivrian.

"I'm glad it worked out," the baron said softly to Ivrian's ear. "She'll need this." The baron pressed a cold, round object into his hand. Ivrian glanced down to find a second ambassadorial medal in his palm.

"Farewell, friends." The baron raised a hand as he stepped away. "I hope to see all of you again."

The humans returned his well wishes. Then, grinning, Mirian held the door and ushered her friends into the carriage. Once everyone was seated, she ordered it onward to her home.

Jekka sat across from his cousin, staring in disbelief. Ivrian wondered if he would ask whether the other dead expedition members might be restored, and readied himself for somber explanations.

But Jekka had other concerns. "I am sorry you missed the lunch," he said. "There was most interesting food."

"I was fed at the temple."

Ivrian passed the medal over to Kalina. "I'm glad you're back with us, my friend."

"I am glad Jekka will not be alone," Kalina said.

"But I am not alone," Jekka countered. "Mirian is my sister now. We are clan."

The lizard woman's head swung to consider Mirian.

"My home is yours, Kalina. If you wish it."

"As is mine," Ivrian said.

Jekka cocked his head at him. "Even if you are not a Raas, I think you, too, are clan."

"Close enough," Mirian agreed.

"What is this object?" Kalina studied the bronze circle Ivrian had handed her.

"You're a friend of Sargava now," Mirian explained. "By order of the baron."

"I never expected that." Her eyes bored into Mirian's own. "Jeneta told me all that you did for me. I cannot thank you enough."

"Jeneta is the one who preserved your body with magic while we rode. It was her people who called you back."

"But she said it took many moneys. Didn't your family need them?"

"Ivrian and I split the cost," Mirian said. "I wish we could have saved the others, but there was no way to recover their remains."

Ivrian would rather not dwell on any of that. He cleared his throat. "Kalina, do you remember anything about what happened between your, uh, passing and your return?"

"No," Kalina answered. "I remember fighting a thing in the water that I did not want to eat, and then I awoke near Priestess Jeneta and other humans I did not know. They were kind to me."

Ivrian tried to hide his disappointment. "I'd hoped you could tell me a little about what the afterlife looked like." What he didn't add was that he'd hoped his mother would pass on a final word to him through Kalina. Or at least tell him that she was all right now, on the other side.

"That would have been unlikely," Jeneta said. "Most who return cannot recall anything at all."

"Kalina," Jekka said, "I have not had much time to study the cones. We have had a mourning day for Mirian's brother, and for you and Heltan."

Ivrian bowed his head. The official funerals were to be held tomorrow.

Jekka continued: "There is mention of an island off a coast, and black ships. I must study them in greater detail."

"Which coast?" Ivrian asked.

"That is not yet clear to me. You will sail with me, to find it?"

"Aye," Mirian said, and Ivrian nodded agreement.

"Me too," Jeneta promised.

"That is good," Jekka said, and let out a long, rattling sigh. Ivrian had never heard the like from him, and he supposed it indicated contentment. The lizard man actually looked relaxed, and Ivrian couldn't recall ever seeing that before, either.

But there was one last item, one that had plagued Ivrian for the last weeks. He took a deep breath. "Mirian, there's something I've been meaning to speak with you about."

"Oh?"

Was that a hint of amusement in her voice?

He faced her squarely. "I'd still like to write our adventure down. I can change your name, if you'd like, but I want to tell this tale, or some version of it."

"Go right ahead. And keep my name."

"Just like that?" He could scarcely believe it. "I thought you hated the idea."

"It's your story now, too."

There was a long silence before he answered, softly and sincerely. "Thank you."

"You might want to leave some parts out, of course."

He chuckled. "You can count on that." He nodded to Jekka. "I'll set it in the Laughing Jungle instead of the Kaava Lands, in case you and Kalina ever want to return to the ruins."

"Perhaps we will," Kalina mused. "But we would need more explorers, and warriors. I should like to slay the drake and remove the rest of our book cones. For now, though, I am most excited to see the words you will write, Ivrian. If you will read them to us."

"Whatever you wish," Ivrian promised.

As the coach rumbled on, Jekka rubbed the circlet now hanging from his neck, then considered everyone seated with him. "It is good to have a medal, and it is good to have drunk sweet wine. But it is even better to have a family, and friends."

"If we had more wine," Ivrian said, "I'd raise a glass to that."

"Then let's open some bottles when we get home," Mirian said. "We'll raise a toast: To friends, family, and our future together."

About the Author

Howard Andrew Jones is the author of two previous Pathfinder Tales novels—*Plague of Shadows* and *Stalking the Beast*—as well as the short stories "The Walkers from the Crypt" and "Bells for the Dead" (both available for free at **paizo.com**). In addition, he's written the creator-owned novels *The Desert of Souls*, *The Bones of the Old Ones*, and the forthcoming *For the Killing of Kings*, as well as a collection of short stories, *The Waters of Eternity*. His books have been honored on the Kirkus New and Notable Science Fiction list and the Locus Recommended Reading List, and *The Desert of Souls* was number four on Barnes & Noble's Best Fantasy Releases of 2011, as well as a finalist for the prestigious Compton Crook Award for Best First Novel.

When not helping run his small family farm or spending time with his wife and children, Howard has worked variously as a TV cameraman, a book editor, a recycling consultant, and a college writing instructor. He was instrumental in the rebirth of interest in Harold Lamb's historical fiction, and has assembled and edited eight collections of Lamb's work. He serves as the Managing Editor of *Black Gate* magazine and blogs regularly at **blackgate.com** as well as at **howardandrewjones.com**.

Acknowledgments

Without a small cadre of dedicated allies, this book would never have been completed. Rich Howard gave me some valuable tips about diving and life in the depths. James Sutter guided me surely through all the edges of the rough draft and pointed me toward the novel I was really trying to write. Dave Gross combed carefully through the later draft and helped me cut out the chaff and punch up the character moments. My wife Shannon gave me Kalina, and book cones, and laumahks and hundreds of suggestions that heightened description, improved flow, and brightened characters. I sincerely thank you all.

Glossary

All Pathfinder Tales novels are set in the rich and vibrant world of the Pathfinder campaign setting. Below are explanations of several key terms used in this book. For more information on the world of Golarion and the strange monsters, people, and deities that make it their home, see *The Inner Sea World Guide*, or dive into the game and begin playing your own adventures with the *Pathfinder Roleplaying Game Core Rulebook* or the *Pathfinder Roleplaying Game Beginner Box*, all available at **paizo.com**. Those interested in learning more about Sargava specifically should check out *Pathfinder Player Companion: Sargava, The Lost Colony*, or explore it themselves in the Serpent's Skull Adventure Path.

Arcane: Magic that comes from mystical sources rather than the direct intervention of a god; secular magic.

Asmodeus: Devil-god of tyranny, slavery, pride, and contracts; lord of Hell and current patron deity of Cheliax.

Avistan: The continent north of the Inner Sea, on which Cheliax and many other nations lie.

Avistani: Of or related to the continent of Avistan.

Bandu: Demon-worshiping tribe native to Sargava, focused on slave-taking and human sacrifice.

Bandu Hills: Mountain range in central Sargava.

Bas'o: Nomadic tribe native to Sargava, known for its skilled warriors and hunters.

Boggards: Froglike humanoids that live in swamps and often attack other sentient races.

Chelaxian: Someone from Cheliax, either ethnically or by legal citizenship.

Cheliax: A powerful devil-worshiping nation located in southwestern Avistan, of which Sargava was formerly a colony.

Chelish: Of or relating to the nation of Cheliax.

Colonial: Sargavan slang term for a Sargavan citizen of Chelish heritage, or anyone in Sargava's primarily light-skinned ruling caste.

Crown's End: Sargavan port city north of Eleder, known for its corruption and rampant smuggling activity.

Custodian: Alternative formal title of the Baron of Sargava, the nation's ruler.

Desna: Good-natured goddess of dreams, stars, travelers, and luck.

Desperation Bay: Large bay around which Sargava wraps.

Devils: Fiendish occupants of Hell who seek to corrupt mortals in order to claim their souls.

Eleder: Capital of Sargava and thriving port city specializing in shipping raw resources north to more powerful nations.

Free Captains: The leaders of the Shackles' legendary pirate bands, paid by Sargava's government to keep Cheliax from retaking Sargava.

Freehold: Ranching town in central Sargava.

Garund: Continent south of the Inner Sea, renowned for its deserts and jungles, upon which Sargava lies.

Garundi: Human ethnic group consisting of dark-skinned people, mostly found in northern Garund.

Gillmen: Race of amphibious humanoids descended from the Azlanti after that empire sank into the sea in a bygone age.

Gozreh: God of nature, the sea, and weather. Depicted as a dual deity, with both male and female aspects.

Halflings: Race of humanoids known for their tiny stature, deft hands, and mischievous personalities.

Harpies: Predatory and intelligent race of human-headed bird women, who use their magical songs to lure intelligent creatures to their deaths.

Her Infernal Majestrix: Formal title of the ruler of Cheliax.

Ijo: Coastal tribe of native Sargavans known for their skill with boats and fishing.

Infernal Dukes: Greater devils who rule Hell beneath Asmodeus.

Inheritor: Iomedae.

Inner Sea: The vast inland sea whose northern continent, Avistan, and southern continent, Garund, as well as the seas and nearby lands, are the primary focus of the Pathfinder campaign setting.

Iomedae: Goddess of valor, rulership, justice, and honor, who in life helped lead the Shining Crusade before attaining godhood.

Kaava Lands: Jungle-covered peninsula north of Desperation Bay.

Kalabuto: Ancient Sargavan jungle city now inhabited primarily by native Sargavans and ruled by a small cadre of colonials.

Kelesh: Empire far to the east of the Inner Sea.

Keleshite: Of or related to the Empire of Kelesh; someone of that ethnicity.

Laughing Jungle: Jungle in southern Sargava.

Lizardfolk: Ancient and tribal race of intelligent reptilian humanoids; often viewed as backward by humans.

Mulaa: Prominent tribe of native Sargavans known for their farming and ranching.

Mwangi: Of or pertaining to the Mwangi Expanse; someone from that region. "Mwangi" as an ethnicity is a catch-all term created by northern humans to describe the wide variety of cultures found in central Garund.

Mwangi Expanse: A sweltering jungle region south of the Inner Sea and north of the Inner Sea.

Native: Sargavan slang term for the nation's indigenous peoples.

Oubinga River: Major river in the Kaava Lands.

Pathfinder: A member of the Pathfinder Society.

Pathfinder Lodge: Meeting house where members of the Pathfinder Society can buy provisions and swap stories.

Pathfinder Society: Organization of traveling scholars and adventurers who seek to document the world's wonders.

Pharasma: The goddess of birth, death, and prophecy, who judges mortal souls after their deaths and sends them on to the appropriate afterlife; also known as the Lady of Graves.

Sargava: Former Chelish colony which successfully won its independence, and maintains it through an expensive arrangement with the piratical Free Captains of the Shackles.

Sargavan: Of or related to Sargava, a citizen of Sargava.

Scrying: Using magic to view something from a distance.

Sea Devil: Intelligent and predatory aquatic race with a resemblance to the sharks they adore.

Sea Drake: Breed of lesser aquatic dragon capable of breathing devastating electrical attacks, but still less intelligent and powerful than a true dragon.

Senghor: Prominent port city northwest of Sargava.

Shackles: Chaotic pirate isles northwest of Sargava, ruled by the Free Captains.

Shelyn: The goddess of beauty, art, love, and music.

Smuggler's Shiv: Dangerous island in Desperation Bay known for both its smuggling activity and the many monsters that inhabit its wilds.

Sorcerer: Someone who casts spells through natural ability rather than faith or study.

Taldane: The common trade language of the Inner Sea region.

Tines: Raised fork on which Chelish criminals are sometimes impaled. Also the name of a rude hand gesture from Cheliax, which suggests that the recipient should be impaled in such a manner.

Varisian: Of or relating to the region of the frontier region of Varisia, or a resident of that region. Ethnic Varisians tend to organize in clans and wander in caravans, acting as tinkers, musicians, dancers, or performers.

Venture-Captain: A rank in the Pathfinder Society above that of a standard field agent, in charge of organizing expeditions and directing and assisting lesser agents.

Wand: A sticklike magic item imbued with the ability to cast a specific spell repeatedly.

Wizard: Someone who casts spells through careful study and rigorous scientific methods rather than faith or innate talent, recording the necessary incantations in a spellbook.

Turn the page for a sneak peek at

Bloodbound

by F. Wesley Schneider

Available December 2015

5
Unwelcome Guests
Larsa

The night's fog was already retreating by the time I reached Thorenly Glen, withdrawing as the first shades of daylight bled over the distant tree line. The walk had taken considerably longer than I'd expected. The city's constables would be on their way soon, following up on Lady Thorenly's distress from the previous night. I wouldn't have much time to investigate without interference, or to deal with what would assuredly ruin a couple of guards' morning.

The blanket of mists receded slowly, and its removal wasn't flattering. A manor house rose across a lake of weeds and shapeless hedges. Porch sagging, windows blinded by shutters, roof shedding shingles like an old man's hair, Thorenly Glen lacked anything in common with the pastoral haven its name suggested. A road-worn coach rested in the weedy turnabout just before the mansion's cracked steps. Whoever the estate's guests were, no one had bothered to prepare for them.

I circled the manor at some distance, following a line of knotty trees. Unbelievably, the estate was putting its best face forward. The roof over the house's back porch had collapsed, blocking doors and windows and burying much of the rear in splinters. Ivy crawled through the ruins. The damage was far from fresh.

Lady Thorenly had been discovered raving along the road leading south. Had she actually been living in this wreck?

Even more outrageously, had she and her husband actually been charging others to board in their ruin? Retreat for the aged indeed.

The baffling nature of what nobles would pay for aside, the house was too still. Were Lord Thorenly, two nurses, and some number of boarders in residence here, there would be some sign— the flicker of a light left burning overnight, a window left open a crack, servants preparing for the day. But instead, nothing. With every window shuttered or boarded over, not even a rustle of curtains or a passing silhouette suggested the manor was anything but abandoned.

I slid out from behind the shell of a disused shed, approached and listened under the windows. There was briefly a noise from inside—an unexpected tromping on the floor above. Booted steps, perhaps. It swiftly faded.

I came upon a servant's door, its threshold at waist height. A soggy barrel and mismatched crates formed makeshift steps. I skirted them and was headed back to the front when a wordless roar burst from within. Somewhere glass shattered. It certainly wasn't the sound of a retired landlord turning down his morning tincture.

It also wasn't anywhere near the servant's door. I carefully scaled the crates to the entry. No one had bothered to lock the door.

The cramped kitchen within was surprisingly clean, a busy array of pans and cooking implements hanging over well-scrubbed countertops. Several tea services stood ready, but the fireplace's hearty kettle wasn't growing any warmer over the ashes. The tromping was louder now, boots practically tumbling down nearby stairs. They passed close by, rattling the cups and saucers. Somewhere a door slammed open.

Someone was in quite a hurry.

I cracked the kitchen's swinging door enough to see a sliver of the hall beyond. Threadbare carpeting stretched to an open door at the end of a gallery of faded portraits. Beyond, a cast-off sheet twisted in the air, sprawling across a floral divan. Stomping and clattering continued inside.

I slipped out, checking the hall in the opposite direction—doors, bad art in cheap frames, blood. Upon steep stairs a mass of wrinkles and shredded robes, hardly recognizable as a man, no longer bled. I ignored it for now—it was one corpse I didn't expect to be a threat. I moved on, the clamor from the hall's end covering the complaints of crotchety floorboards and the hiss of drawing my blade.

A brass candelabra skipped across the floor as I reached the doorframe. The room had been closed up early—or never opened at all—its furniture, paintings, and fireplace all covered in linens. Stale air suggested it hadn't been used for some time—and even then it surely hadn't received the rough treatment it was getting now.

At the opposite end of the room, a figure in a coal riding coat pulled the covers from a pair of mismatched bookcases. With one swipe, he scattered a shelf's contents to the floor. Delicate figurines and silhouettes in tiny frames cascaded down amid an avalanche of decorative tomes.

I stepped into the room, trying to start things lightly. "I don't think the owners would appreciate their—"

"Where is it?" He spun with inhuman speed, his shout shooting cracks through colorless skin. Before I could reply he stormed over. His fingers shriveled into claws, already stained from feeding.

Only half surprised, I brought my blade up. He swiped for my gut, but I slid aside. "Is this how you treat your elder's agent?"

That should have slowed him down, but it didn't.

"You're not him." His claws came up for my face. My blade slapped his forearms but the blow pushed me back, heels and spine slamming against the hearth. Who had he been expecting?

I made a show of it, my sword slicing a broad warning between us. Having no clue what he was talking about, I bluffed. "Plans changed."

"Liar!" His rage surged between us, red thoughts roiling at the edge my sight. As was the case with most of his kind, his will wasn't entirely fettered to his mind—something in death had jarred it free. Few humans know what it is to have their thoughts invaded, but once you've been a captive inside your own head, you recognize trespassers.

I wrenched my eyes away and lunged. He was fast enough that his throat wasn't pierced cleanly, but the wound looked like a woodcutter's first chop—and was just as bloodless. He hissed, dashing into the wall and up, his claws not even marking the faded floral paper. I sliced the sheet covering some wall hanging. Suddenly the surface he clung to was sliding. He scrambled, then hit the ground solidly. I delivered the woodcutter's next strike.

The body burst into a cloud of pyre smoke. My sword screeched across the floor, momentum thrusting my face into that blast of dry death. I twisted away, grimacing as I regained my balance. I hated that smell. The young ones smelled wet, the old smelled dry, but both had that throat-clogging bitterness.

Like a shadow given shape but not substance, the smoke fell but refused to disperse. It pooled across the floor, seeking cracks in the boards, trying to seep into the dark below. I hadn't ended the stranger—his head hadn't severed cleanly—just panicked him. Instincts were powerful things, even more so when immortality was at stake. He'd search out a dark place to recover, but he wouldn't be bothering me again soon.

I scanned the room for whatever he might have been looking for, but the woman caught my attention.

The cloth I'd cut from the wall revealed a portrait of a noble family: two arch-looking young women in matching floral dresses, plus a mother and father. My slice had cut a mortal wound across the chest of one daughter, but it was her near-twin who caught my attention. Red strands strayed from beneath her broad sun hat.

The traumatized canvas distorted her face, but it was clear she was a fragile thing, with her father's calm expression . . .

I raised my hand to the portrait. Something about that woman seemed . . .

I pinched the limp canvass back into place.

It was me.

Somehow, impossibly, the other woman seated in the picture was unmistakably me. The dress was some pampered socialite's, the hair impractically styled, and the scene's other occupants utter strangers. But everything else was absolutely me.

The creak on the steps brought me back to the moment. Down the hall, another man in a dark coat and hat peered from the stairs. He'd already seen me, and maybe the last wisps of his companion settling into the floorboards. Our gazes barely met before he launched back upstairs.

"Damn it." The portrait's eerie occupant would have to wait. I vaulted the banister, swinging myself over the bloody mess staining the steps. Battered doors and artless decorations lined the upper hall. The houseguest was nowhere in sight, but most of the doors were open.

Inside the nearest room spread remnants of a gory debauch, a slaughter framed in nurse's white. The resident was in but wouldn't be receiving guests, butchered in what she must have known would be the last bed she'd ever own. Nothing stirred. I moved on. Each room presented a similar tableau, though the framing was different in each—a hunter, a debutant, a collector of glass figurines sprawled amid his shattered collection. Despite myself, my tongue was starting to feel dusty.

The last door was open only a crack, though the wood around the lock had been shattered. I checked behind me, then pushed into what was clearly the master bedroom. Dawn's light drowned beneath thick, sea foam curtains, casting everything in shades of sunken green. A bulky vanity lay wrecked against one wall, its hinged mirror shattered. There was certainly truth to the vampiric aversion to mirrors, but few knew how personally some took their weaknesses.

A lavish mahogany hat box sat open upon the bed, brass clasp gleaming. Inside, white satin cushioning and nothing more.

I smelled him the instant before he struck. Rolling across the bed corner, I rounded on him, sword still in hand, my back to the window. He was already on me, fangs like a snake's striking for my face. He was too close. I dropped my sword and grabbed the loose flesh of his forearms. My grip did little to slow his charge, a power stronger than death driving him on—but I didn't have to be stronger.

Adjusting my footing, I pulled him to me, adding my weight to the force of his rushing frame. We toppled back. His wide hat shadowed his face except for bloodless lips. They twisted into a smile the moment before the glass shattered.

We crashed onto the sloped porch roof, glass and loose shingles slipping beneath us as our bodies slid on the tearing curtain. His victorious expression vanished and I rolled hard, forcing him beneath me. He shrieked and flailed his arms in an attempt to simultaneously throw me off and slow his slide into the dawn light. The smell came first, appropriately like sulfur and burning garbage as his fleshier features charred.

We hit the edge of roof. I let my body go limp, crashing upon him as we hit the ground. His chest gave way, crackling as though I'd fallen upon a bundle of brittle twigs. Ash and the echoes of another shriek burst into the air. As flesh or as smoke, for him this was immortality's end.

He burned quickly.

Standing, I brushed ashes off of my hands. The house and drive were still, looking far less ominous without their veils of morning fog. Whippoorwills warbled in the distant trees.

A shadow settled near the stranger's cinder-filled coat. His traveling hat landed gently, a wide-brimmed slouch common to the riders of Amaans. Supposedly the horsemen wore them to keep the sun out of their eyes when riding valley trails.

"Huh. Not your worst idea, friend." I tried it on.

I checked the height of the sun from under the shady brim. The city constables were already late and might arrive at any moment, but I still had questions. Questions with answers I might learn from a torn canvas, or from a coward hiding in basement shadows. I started back toward the manor's front door, pulling a sturdy stake from the holster on my thigh.

6

The Exorcism of Elistair Wintersun

Jadain

Pain pierced my fear, forcing me back into the moment. Still the essence of the asylum's insanity bled into the room, babbling its shattered psyche as it reached for me. My amulet, slipping in my grip, forced the edges of the goddess's spiral into my palm.

I thrust the holy icon before me, nearly plunging it into the core of the shrieking thing.

"Get back!" I poured my swallowed scream into my words, lending them something like force. "In Pharasma's name, get back!"

A measure of conviction, of my faith in the goddess, must have shone through my words. The carved image of the Lady's spiral shivered to life, its cold radiance washing over the blot of murmurs and shadowy limbs.

The stray soul refused to be lit, but its inky mass diminished, flagging in the goddess's light.

I sought sanctuary in remembered lessons. What was this? A spirit shackled to the world by its own broken mind? Literally a stray soul? As a servant of the goddess, wasn't it my duty to banish the remnants of just such a thing? Was my fear nothing more than a novice's unease? Could all hunters feel such dread upon first drawing their bows?

The high exorcist must have been watching me through the door—testing me.

I raised the icy blue spiral, letting its radiance fill the room. The apparition withered, and I addressed it as I knew a Kellid would prefer. "Elistair, son of Clan Wintersun—your gods and ancestors wait for you."

The thing shuddered upon hearing the name. The babbling slowed, features congealing in the blot's depths.

"Leave here, son of the North. The Lady of Graves waits for you. You'll not travel the River of Souls alone."

Eyes, lips, hands strained from the oily dark—signs of reason. The features of an aging northman fought for form beneath unlife's stain.

"Join your lieges and the spirit of the land that once was. Your path—"

Shrieking, its form tore back open. The tarry pollution of soul surged, consuming any semblance of sanity. A lash of intangible dark defied the goddess's light. Before I could jerk away, a corrupt limb boiled over my holy symbol. In an instant-eternity, death was inside me. It consumed my hand, and the goddess's symbol fell from numb, colorless fingers.

"No."

As the icon slipped, so did the goddess's light. Shadows crashed back into the room. The madness that was Elistair Wintersun filled the cell. I groped after my holy symbol, trying to keep my desperation separate from the insane jabbering forcing into my head. The cell was not large—the thing was over me. Frozen fingers—a dull weight hanging from my wrist—scraped over stone encrusted with the madman's blood. In the blackness, I found nothing of the goddess.

Lightning flashed. The spirit's shriek clawed to unearthly pitches of pain. In the moment my body was still my own, I scrambled away, slamming into a wall. The flash came again, fast and limned in crimson. Behind it was the hint of the cell door, the screeching of its opening lost amid the howling. An ember-colored cloak and a glowing blue blade flared. The stained soul twisted, its shadows weakening before this new vicious light. Its song shot through every pitch of confused pain. Dark tendrils whipped toward the dancing blade only to be cut away. With every slash, the black madness lost form. Seeking to escape, it surged upward, soiling the ceiling.

High Exorcist Mardhalas stepped beneath it and plunged her cold blue longsword up, skewering the shadow and impaling what remained. A thousand frantically babbling voices gasped, the form shuttering as the sword's glow burned through.

"Go," the high exorcist commanded. "And be damned."

What remained of Elistair Wintersun burned like a page cast into a bonfire. The ashes of shadows scattered, rained down, and faded away.

Next, the exorcist came for me. She reached down.

"Thank you, Sister," I practically panted. My head pounded, my fractured thoughts slowly recrystallizing. "I don't—"

A rough hand clamped around my throat. The sound I choked wasn't a word. My hands sought to loosen her grip, but years of flipping hymnal pages made even my uninjured fingers poorly suited to breaking a soldier's grip. My heartbeat pounded in my neck, frantically trying to break the high exorcist's hold from inside.

She released me. My effort to tear away threw me back, knocking my head soundly against the wall and shooting sparks across my vision.

"Lady's tears! Have you lost your mind?" I rubbed my throat against the sudden hoarseness.

Mardhalas looked down at me unapologetically. "Your heart still beats. As poorly as you handled that, I couldn't be sure it hadn't drained you and left something else."

I was dimly aware of Doctor Linas entering the room behind her, holding the other lantern.

"Had it been a living thing, I might have let the goddess take you." She retrieved my holy symbol, inches from my foot. I snatched for it as she stood, missing thoroughly. "But stray souls are not of Her nature."

She held my simple amulet before her eyes, examining it suspiciously. "Bringing you here confirmed my suspicions, though. You're too weak and sentimental to serve the goddess."

Another cold wave crashed over me. I mouthed a word, but the sound didn't come out.

"The cycle of life and death isn't your rosy path of hope and wishes. It's cold and brief. You can tell yourself otherwise, but such fairytales have no place tainting the Lady's teachings. I had hoped to show you that here tonight, but the lesson almost cost you your life."

She twisted the twine holding the amulet, setting it spinning. "I know you don't accept it yet, but deep within, you agree. You know you're not fit. In the face of that abomination, your faith proved wanting. The goddess's own mark abandoned you."

She tossed the holy symbol onto my lap. "A true priestess wouldn't be separated from this, no matter the cost."

I swallowed deeply, mining whatever stone I had to buttress my voice. "I know I'm not a warrior like you, but I *am* a servant of the goddess." Still my words cracked. "I'm every bit as devoted as you."

Somehow she took that as an insult. "You think I've ever shrieked and fled? Begged an abomination to leave by the whim of its blasphemous soul? Cowered?" She laughed—actually laughed. "No, Miss Losritter, you and I do not share the same devotion."

The high exorcist turned.

Doctor Linas had been watching intently. "This is not a usual part of the exorcism."

"No. But we're done here." Mardhalas's words seemed as much for me as the doctor. I struggled to my feet, a challenge with trembling legs and one hand still numb from the spirit's attack. I gripped my holy symbol. It felt tepid.

"Good," Linas said. "Should we take any special precautions before assigning this room a new occupant?"

"No."

"Excellent. I'll have your payment sent in the morning—or donation, whatever your order prefers to call it." Linas stepped back into the hall, ready to show us the way out.

"That will be fine." Mardhalas followed without looking back.

We returned to the asylum's entry in silence. Even the lunatics seemed more subdued.

Only once the door was in sight did the high exorcist acknowledge me. "Miss Losritter. Upon returning to the cathedral, I'll be leaving a message for the holy mother. In the morning, I will discuss with her the unsuitability of your performance and advise we dismiss you from the order. Whether this means relocation or excommunication will be her decision, though I will make my recommendation plain. Expect a summons to interrupt your afternoon routine." Her words were casually formal, as though she were discussing the weather with a respectable stranger—not promising to shatter a life. "Now go fetch the coach."

"No." The incredulous word escaped before I could think better of it. The idea of sharing the ride home with this vicious woman, of enduring her company a moment longer, twisted my stomach.

She looked back as though I were an impetuous child. "This sort of behavior certainly won't encourage the holy mother to look upon you more favorably. Go get the coach."

I ignored her, turning to Doctor Linas, pausing upon the front steps. "Doctor. Does the asylum have a shrine or other place of worship?"

Her brows lifted. "Yes."

"Might I make use of it?"

"For what?" She asked, clipped and clinically.

"I find myself in need of the goddess's counsel, and feel the need to pray for temperance."

Mardhalas scoffed.

The doctor considered over the course of several slow blinks. "Through there." She pointed to a pair of sliding wooden doors, just off the foyer.

"Thank you, Doctor." I said as politely as possible, restraining the slurry of emotions roiling in my stomach. Something boiled over, though. I turned on the high exorcist. "And thank you as well, Miss Mardhalas. I don't—"

The slam of asylum's front door cut me off. The high exorcist had left, taking with her my life as a priestess.

When a mysterious monster carves a path of destruction across the southern River Kingdoms, desperate towns-folk look to the famed elven ranger Elyana and her half-orc companion Drelm for salvation. For Drelm, however, the mission is about more than simple justice, as without a great victory proving his worth, a prejudiced populace will never allow him to marry the human woman he loves. Together with a fresh band of allies, including the mysterious gunslinger Lisette, the heroes must set off into the wilderness, hunting a terrifying beast that will test their abilities—and their friendships—to the breaking point and beyond.

From acclaimed author Howard Andrew Jones comes a new adventure of love, death, and unnatural creatures, set in the award-winning world of the Pathfinder Roleplaying Game.

Stalking the Beast print edition: $9.99
ISBN: 978-1-60125-572-3

Stalking the Beast ebook edition:
ISBN: 978-1-60125-573-0

PATHFINDER TALES

Stalking
the Beast

HOWARD ANDREW JONES

PATHFINDER®
CAMPAIGN SETTING™

THE INNER SEA WORLD GUIDE

You've delved into the Pathfinder campaign setting with Pathfinder Tales novels—now take your adventures even further! *The Inner Sea World Guide* is a full-color, 320-page hardcover guide featuring everything you need to know about the exciting world of Pathfinder: overviews of every major nation, religion, race, and adventure location around the Inner Sea, plus a giant poster map! Read it as a travelogue, or use it to flesh out your roleplaying game—it's your world now!

EXPLORE YOUR WORLD!

paizo.com